Gregory L. Reece is an independent Alaba
with special interests in new religious move
previous books include *Elvis Religion: The Cult of the King* (2006), *UFO Religion: Inside Flying Saucer Cults and Cultures* (2007) and *Weird Science and Bizarre Beliefs* (2008), all published by I.B.Tauris.

'In *Creatures of the Night* Gregory Reece takes us on a fascinating journey: into the dark forests of our imaginations and through the haunted castles of our deepest fears. Searching for the things that have terrified us for centuries, he peels back the pop culture skin of fantasy to reveal the flesh and bones of myth and history. Vampires, demons, and werewolves are just some of the creatures we encounter in his very entertaining book. More than them, though, he reveals how we meet ourselves, albeit in the oft-warped mirror of literature, film, and the everyday stage.'

Douglas E. Cowan,
Professor of Religious Studies, Renison University College/
University of Waterloo; author of Sacred Terror: Religion and Horror on the Silver Screen *and* Sacred Space: The Quest for Transcendence in Science Fiction Film and Television

Creatures of the Night

In Search of Ghosts, Vampires, Werewolves and Demons

Gregory L. Reece

I.B. TAURIS

LONDON · NEW YORK

Published in 2012 by I.B.Tauris & Co Ltd
6 Salem Road, London W2 4BU
175 Fifth Avenue, New York NY 10010
www.ibtauris.com

Distributed in the United States and Canada Exclusively by Palgrave Macmillan
175 Fifth Avenue, New York NY 10010

ISBN: 978 1 84885 385 0

A full CIP record for this book is available from the British Library
A full CIP record is available from the Library of Congress

Library of Congress Catalog Card Number: available

Typeset in Caslon by JCS Publishing Services Ltd, www.jcs-publishing.co.uk
Printed and bound in Sweden by ScandBook AB

Contents

This book is for my parents

Henry Floyd Reece (1928–1989)
and
Mary Corinne Fain Reece (1931–2011)

Illustrations

Acknowledgments

I wish to express my thanks to the many people who helped me find my way in the dark, but especially to Wolf VanZandt and Druwydion Pendragon.

I also wish to thank Kristen, Sam and Olivia, my lights in the darkness.

Introduction
Oz the Great and Terrible

[This book] aspires to be a modernized fairy tale, in which the wonderment and joy are retained and the heart-aches and nightmares are left out.

L. Frank Baum, *The Wonderful Wizard of Oz*

It's probably wrong to believe there can be any limit to the horror which the human mind can experience. On the contrary, it seems that some exponential effect begins to obtain as deeper and deeper darkness falls – as little as one may like to admit it, human experience tends, in a good many ways, to support the idea that when the nightmare grows black enough, horror spawns horror, one coincidental evil begets other, often more deliberate evils, until finally blackness seems to cover everything. And the most terrifying question of all may be just how much horror the human mind can stand and still maintain a wakeful, staring, unrelenting sanity. That such events have their own Rube Goldberg absurdity goes almost without saying. At some point, it all starts to become rather funny. That may be the point at which sanity begins either to save itself or to buckle and break down; that point at which one's sense of humor begins to reassert itself.

Stephen King, *Pet Sematary*

[O]ut of shudder a holy awe.

Rudolf Otto, *Das Heilige*

Human eyes peer from the blue faces of the flying monkeys, human eyes, deep-set and hollow. The friendly organ-grinder costumes are made menacing by the Mohawk haircuts and buzzard wings, inexplicably feathered and sprouting from their furry backs. They are silent, except in flight, except when swooping down upon their victims. Then their whoops sound not human, not simian, but avian, like a flock of cranes, like Crëyr, the Welsh crane-god, creator and bringer of death. The scene shot from above, they look like vultures landing, drawn to carrion. But their prey, of course, is alive. Dorothy runs from them, really runs, fast and furiously. The Tin Woodman strikes at them with his axe. Is that his cry that is heard? Does he say 'Awful! Awful!'? The Scarecrow is on the ground, his insides being ripped out. The Lion is barely glimpsed, surrounded by the winged things, overrun and overwhelmed. What must his fear be like, this coward, this phobic feline who cowers at his own shadow and now has something real to fear? Dorothy is captured from behind, two winged monkey-things sweeping down on her and carrying her away, kicking and screaming through the barren treetops and across the gray sky.

1. Margaret Hamilton as the Wicked Witch of the West plots the destruction of Dorothy with one of her winged monkeys in *The Wizard of Oz* (1939).
Notice the monkeys adorning the stand for the crystal ball (Turner Entertainment Company).

* * *

This is terror, the stuff of nightmares and childhood fears. The Witch we can stand, with her green face-paint and improbable weakness: hiding, we imagine, from the very rain lest she fade away in a pool of wax and a puff of steam. But the monkeys are terrifying. They are outside our understanding, part monkey, part bird, and – most terrifying of all – part human. Their eyes reveal that there are human souls inside these nightmare things and human souls hold cunning and malice and wickedness. Generations of children have shuddered at the sight of these blue demons, hidden their heads under covers or behind their hands, run from the room screaming, wakened in the night crying for help when the things which had invaded their television screens and family rooms now invade their dreams.

The flying monkeys made their first, and far less terrifying, appearance at the dawn of the twentieth century in L. Frank Baum's *The Wonderful Wizard of Oz*. In W.W. Denslow's color illustrations of Baum's classic, the monkeys appear without the Mohawk haircuts and uniforms, their huge round eyes and smiling mouths beaming with friendliness. They make a very different impression from the menacing primates of Metro-Goldwyn-Mayer and, although their first appearance does produce a frightening moment, the goose-bumps quickly fade.

> The sky was darkened, and a low rumbling sound was heard in the air. There was a rushing of many wings; a great chattering and laughing; and the sun came out of the dark sky to show the Wicked Witch surrounded by a crowd of monkeys, each with a pair of immense and powerful wings on his shoulders.
>
> One, much bigger than the others, seemed to be their leader. He flew close to the Witch and said,
>
> 'You have called us for the third and last time. What do you command?'
>
> (Baum 1900, 147)

Baum's original monkeys are forced to do the bidding of the Witch by the power of a magic cap that granted its bearer power over them in the form of three commands. They capture Dorothy because they are under a magical spell and not, as it appears in the film, for the sheer joy of the hunt. (Though, in one brief scene in the movie the Witch can be seen holding the magic hat, a remnant of a scene lost to editing in which her control over the monkeys was explained. Better that it was cut. These winged nightmares need no such compulsion.)

When Baum published his tale of winged monkeys and wicked witches, by his own account terrorizing children was the furthest thing from

2. W.W. Denslow's illustration of Dorothy and the flying monkeys for the first edition of Baum's *The Wonderful Wizard of Oz* (1900).

his mind. In the preface to the original 1900 edition of the book Baum proposed a new kind of children's story, free from the terror and horror of what he called the 'historical' tales of folklore, legends, myths and fairy tales. He wrote:

> every healthy youngster has a wholesome and instinctive love for stories fantastic, marvelous and manifestly unreal. The winged fairies of Grimm and Anderson have brought more happiness to childish hearts than all other human creations.
>
> Yet the old time fairy tale, having served for generations, may now be classed as 'historical' in the children's library; for the time has now come for a series of newer 'wonder tales' in which the stereotyped genie, dwarf and fairy are eliminated, together with all the horrible and blood-curdling incidents devised by their authors to point a fearsome moral to each tale. Modern education includes morality; therefore the modern child seeks only entertainment in its wonder tales and gladly dispenses with all disagreeable incident.
>
> Having this thought in mind, the story of *The Wonderful Wizard of Oz* was written solely to please children of today. It aspires to being a modernized fairy tale, in which the wonderment and joy are retained and the heartaches and nightmares are left out. (Introduction)

Despite the gentler nature of the winged primates, Baum's promise to stay away from nightmares and terrors does not ring true. As a matter of fact, before she calls upon her monkey minions, the Witch tries various other methods to destroy her enemies. The results are some pretty frightening scenes. The Witch sends forty wolves to tear Dorothy and her friends to pieces, only to have the Tin Woodman chop off their heads with his axe. She sends a flock of crows to peck out their eyes but has to watch as the Scarecrow catches the birds in his hands, twists their necks and tosses their lifeless bodies aside (Surely no scarecrow has ever done its job in quite this way before!). The Witch sends bees to sting them to death and Winkie soldiers armed with spears to kill them, only to have the heroes escape time and again, until the monkeys find success in their mission.

These are not the only frightening moments in *The Wonderful Wizard of Oz*; the most frightening is associated with the Wizard himself as he is first encountered by Dorothy and her three companions. While Dorothy encounters the giant disembodied head made famous by the movie (though in a much less frightening form than in the film) and the Scarecrow sees the Wizard as a beautiful woman, the Tin Woodman and the Lion have much more of a shock. The Lion sees the Wizard in the form of a great ball of fire and the Woodman perceives him as a horrifying beast fit for the Book of Revelation, fit to herald the end of the world and the coming of eternal darkness:

> But when the Woodman entered the great Throne Room he saw neither the Head nor the Lady, for Oz had taken the shape of a most terrible Beast. It was nearly as big as an elephant, and the green throne seemed hardly strong enough to hold its weight. The Beast had a head like that of a rhinoceros, only there were five eyes in its face. There were five long arms growing out of its body, and it also had five long, slim legs. Thick, woolly hair covered every part of it, and a more dreadful-looking monster could not be imagined. It was fortunate the Tin Woodman had no heart at that moment, for it would have beat loud and fast from terror. But being only tin, the Woodman was not at all afraid, although he was much disappointed.
>
> 'I am Oz, the Great and Terrible,' spoke the Beast, in a voice that was one great roar. 'Who are you, and why do you seek me?' (132)

It is Oz the Great and Terrible who gives the clearest indication of Baum's strategy of removing the horror from the children's tale, however: the terrible monster faced by the Tin Woodman (as well as the other forms taken by the Wizard) is unveiled to be nothing more than a hoax. When the screen falls, all is revealed.

For they saw, standing in just the spot the screen had hidden, a little old man, with a bald head and a wrinkled face, who seemed to be as much surprised as they were. The Tin Woodman, raising his axe, rushed toward the little man and cried out, 'Who are you?'

'I am Oz, the Great and Terrible,' said the little man, in a trembling voice. 'But don't strike me – please don't – and I'll do anything you want me to.' (183)

There was never any real reason for Dorothy and her companions to be afraid. The Wizard, after all, was nothing more than a humbug. The Witch could be destroyed with a bucket of water. The monkeys, freed from their spell, would give aid to Dorothy and would finally be freed by the good witch Glinda from control by the magic cap.

But I know better – don't you? I've seen that look in their eyes. I've seen them, time and again throughout my childhood, swoop down on Dorothy and Toto, lifting them from the earth with the flapping of their wings, clutching them in their hideous little monkey paws.

Within two years of the publication of Baum's 'modernized fairy tale', W.W. Jacobs published a horrifying little masterpiece that was itself a fairy tale for the modern age, complete with a charmed object able to grant its bearer three wishes. Despite Baum's assertion that children's stories should be without 'disagreeable incident', this short story is all about an incident that is most assuredly disagreeable. Of course, Jacob's 'The Monkey's Paw' was not intended for children but rather for an audience more mature than the freckled-faced Midwestern farm boys and girls that Baum had in mind. Nevertheless, I first read the story as a child, published in *Ten Tales Calculated to Give You Shudders* – one of the cardboard-backed Whitman Classics volumes devoured by children of the 1970s, along with abridged versions of *Tom Sawyer*, *Treasure Island*, *Heidi* and, yes, *The Wonderful Wizard of Oz*. I can still see the cover of my copy of the book: two kids in overcoats walking through an overgrown yard and away from a spooky old house, a silhouetted figure watching them from an upstairs window, the whole picture awash in greens and blues. I can also still remember the shocked horror that swept over me, the sick feeling in the pit of my stomach, when I first read the tale and imagined the terrible sound of the knocking at the door.

The monkey's paw is cursed by an Indian fakir, cursed with the ability to grant its bearer three wishes. It is a hellish version of Aladdin's magic lamp. The paw is given to a family in industrial England by Herbert, a friend

3. The cover of *Ten Tales Calculated to Give You Shudders* (1972) (Whitman Publishing).

returning from India, a friend who cannot dissuade the new owners from using the thing's accursed power. The father makes his first wish just to test the thing's ability. He wishes for two hundred pounds. He is warned again as Herbert leaves the house: "'I expect you'll find the cash tied up in a big bag in the middle of your bed,' said Herbert, as he bade them good-night, 'and something horrible squatting up on top of the wardrobe watching you as you pocket your ill-gotten gains'" (Jacobs, 38). But, of course, before the tale is over, before the horror is done, the father can only wish that the money had come with only something horrible squatting.

The next afternoon a stranger comes to the door of the house of the old man and woman, the father and the mother. He comes with news of their son's death, the explanation for which is given in just a few terrible words: 'He was caught in the machinery.' (I imagine Charlie Chaplin in *Modern Times*, tangled up in the gears and belts of some mechanized terror, only with Technicolor blood gushing from between the cogs.) In

4. Charlie Chaplin in *Modern Times* (1936).

recompense for the tragedy the company is prepared to offer the couple 'a certain sum.'

> Mr. White dropped his wife's hand, and rising to his feet, gazed with a look of horror at his visitor. His dry lips shaped the words, 'How much?'
> 'Two hundred pounds,' was the answer.
> Unconscious of his wife's shriek, the old man smiled faintly, put out his hands like a sightless man, and dropped, a senseless heap, to the floor. (44)

A week later, in the horrible loneliness of the night, the mother pleads with the father to use the paw again, to use its magic to bring their son back to them, back from the grave. Together they call their son forth and then return to bed to wait for the wish to be granted. I remember being in my bedroom, lying in my bed, reading the story for the first time, listening for the sounds that were heard by the old couple, listening for 'a knock, so quiet and stealthy as to be scarcely audible' (51). The sound brings the mother from the bed, sends her running downstairs to open the door for her returning child: her prodigal son who was dead, and is alive again. She releases the bottom bolt, but cannot reach the top one. She cries out for her husband to come down, to help her, to join her in the homecoming, to bring the best robe, to kill the fatted calf.

> But her husband was on his hands and knees groping wildly on the floor in search of the paw. If he could only find it before the thing outside got in. A perfect fusillade of knocks reverberated through the house, and he heard the scraping of a chair as his wife put it down in the passage against the door. He heard the creaking of the bolt as it came slowly back, and at the same moment he found the monkey's paw, and frantically breathed his third and last wish.
>
> The knocking ceased suddenly, although the echoes of it were still in the house. He heard the chair drawn back and the door opened. A cold wind rushed up the staircase, and a long loud wail of disappointment and misery from his wife gave him courage to run down to her side, and then to the gate beyond. The street lamp flickering opposite shone on a quiet and deserted road. (52–3)

As a child, the ending of this tale came as a relief. The threat had dissolved, melted away like the Wicked Witch. The third wish had undone the second. I might have had nightmares after reading the story, but at least I could sleep. Now is another story. Now, I don't know what would be more horrible: the sight of the broken son, mangled by the machine, a week dead ('Lord, by this time he stinketh,' said Martha to Jesus), or the lamplight shining on the 'quiet and deserted road', the son still in the grave, still gone from life, never to be seen or touched again. Now, I stay awake at night listening for the sounds of my children, holding my breath until I hear them breathe. I strap them tight into car seats and make them wear bicycle helmets because I have learned to fear the machine and what it can do to soft human flesh, defenseless against the hardness of steel and asphalt. I wonder if there is any way that the thing knocking on the door, the unknown terror, could be any worse than seeing that deserted road that runs by the factories and the farms, from London to Kansas, paved not with yellow bricks, but with blood.

In 1917 Baum published the eleventh in his series of Oz books, *The Lost Princess of Oz*, and included a note 'To My Readers,' praising the imagination of children.

> Imagination has brought mankind through the Dark Ages to its present state of civilization. Imagination led Columbus to discover America.

Imagination led Franklin to discover electricity. Imagination has given us the steam engine, the telephone, the talking machine and the automobile, for these things had to be dreamed to become realities. (14)

Baum wrote as if the worst days of the world were behind it, as if humanity was on the road to the great city of tomorrow, as if imagination had provided us with the machinery to make our dreams become realities. Perhaps, writing from his home in Hollywood, where his books were being translated for the silver screen, it seemed that way. Or perhaps he just thought it inappropriate in a book for children to comment on the horrors that human imagination can dream up, on the terrors that technology can make come true.

The year 1917 marked the official beginning of the United States' involvement in World War I. Spurred to action by a leaked telegram from Germany seeking Mexico's support should the U.S. enter the war and by the attack on American ships by German submarines, human imagination and invention seemed to breed death and destruction. The war joined by the U.S. was already being fought with the grinding gears of machinery, underwater and in the air. Parents lost their children or saw them returned wounded and maimed. The horror at the heart of 'The Monkey's Paw' came frightfully to life, a horror that was captured on film by Abel Gance in *J'Accuse*. This film, a love triangle set in France during the war, shocked audiences with its terrifying finale in which the war dead arise from their graves and return to their homes, a shambling army of horrors marred by

5. A scene from Abel Gance's *J'Accuse!* (1919).

6. Lon Chaney as *The Phantom of the Opera* (1925) (Universal Pictures).

the scars of war. Many of the reanimated soldiers in the film were played by enlisted men who would soon return to the front to face the machine of war anew. Others marching in the parade of the damned were war veterans, the horrifying masks they wore their own real flesh and blood, their broken faces and scarred features capturing the horror that had been waiting behind the door for countless mothers, fathers, wives and lovers when their war heroes returned home. The same shocking experience was captured in 1925 by the great Lon Chaney in *The Phantom of the Opera*; his mask was removed to reveal a face remarkably like those uncovered by Gance, remarkably like thousands of faces scarred by the war. Men looked away. Women fainted. Then, families everywhere welcomed the horror home.

It was also in 1917 that German theologian Rudolf Otto published his classic work, *Das Heilige*. Otto's work immediately struck a chord with the war-weary and shell-shocked public. Following its publication, students flocked to the University of Marburg for the chance to hear Otto lecture and to study with him. The book went through a rapid series of reprints. An equally successful English edition of the book, *The Idea of the Holy*, was published in 1923. Although Otto's reputation among scholars and intellectuals never matched his book sales (he is often treated by historians as little more than a transitional figure between the theological speculations of the nineteenth century and those of the twentieth), the fact remains that Otto is arguably one of the most popular theologians of the last century. Reacting against the Rationalist and Romantic philosophy and theology of the nineteenth century which had, in effect, rendered religion a product of the rational mind, as in Hegel, or, as in Schliermacher, a product of human emotional dependence, Otto sought religion's heart in a far more frightening place. It was an approach that the Western world was more than ready to hear.

The essence of religion, he argued, cannot be expressed purely in terms of rational attributions. Accordingly, it is not something that can be taught. Religion must be invoked, it must be awakened as the emotions are awakened, not by rational argument but by the living of life. The 'holy' is not reducible to moral concepts, despite the fact that it is a term that is often used in a purely moral sense. The idea of holiness may indeed include morality, but it certainly contains elements not ascribed by moral terms. Otto believed that these are the elements that point toward the divine.

Struggling for a way to express his point in language, Otto coined his own terminology. As the Latin word *omen*, referring to the sign of the divine presence, gives us the term 'ominous,' a term that expresses the sense of foreboding contained in that sign, so he suggested that the Latin *numen*, referring to the divine presence itself, might give us the term 'numinous.' 'Numinous,' like 'ominous,' is also meant to express a sense of dread and awe. Otto argued that the numinous is experienced primarily as what he called *mysterium tremendum*, a tremendous mystery. This tremendous mystery is experienced in a variety of ways.

> The feeling of it may at times come sweeping like a gentle tide, pervading the mind with a tranquil mood of deepest worship. It may pass over into a more set and lasting attitude of the soul, continuing, as it were, thrillingly vibrant and resonant, until at last it dies away and the soul resumes its 'profane', non-religious mood of everyday experience. It may burst in sudden eruption up from the depths of the soul with spasms and convulsions, or lead to the strangest excitements, to intoxicated frenzy, to transport, and to ecstacy. (12–13)

There is little in Otto's argument thus far that would have seemed remarkable to his readers, little that was not expressed earlier by the Romantic theologian Schliermacher or known by countless religious believers. Religion is not a matter of facts and knowledge, but of personal and emotional experience. But Otto was not done. In addition to these commonplace expressions of religious emotion, Otto also noted that religion 'has its wild and demonic forms and can sink to an almost grisly horror and shuddering' (13). Of course it can; his readers knew. 'There are no atheists in foxholes,' the old saying goes, but what must it have been like to meet God in the trenches, to hear his voice in the sound of rifle fire, to see his face in the ghastly grinning cadaver that moments ago was your living, breathing friend?

Otto told his readers that the word 'tremendous' had its roots in the word 'tremor,' and that 'tremor is in itself merely the perfectly familiar and "natural" emotion of *fear*' (13). Likewise, the English language has the terms 'awe,' which is often taken in a worshipful and religious sense, and 'awful,' which denotes something more terrible. Indeed, the root and origin of religion is, Otto argued, to be found in the human feeling of fear, horror, terror and awe. Otto believed that the evolution of religion, first experienced by primitive societies as 'daemonic dread,' had been a movement through 'fear of the gods' to 'fear of God.' In the highly evolved state of modern man, the holy shudder might hardly be felt at all. But, Otto confessed, this pure form of religious experience can still show itself:

> **(TREMOR IS IN ITSELF MERELY THE PERFECTLY FAMILIAR AND "NATURAL" EMOTION OF *FEAR*.)**

> the potent attraction again and again exercised by the element of horror and 'shudder' in ghost stories, even among persons of high all-around education. It is a remarkable fact that the physical reaction to which this unique 'dread' of the uncanny gives rise is also unique, and is not found in the case of any 'natural' fear or terror. We say: 'my blood ran icy cold', and 'my flesh crept'.... [T]here is something non-natural or supernatural about the symptom of 'creeping flesh'. (16)

> [O]ut of 'shudder' [grows] a holy awe. (110)

Note that Otto distinguished between natural fear and something he called uncanny dread. The former is a physical and emotional state that we all understand. We find ourselves standing too close to a dangerous precipice and step back in alarm, our heart pounding, our palms sweating, afraid that we might fall. A snake slithers across the path in front of us; a car horn blares as we unthinkingly step out into oncoming traffic; tornado sirens wail, warning us of an approaching storm, warning us of the cyclone that is tearing its way across the fields. While this type of fear may be related to Otto's concept of uncanny dread, it is not quite pure enough, not quite holistic enough, not quite nauseatingly horrible enough. This fear is a natural fear, shared by human beings and other animal species. Otto spoke of a terror that is known to humanity alone. As he wrote, '"shuddering" is something more than "natural", ordinary fear' (15).

What Otto had in mind was more like the sense of terror that is felt at a ghost story told around a campfire. There is nothing there, nothing tangibly in front of us that might cause us harm, but still we tremble. This terror is hard to define. It seems to lie beyond the realm of rational explanation, of rational causes. We hear a quiet knock on our door late at night when we know there is no one there. The wind whispers. We catch sight of a strange movement out of the corner of our eyes. Our flesh crawls, the hair on our neck bristles, our palms sweat even though there is nothing there, even when we are sitting peacefully in our easy chair, in our living rooms, in our homes, safe and secure.

The terror that Otto has in mind, in its simplest and most primitive forms, is the fear of ghosts, of demons, of the beasts of ancient folklore. It is the fear of the howling wolf, the sound of the uncanny canine, a fear that reaches us even when we are safe and secure. It is the fear of the walking dead, the reanimated corpse, the bloodsucking vampire. It is the fear of the dread unknown, of the nonrational, of the invisible, the fear of the thing scratching at the door, the thing behind the mask, the thing behind the curtain. In its more developed form, this dreadful fear may break through into all parts of our lives, may not be kept carefully locked away inside the pages of *Weird Tales* or the latest Stephen King novel. It is the fear of the unknown, of the forces of the universe that are arrayed against us, the dread that keeps us awake at night, uneasily focused on nuclear bombs and madmen in airplanes, on pink slips from our boss, on the child that disappears down the lonely road, on the specter of war and disease and death. There is no wonder that Otto's reflections on religion found resonance in the twentieth century, that age of world wars, nuclear terrors, bone-crushing machinery, alienating technology, economic depression, influenza and AIDS. Any religious theory that fails to come to terms with the knot of fear in the bottom of countless human guts is surely a failure. Otto embraced this fear,

> **❲IT IS THE FEAR OF THE HOWLING WOLF, THE SOUND OF THE UNCANNY CANINE, A FEAR THAT REACHES US EVEN WHEN WE ARE SAFE AND SECURE.❳**

saw it for what it was and argued that religion is, at its heart, a response to this fear, a recognition of this fear. It is a shudder in the presence of the seemingly malevolent unknown.

For Otto, *tremendum* does not stand alone; its essence is shaped by the mystery before which it stands. It is precisely trembling before the *mysterious* that makes this awfulness so very awful. He wrote:

> Taken in the religious sense, that which is 'mysterious' is – to give it perhaps the most striking expression – the 'wholly other', that which is quite beyond the sphere of the usual, the intelligible, and the familiar, which therefore falls outside the limits of the 'canny', and is contrasted with it, filling the mind with blank wonder and astonishment. (26)

And,

> The truly 'mysterious' object is beyond our apprehension and comprehension, not only because our knowledge has certain irremovable limits, but because in it we come upon something inherently 'wholly other', whose kind and character are incommensurable with our own, and before which we therefore recoil in a wonder that strikes chill and numb. (28)

Again, Otto found the modern shape of the primitive expression of this fear of the unknown in the world of Gothic horror tales. The fear of ghosts he called a 'degraded offshoot and travesty of the genuine "numinous" dread or awe,' (28) and noted that part of the attraction of the ghost story is found in the simple pleasure experienced with the release of tension that the story builds. The resolution of the story, the mind's relief when realizing it is 'only a story,' provides a pleasant experience that makes the story enjoyable. This explanation, however, Otto thought insufficient.

> The ghost's real attraction rather consists in this, that of itself and in an uncommon degree it entices the imagination, awakening strong interest and curiosity; it is the weird thing itself that allures the fancy. But it does this, not because it is 'something long and white' (as someone once defined a ghost), nor yet through any of the positive and conceptual attributes which fancies about ghosts have invented, but because it is a thing that 'doesn't really exist at all', the 'wholly other', something which has no place in our scheme of reality but belongs to an absolutely different one, and which at the same time arouses an irresistible interest in the mind. (28–9)

It is because the ghost, the ghoul, the demon is wholly other from our everyday reality that the story attracts us, compels us to listen and read.

The ghost story, in its simple way, reveals the numinous to us, awakens our fear of the unknown, makes us to tremble before the mysterious, the hidden, the wholly other. The ghost story is a poor substitute for the genuine religious experience of the numinous, but it at least gives us hints of what the experience is like in its simpler forms.

Otto may have been able to dismiss the horror tale so easily as a travesty of genuine dread only because he had not read the tales of H.P. Lovecraft. In his essay 'Supernatural Horror in Literature,' first published in 1927, horror master Lovecraft described the place of horror in much the same way as Otto had. Lovecraft wrote, 'The oldest and strongest emotion of mankind is fear, and the oldest and strongest kind of fear is fear of the unknown' (105). The 'spectrally macabre,' as he calls it, stands side by side with the religious impulse. The first emotions of human beings were formed in response to our environment, Lovecraft proposed, and were shaped by the rewards of pleasure and pain. Predictability of outcomes was the boon to human civilization. Humans learned to avoid pain and to seek pleasure. But there always remained parts of the environment that were unpredictable, always calamities and unforeseen tragedies that humans could do nothing about. The fearful dread associated with these became the basis of religion: sacrifices and rituals were an attempt to appease the unknowable forces that struck without rhyme or reason.

Lovecraft's definition of the essence of the 'weird' story as a genre of literature is reminiscent of Otto's definition of the essence of religion:

> The one test of the really weird is simply this – whether or not there be excited in the reader a profound sense of dread, and of contact with unknown spheres and powers; a subtle attitude of awed listening, as the beating of black wings or the scratching of outside shapes and entities on the known universe's utmost rim. (Lovecraft, 108)

It is precisely this 'profound' sense of dread, this attitude of 'awed' listening, this contact with 'unknown spheres and powers' that Otto believed lay at the core of religion and that Lovecraft sought to convey in his stories of the weird and macabre, stories calculated to give you shudders.

Lovecraft's tales of dread Cthulhu and the other elder gods brought horror into the twentieth century. The horrors brought to the surface in his tales are horrors of a deep and universal nature. From the depths of the ocean, from beneath the frozen polar icecaps and from the darkness of space, Lovecraft's horrors threaten humanity. They represent the ancient incomprehensibility of the universe, the aggressive alien presence at the heart of the cosmos. For Lovecraft, the wholly other is the universe itself.

In Lovecraft's classic story 'The Call of Cthulhu,' the narrator, Francis Thurston, summarizes and philosophizes about the horror that he faces. He says, 'The most merciful thing in the world, I think, is the inability of the human mind to correlate all its contents. We live on a placid island of ignorance in the midst of the black seas of infinity, and it was not meant that we should voyage far' (1). The gigantically loathsome creature Cthulhu, ancient visitor from a distant star, sleeps at the bottom of the ocean in his ancient city of R'lyeh waiting for a chance to arise ('In his house at R'lyeh dread Cthulhu waits dreaming,' the members of his primitive cult chant in the darkness). It is a horror to make souls shudder. The universe is a place of ancient

> ❝I SHALL NEVER SLEEP CALMLY AGAIN WHEN I THINK OF THE HORRORS THAT LURK CEASELESSLY BEHIND LIFE.❞

evil. Humans are but a speck in the cosmic drama. The world is not as we think it. Thurston expresses his fears this way: 'I shall never sleep calmly again when I think of the horrors that lurk ceaselessly behind life in time and in space, and of those unhallowed blasphemies from elder stars which dream beneath the sea . . .' (22).

Or, as Lovecraft himself wrote in a letter from 1927, describing his philosophy for writing what he called 'weird' fiction,

> Now all my tales are based on the fundamental premise that common human laws and interests and emotions have no validity or significance in the vast cosmos-at-large . . . To achieve the essence of real externality, whether of time or space or dimension, one must forget that such things as organic life, good and evil, love and hate, and all such local attributes of a negligible and temporary race called mankind, have any existence at all. (quoted in Joshi, xvi)

Lovecraft's stories rang true to the post-World War I readers of the pulp magazine *Weird Tales* and to his even larger audience after World War II and beyond, in large part because Lovecraft succeeded so well in the development of tales that provoked these feelings of cosmic horror in his readers – the same feelings that, according to Otto, opened the door to the holy.

* * *

In the year 2000, a century after the publication of Baum's *The Wonderful Wizard of Oz*, the master of the twentieth-century horror novel, Stephen King, wrote in the introduction to the 2001 edition of *Pet Sematary*:

> When I'm asked (as I frequently am) what I consider to be the most frightening book I've ever written, the answer comes easily and with no hesitation: *Pet Sematary*. . . . All I know is that *Pet Sematary* is the one I put away in a drawer, thinking I had finally gone too far. . . . Put simply, I was horrified by what I had written, and the conclusions I'd drawn. (ix)

I agree with King. *Pet Sematary* was first published in 1983. I read it in paperback over Thanksgiving break in 1984 during my senior year in high school. It scared me then. It scares me now.

The story is not original. The most frightening tales never are. They touch something ancient and primitive, something universal. It is, in its heart, a retelling of 'The Monkey's Paw' with a little Lovecraft and *The Wonderful Wizard of Oz* thrown in. It is the story of a family that moves into an old farmhouse on a busy two-lane highway. It is the story of the tragic death of a child, crushed under the wheels of a log truck, caught in the machinery of progress. Like the father in 'The Monkey's Paw,' this father has access to a supernatural gift. In this case he knows of the existence of a cemetery deep in the woods near his home, beyond the place where children bury their pets, an old place filled with ancient cosmic power, filled with primal force. The burial ground of the Micmac Indians, though undoubtedly much older than the tribe, much older than humanity itself, had the power to bring the dead back to life.

'THE BURIAL GROUND OF THE MICMAC INDIANS, THOUGH UNDOUBTEDLY MUCH OLDER THAN THE TRIBE, MUCH OLDER THAN HUMANITY ITSELF, HAD THE POWER TO BRING THE DEAD BACK TO LIFE.'

> The graves in the Pet Sematary mimed the most ancient religious symbol of all: diminishing circles indicating a spiral lead down, not to a point, but to infinity; order from chaos or chaos from order, depending on which way your mind worked. It was a symbol the Egyptians had chiseled on the tombs of the Pharaohs, a symbol the Phoenicians had drawn on the barrows of their fallen kings; it was found on cave walls in ancient

Mycenae; the guildkings of Stonehenge had created it as a clock to time
the universe; it appeared in the Judeo-Christian Bible as the whirlwind
from which God had spoken to Job.

The spiral was the oldest sign of power in the world, man's oldest
symbol of that twisty bridge which may exist between the world and the
Gulf. (387)

Overcome by grief and possessed by the cursed earth, the father
unearths his son, digs him up from his grave, wraps his body in a tarp,
and carries him through the woods to the stinking place. Then, he goes
home to wait.

The mother, too, is blinded by sorrow and haunted by memories of her
sister Zelda's childhood death, haunted by the months of watching her sister die slowly of spinal meningitis, seeing her transformed into a screaming
monster, with her mind growing as twisted as her back. She was alone with
Zelda when she died; the memory remains burned into her soul.

> I backed across the room. I guess I wanted to back out the door, but I hit
> the wall and a picture fell down – it was a picture from one of the Oz books
> that Zelda liked before she got sick with the meningitis, when she was well,
> it was a picture of Oz the Great and Terrible, only Zelda always called him
> Oz the Gweat and Tewwible because she couldn't make that sound, and so
> she sounded like Elmer Fudd. My mother got the picture framed because
> . . . because Zelda liked it most of all . . . Oz the Gweat and Tewwible . . .
> and it fell down and hit the floor and the glass in the frame shattered and
> I started to scream because I knew she was dead and I thought . . . I guess I
> thought it was her ghost, coming back to get me. (273–4)

Oz the Gweat and Tewwible looms over the mother's life, like a god
of chaos. The father too sees the deity's handiwork everywhere. Looking
into a drainage ditch outside the cemetery before he unearthed his son's
remains, he sees a decaying mass of flowers, removed from someone's grave
and thrown away, their beauty turned into a stinking rot.

> Christ.
> No, not Christ. These leavings were made in propitiation of a much
> older God than the Christian one. People have called Him different
> things at different times; but Rachel's sister gave him a perfectly good
> name, I think: Oz the Gweat and Tewwible, God of dead things left
> in the ground, God of rotting flowers in drainage ditches, God of the
> Mystery. (469)

Less than a century after Baum wrote his optimistic introduction to *The Wonderful Wizard of Oz* and revealed the Wizard to be nothing more than a humbug, sought to remove the nightmare from the children's story – less than a hundred years later, Stephen King transformed the lovable old humbug from Omaha into Oz the Gweat and Tewwible, a Lovecraftian cosmic deity, the Wholly Other. But, then again, it was a century fit for King's kind of deity, fit for Otto's shuddering terror. And those monkeys, those monkeys never could be trusted, with the beating of their black wings heard forever over our shoulders.

'Sometimes dead is better,' Stephen King's weird tale tells us: a lesson the mother learned in childhood at her sister's bedside; a lesson the father learned in the end. It is a lesson that is only learned the hard way, a lesson that shakes us to our core. King tells us in *Pet Sematary* the lesson we should have learned from 'The Monkey's Paw': 'What comes when you're too slow wishing away the thing that knocks on your door in the middle of the night is simple enough: total darkness' (537).

In that darkness squats the creature of the night. Its identity is a mystery, its shape seemingly changing with the shadows in the drifting wind. For a moment it seems human, though far too transparent, far too shallow to be real. Then it opens its mouth in a snarl, it bares its teeth to the moonlight, and its humanity vanishes with its glistening canines. Is that hair bristling on its neck? Does it arch its back as if preparing to howl? Its beastliness shifts as did its humanity. It is something more, something from the pit, something from the mouth of hell, something stinking and foul and powerfully evil. It is a demon. It is a god. It is both.

The creatures of the night are the prowlers of the forest and the dark city streets. They are the haunters of castles, the risers from the dead, those who run on four feet and on two. They are the ones with dripping fangs, the ones with bloody claws. They show no mercy. They show no fear. They live in our folktales, told to children around campfires. They dwell in our literature, raging between the pages of our books. They stride across our movie screens, ephemeral, flickering giants drenched in blood and gore. They live in our basements, in our attics, in the house on the corner, in the cemetery overgrown with weeds, in the dark woods. They live in our minds, in our hearts, in our souls.

The creatures of the night, whether ghost, vampire, werewolf or demon, have haunted humanity for as long as we have been human. Their features change with culture and time but they remain in so many ways the same. They are the opaque spirits of the dead. They are the stinking corpses that burst from the earth. They are the beasts of the forest and of the human heart. They are the thing from the beyond, the demons from the depths. Today, as at all other times in human history, they walk the earth, bringing fear and damnation, shaping nightmares and shattering dreams.

We have shone the light of science in the dark corners in an attempt to evaporate the threat with our knowledge. They have found deeper shadows in which to dwell. We have resolved them with psychotherapy and treated them with drugs. They always return, grinning wider than before. We have cast them out by the power of our faith, denounced them with our religions, prayed for their defeat. They rise from the dead, again and again, as if they are themselves dark messiahs, reborn, not at the first light of Easter morn, but in the deepest midnight, at the witching hour, bringing their own gospel, pointing the way to the Other with their long bony fingers.

The horror personified by these creatures of the night is a fundamental trait of human life, but is it possible that these monsters of myth and media are also bearers of religious revelation, reflecting humanity's struggle to find meaning in the midst of horror, themselves shadowy prophets of the dark gods we tremble before? This book is an exploration of these horrors – these creatures of the night – from this religious point of view. Chapter One, 'The Holy Ghost and Fire,' examines the cultural and religious significance of ghosts and hauntings: those spirited survivors of death that point us toward the fears inherent in our own mortality, and beyond. Chapter Two, 'It Was a Dark and Stormy Night,' examines the more fleshy components of that mortality, those parts that we try to hide with make-up and embalming fluid, the rotting corpses and stinking graves from which vampires rise and stalk the night. Chapter Three, 'Oh Grandmother, What Big Teeth You Have,' moves from fears of death to fears of life, the life beyond our human community, the howling beasts of forest and field, and the howling beasts who stand much closer, inhabiting our civilizations, our homes, our hearts. In Chapter Four, 'This Little Piggy,' and Chapter Five, 'Speak of the Devil,' the religious significance of horror (or, the horrific significance of religion) becomes even more explicit. Demons that possess our bodies transition to demons before whom we bow. Exorcists give way to Satanists. Fear and faith stand hand in bony hand, hand in hairy paw, hand in horny claw. As they always have and always will.

The Holy Ghost and Fire

I indeed baptize you with water unto repentance: but he that cometh after me is mightier than I, whose shoes I am not worthy to bear: he shall baptize you with the Holy Ghost, and fire.

Matthew 3:11

The story had held us, round the fire, sufficiently breathless, but except that the obvious remark that it was gruesome, as, on Christmas Eve in an old house, a strange tale certainly should be.

Henry James, *The Turn of the Screw*

She was burning. Her nightgown ablaze, she ran down the long hallway, screaming in terror and in pain. The air was pungent with the smell of burning cotton, burning hair, burning flesh. The girls on the hall stood in their doorways and watched the flaming comet, the blazing meteor, streak by their door. She was a banshee, crying out the warning of her own death, a will-o'-the-wisp with a jack-o'-lantern skull.

It was 1908 when Condie Cunningham combusted in Main Hall, the dormitory of what would become the University of Montevallo. She was cooking fudge with her friends, heating the chocolate with a Bunsen burner, when the head resident called for 'lights out.' A bottle of alcohol was upset in the excitement and Condie burst into flames. She ran down the long hallways, down the stairs, and into the open air. Too frail for transport to her home or a hospital, she lived her last days in a ground-floor room of Main Hall. Soon after her death, residents of the dormitory reported seeing Condie ablaze and again running down the hallways, screeching down the stairs. I imagine that they would not be able to stop seeing her. I imagine that her screams would ring in the ears of the witnesses for the rest of their lives, that the sight of that blazing phantom would haunt the memories of the young girls of Main Hall long after they had left the school and grown to adulthood. Wouldn't you see her every time you closed your eyes, every time the lights went out, every time you smelled chocolate cooking or saw a candle flame?

The image of Condie kept appearing long after her friends had moved on with their lives. New generations of girls attending the small Alabama college had their vision haunted by the specter of Condie aflame, Condie ablaze, Condie afire. Bunsen burners would turn into microwave ovens, but Condie's flame kept burning, kept lighting up the night, kept singeing the nerves of the young women of Main Hall.

For those who doubted that the presence of the unfortunate girl could live on after her body was gone, for those who laughed at the imagination of the young foolish women, there was always Condie's door as a reproach,

7. Condie's door at the University of Montevallo, Alabama (photo by R. Hendrix).

as circumstantial evidence that there was something hauntingly real about Condie's ghost. There, on the doorway that led into Condie's old bedroom, as if burned into the wood grain, was the image of the burning girl. The door, long since removed from its place at Condie's threshold, is now kept in storage by the university for most of the year, brought out and displayed at Halloween when anyone is free to see for themselves Condie's face, her exposed teeth giving her a look of macabre joy, her flaming hair billowing atop her head. I have seen the door, looked into the frightened and frightening face, felt the heat from the century-old fire, felt my skin crawl at the thought of the young girl burning, burning still.

The University of Montevallo campus sits just across the street from my home. I walk its red-brick streets regularly. My wife lived in Main Hall when she was a student. We dated in its expansive lobbies and drawing rooms when we were young. Now, my children run up and down its front steps on their way to piano lessons. In the spring, we see the wisteria that entwines its front columns burst into bloom (like Condie, I sometimes think, bursting into flames), its great clusters of purple flower-grapes blowing in the breeze and dropping petals on the steps and stones (the same wind, perhaps, that fanned Condie's flames). Condie is a very personal ghost, someone we know on a first name basis, an old friend, a spectral acquaintance.

Condie is not alone. Mr. Edmund King, whose 1823 home stands within sight of Main Hall, still prowls the campus, wandering between his former home and his burial site (also on the campus), carrying a lantern and shovel. He is said to be looking for his treasure, which he buried somewhere in the area to protect it from Yankee soldiers during the American Civil War. His greed keeps him alive long past his appointed time.

The horrors of the old war also provide the setting for the haunting of Montevallo's Reynolds Hall, a ghostly white building next door to Main. It was here that, according to legend, Captain Reynolds of the Confederate army was stationed to guard the sick and wounded troops housed in the building, which was being used as a makeshift hospital. Upon receiving news of an imminent attack by the Northern army on a local ironworks, Captain Reynolds left his post at the hospital and took his men to defend the plant at Brier Field. While Reynolds and his men were away, General Sherman's soldiers slaughtered the patients in the unprotected hospital. When Reynolds discovered the horror caused by his actions, he vowed to stand guard over the building forever, even after his death. According to witnesses who have seen the soldier standing guard still, this is exactly what he has done, his guilt a barrier to his eternal rest.

So Captain Reynolds and Mr. King, haunted by their greed and their guilt, haunt the world in turn. Mr. King wanders lost, his lantern fire too dim to lead him to his lost wealth, his lost life. Captain Reynolds stands guard awaiting Sherman's army that will never again come this way, their fires long died out, extinguished by the passing years. Along with Condie, eternally aflame in her private hell, they haunt the night.

Around the world, ghosts haunt. None of us has to travel far to find their like. They haunt cities and towns, farmhouses and mansions, lonely meadows and busy streets. Ghosts are not distant and exotic phenomena. They are our neighbors, inhabiting the landmarks of our lives, the building across the street, the room down the hall. They are universal, a common theme in human life. The dead do not go away; they remain with us. They haunt us. I tell Condie's story, the story of her burning death and her burning afterlife, because it is my story. We all have one. We are all haunted.

Perhaps it should be obvious, this universal haunting, perhaps it should come as no surprise. Edward Burnett Tylor, an English anthropologist, theorized in 1871 that ghosts have their origins in the most primitive and ancient of human cultures. Indeed, ghosts haunt, according to Tylor, the very origins of religious belief. Tylor's influential work, *Primitive Culture: Researches into the Development of Mythology, Philosophy, Religion, Language, Art and Custom*, offered an evolutionary view of culture and religion. Eschewing the idea espoused by conservative churchmen – that the original religion was the monotheism revealed by Jehovah and contained in the Bible – Tylor argued that the origins of religion could instead be found in some simple features of human existence.

As Tylor put it,

> It seems as though thinking men, as yet at a low level of culture, were deeply impressed by two groups of biological problems. In the first place, what is it that makes the difference between a living body and a dead one; what causes waking, sleep, trance, disease, death? In the second place, what are those human shapes which appear in dreams and visions? (vol. 1, 428)

Faced with these two phenomena, the ancients, according to Tylor, developed the theory that every person has two mysterious features: 'life' and a 'phantom existence.' Both of these features of the human experience appear to have existence separate from the body. Life can clearly depart the body upon death, while the phantom-self leaves the body while it is alive and can be seen by others in dreams or visions. Over time, primitive cultures combined these two features into one, something Tylor called an 'apparitional-soul' or 'ghost-soul.' These early cultures came to believe, to put it simply, that every human being possessed a spirit, something Tylor described as:

> a thin unsubstantial human image, in its nature a sort of vapour, film, or shadow; the cause of life and thought in the individual it animates; independently possessing the personal consciousness and volition of its corporeal owner, past or present; capable of leaving the body far behind, to flash swiftly from place to place; mostly impalpable and invisible, yet also manifesting physical power, and especially appearing to men waking or asleep as a phantasm separate from the body of which it bears the likeness; continuing to exist and appear to men after the death of that body; able to enter into, possess, and act in the bodies of other men, of animals, and even of things. (vol. 1, 429)

Tylor proposed that such a conception of human beings is found universally among primitive cultures, a fact that need not be attributed to the spread of the idea of the soul from one culture to another. Rather, he believed this idea of the spiritual nature of humanity is a universal feature of early cultures' attempts to understand some basic phenomena associated with human life in the world. It is a simple fact of life that humans sometimes see other people – whether in dreams, visions, or by dark of night – that they have no business seeing. It is a simple fact of life that people sometimes see ghosts.

'IT IS A SIMPLE FACT OF LIFE THAT HUMANS SOMETIMES SEE OTHER PEOPLE – WHETHER IN DREAMS, VISIONS, OR BY DARK OF NIGHT – THAT THEY HAVE NO BUSINESS SEEING.'

Tylor saw this basic human experience of 'seeing a ghost' as the central impetus for the origin of religion. From the belief that human spirits lived on after death, early cultures developed beliefs about the afterlife. Since loved ones were called upon for assistance during their lifetimes, it was only natural that they should be called upon after they had entered the spirit world. In this way the practice of prayer and offerings arose. Over time, the most famed ancestors were elevated above others, becoming deities that demanded worship. In time, primitive cultures developed techniques and practices for contacting the spirit world. Fasting, extreme penance, and the use of narcotics were all means for opening up paths to the world of the spirits and allowing devotees to 'obtain the sight of spectral beings' and 'gain spiritual knowledge and even worldly power' (vol. 1, 446). The features of religion, the belief in spiritual survival after death and the belief in gods and goddesses arose, according to Tylor, because ancient cultures, like modern ones, were haunted by ghosts, because in ancient times and amid primitive peoples specters appeared in the dark of night.

Religion, historically for Tylor as existentially for Otto, had its origin in the ghostly, though Tylor's thoroughly modern sensibilities meant that he saw belief in ghosts as the result of a logical mistake made by early theorists, as if primitive humanity sat around campfires and hypothesized about the origins of their dreams and developed explanations for their visions of dark and hooded ghosts. For Otto, on the other hand, before there was theory there was the shudder, the terror, the fear. For Otto, it was here that the origin of religion is truly found. He wrote in reference to Tylor's theory,

> the important point is not the origin of 'spirits' in their ideational aspect, but the qualitative element of feeling relative to them. And this does not consist in the fact that 'spirits' or 'souls' are thinner or less easily visible than the body, or quite invisible, or fashioned like air: often all of this is true of them; no less often none of it is; most frequently all of it is both true and false. The essence of the 'soul' lies *not* in the imaginative or conceptual expression of it, but first and foremost in the fact that it is a *spectre*; that it arouses 'dread' or 'awe'. (120)

Missing from Tylor is the clammy sweat, the goose-bumps, the racing heart of the haunted house, the séance room, the dark woods, all of which must surely precede theory and hypothesis. For Tylor, there was no reason that modern cultures should continue to be haunted by ghosts. We have better theories to explain the phenomena that frightened our ancestors. Otto, however, knew this was not true. For as long as we are human we will be haunted, and no theory will take away the shuddering awe that lies in the pit of our stomachs and at the base of our spines.

Sacheverell Sitwell, in writing about the ghost known as a poltergeist, drew distinctions between the spirits of religion and the spirits that haunt, of which he wrote,

> They come from the underworld, from caverns or cesspools covered up or hidden. These things creep underground; they are blind like the mole, sightless and pale from their imprisonment, with long rodent fingers, cold,

and as a dead man's hand. . . . Every religion, and all superstition, serve one another and are sealed in compact. But, at this moment, our meeting is with the lesser shades. Noble lives, passed in true religion, do not concern us here. It is the scullions, or scavengers, the stragglers and camp followers, those who strip dead bodies, who have come upon the earth. They have grown up behind us, in our footsteps. They gather, like a choking weed, and only care can keep them down. (78)

But is it possible that Sitwell's demarcation between the 'noble lives, passed in true religion' and 'the lesser shades' is not a clear line at all, that the spirits of the righteous can cause us to quake just as readily as the spirits of the damned, that even the Holy Ghost overwhelms us with fear and trembling? Is it possible that the 'lesser shades,' the malicious spirits that Sitwell wished to address – those ghosts that come not with kind words but with dire warnings and shrill cries – may themselves lie close to the heart of the divine?

Jesus was thought by his disciples to be a ghost as he walked to them across the stormy sea. They shuddered in horror as his spectral form came toward them through the storm. He called to them, 'It is I, be not afraid.' But they were afraid. After his resurrection he had to insist to them again that he was not a ghost, an immaterial specter, had to make them feel his flesh and poke their fingers into his wounds. 'I am not a ghost,' he told them, 'handle me and see.' But the figure dressed in grave clothes with scarred hands and feet must have been a terrifying sight, must have seemed a ghost in all but name. He promised to leave his spirit with them, his Holy Ghost, and to baptize them, not with water, but with the Holy Ghost and fire. If Tylor is correct, then all ghosts are holy, for all gods were but ghosts in the ancient, primitive heart of human history. Like Condie, ghosts and gods come rushing at us, engulfed in flames, reminding us of our mortality and our loss, preying on our fear of the unknown, scaring us out of our minds. Mr. King seeks his gold. Captain Reynolds stands guard. But Condie, flaming terror, blazing banshee, opens the door and leads the way.

Ghosts, I suppose we could say, are survivors. They refuse to go away, refuse to give up their place in the world, despite ghastly deaths, deep burials and the relentless flow of time. They hang around and beat the odds. They survive. This is true not only of individual phantoms, the wandering souls of Condie Cunningham and Mr. King, but also of the experience of ghosts in culture, the persistence of the ghost story as a cultural form. Unsurprisingly, the survival of ghosts was of great interest to E.B. Tylor, who argued that belief in such things was the result of the primitive logic of primitive culture. But if one form passes into another, if ghost stories turn into myths and wraiths into gods, then why does the ghost story remain? Why does belief in such things persist, not just in primitive cultures, but in the advanced cultures of the world as well? Ghosts, like ghosts, are survivors.

Tylor was particularly intrigued by the development, in his own nineteenth century, of spiritualism as a popular movement. As he wrote in the pages of *Primitive Culture*, a careful analysis of the phenomena

> shows modern spiritualism to be in great measure a direct revival from the regions of savage philosophy and peasant folklore. It is not a simple question of the existence of certain phenomena of mind and matter. It is that, in connexion with these phenomena, a great philosophic-religious doctrine, flourishing in the lower culture but dwindling in the higher, has re-established itself in full vigour. The world is again swarming with intelligent and powerful disembodied spiritual beings, whose direct action on thought and matter is again confidently asserted, as in those times and countries where physical science had not as yet so far succeeded in extruding these spirits and their influences from the system of nature. (vol. 2, 142)

As in ancient times, Tylor noted, there was again in his day intercourse between human beings and the spirits of the dead. Despite the dawn of the natural sciences, despite the growing understanding of the world around us, despite the development of better theories, ghosts had survived. The spiritualist movement that Tylor observed was indeed something of a phenomenon, attracting believers from all walks of life and intriguing members of both the

‹STILL THE MAN DOES NOT DIE; HE IS ONLY SEPARATED FROM THE BODILY PART WHICH WAS OF USE TO HIM IN THE WORLD.›

ecclesiastical and scientific worlds. Nor did it go away with the forward march of science and technology, surviving still today at the start of the twenty-first century.

Tylor, like many other observers past and present, saw the origins of the spiritualist revival in the life and work of Emanuel Swedenborg, the eighteenth-century Swedish naturalist, theologian and philosopher. Swedenborg began his career as a relatively orthodox thinker, but, after a series of visionary experiences, developed a philosophy that was instrumental for the growth of the spiritualist movement that followed. This was particularly true in regards to his descriptions of the afterlife. Swedenborg started with assumptions common to most Christians. For example, he wrote,

> When the body is no longer able to perform its functions in the natural world, a man is said to die. Still the man does not die; he is only separated from the bodily part which was of use to him in the world. The man himself lives. He lives, because he is man by virtue, not of the body, but of the spirit; for it is the spirit in man which thinks; and thought together with affection makes the man. It is plain, then, that when a man dies, he only passes from one world into the other. (270)

In itself, there is nothing in this description that is unique. It is indeed just a modernized version of what Tylor saw in primitive cultures. Swedenborg, however, made other more detailed claims about life after death.

For example, Swedenborg claimed that the deceased possess a fully formed spiritual body that mirrors their material body, complete with the physical senses:

> A human spirit also enjoys every sense, external and internal, which he enjoyed in the world. He sees as before, hears and speaks as before, smells and tastes as before, and feels when he is touched. He also longs, desires, craves, thinks, reflects, is stirred, loves, wills, as he did previously. . . . In a word, when a man passes from the one life into the other, or from the one world into the other, it is as though he had passed from one place to another; and he carries with him all that he possesses in himself as a man. It cannot, then, be said, that after death a man has lost anything that really belonged to him. He carries his natural memory with him, too; for he retains all things whatsoever which he has heard, seen, read, learned and thought in the world, from earliest infancy even to the last of life. (291)

Swedenborg claimed that the experiences of the spirits seem so remarkably like those of earthly life that they may not even be aware that they are dead. In the initial state after death the spirits exist on a plane of existence midway between heaven and hell, from which the spirits are prepared for one or the other, depending on the merits of their lives. It is with spirits in this intermediate state that contact by the earthly realm is most easily made.

Swedenborg believed that human life in the world is one of constant contact with these spirits, as well as with angels and demons. Most of the influence from the spirit realm goes unnoticed, but is there for those able to see it. Swedenborg himself claimed that he had developed a keen awareness of these spirits and that he was able to converse with them quite readily. He wrote on one occasion that a friend who had died on Monday had spoken to him on the following Thursday, visiting with Swedenborg during his own funeral services. According to Swedenborg, the friend watched as the hearse arrived and as his body was lowered into the grave, prompting him to ask why he was being buried alive. Swedenborg reported that another friend had died at ten in the morning and spoken to him at ten that night. Swedenborg cautioned that there could be danger in contact with the beyond, because not all spirits are of a godly nature. Bad people make bad ghosts. They can fill the mind of the medium with evil thoughts, both intentionally and unintentionally, if they themselves are uninformed. Communicating with ghosts no more guarantees truth than does communicating with living, breathing men and women.

Swedenborg's contribution, according to Tylor and others, was to provide a theoretical framework for understanding ghosts and contacts with the spectral world. In doing so, one might say, he provided a way for ghosts as cultural phenomena to move into the modern world. His insistence that spirits maintain the personalities and characteristics that they possessed in life, and that communication with them is almost as easy as communicating with a living friend, opened the door for the treatment of ghosts as phenomena subject to the controls of experimentation and science. Swedenborg, as a medium, not only helped to usher spirits into the presence of living men and women but also helped to usher ghosts into the modern world.

Arthur Conan Doyle, creator of Sherlock Holmes, defender of the Cottingley fairy photographs and advocate of spiritualism, claimed that Swedenborg thus laid claim to the title of father of 'our new knowledge of supernal powers.' Conan Doyle says of Swedenborg in his *The History of Spiritualism* of 1926,

> When the first rays of the rising sun of spiritual knowledge fell upon the earth they illuminated the greatest and highest mind before they shed their light on lesser men. That mountain peak of mentality was this great religious reformer and clairvoyant medium, as little understood by his own followers as ever the Christ has been. (1)

8. 'Fairy Offering Posy of Harebells to Elsie' (1917), Elsie Wright and one of the Cottingley fairies, whose existence was endorsed by Conan Doyle.

While Conan Doyle saw Swedenborg as the deep well from which spiritualism sprang, he found the birth of the new movement in the Fox sisters of Hydesville, New York. Their encounters with spirits from beyond the grave constituted for Conan Doyle a 'rift in the veil' through which countless contacts between the worlds would thereafter be made. The Fox home was inhabited by the two sisters, Margaret, aged fifteen, and Kate, aged twelve, and their parents. Early in 1848 (or 1847 in some accounts) the family began to hear strange 'knocking' sounds at day and night. At first it was thought that the sound was caused by rats or by neighbors, but these theories were soon dismissed. Finally, on March 31, Kate, the younger of the sisters, made a breakthrough that opened the veil for contact with the beyond.

Conan Doyle wrote in his book *The Edge of the Unknown*:

It was upon this evening that one of the great points in the history of psychic evolution was reached, for it was then that young Kate Fox, having lost all sense of fear in the presence of that which use had made familiar, challenged the unseen power to repeat the snaps of her fingers. This challenge, though given in flippant words, was instantly accepted. Each snap was answered by a knock. However humble the operator at either end, the spiritual telegraph was at last working, and it was left to the patience and moral earnestness of the human race to determine how high might be the use to which it was put in the future. Unexplained forces were many in the world, but here was a force claiming to have independent intelligence at the back of it. This was the supreme sign of a new departure. 'Fancy a new spiritual departure in a frame-house in an American hamlet!' Yes, and fancy a previous one in a camel-driver's tent in Arabia, and before that the greatest of all in a carpenter's shop in Judea! (178)

Tylor saw the sisters in a slightly different light and recognized that spirit rappings, despite Conan Doyle's claims, were not some new thing, but rather a survival from earlier times, especially seen in the German 'poltergeist': a spirit, or sometimes an elf, known for causing mischief around the house. Conan Doyle thought of the birth of spiritualism as something new; Tylor saw it is as the rebirth of something old, as the continual haunting of culture by the ghosts of the past. The Fox family, according to Tylor, had 'only to revive the ancient prevalent belief in spirit rappings, which had almost fallen into the limbo of discredited superstitions' (vol. 1, 146).

One of the things that made the spirit rappings of the Fox house unique, however, was the system of communication with the spirits that was developed based on the rappings. By coordinating the number of knocks with the letters of the alphabet, the sisters claimed that they were able to communicate with the spirit. The spirit world could talk to them, not in some internal vision, as with Swedenborg, but in a clearly audible way, subject to verification and public demonstration. It was this that really made the Foxes unique.

When word spread about the strange activities in the household neighbors came from all around to hear the messages from beyond and to ask questions themselves. What came to light was a rather startling claim. The knocker claimed to be the ghost of a thirty-one-year-old man, by the name of Charles Rosma, who had been murdered in that very house and buried in the cellar. Seeking to verify the claim, a group of townspeople excavated the cellar and reportedly discovered human hair, human bones and part of a human skull.

Following this initial communication, the floodgates opened. Charles Rosma had been but a pioneer. His story was really just a good old-fashion ghost tale. The ghost of a murdered man could not rest until justice was done. The bones in the cellar, like Condie's door, was the twist at the end to sell the tale, to make it real. But now there were countless spirits wishing to communicate through the Fox sisters. The deceased friends and relatives of the townspeople began to send messages to the earthly plane, most of them consisting of pedantic well wishes and greetings from the beyond. Word spread, and soon the Fox sisters were nationally famous. Leaving the house and traveling made little difference to their ability to communicate with the spirit world: wherever they went, the messages came through, knock by knock, letter by letter. Helped along by their appealing looks and their shy, honest demeanor, the sisters were a sensation. According to Conan Doyle, the veil had been torn, like the curtain of the temple at the passing of Jesus; something new was afoot in the world. According to Tylor, something old and almost dead had managed to survive, had crawled out of the grave to haunt the world anew. Either way, with the advent of spiritualism, the ghosts that modernity had sought to confine to folklore came, like Condie, screaming back into the world.

In 1932, a spirit medium produced a white substance from her mouth identified as ectoplasm. In a photograph taken of the phenomenon a clear likeness of Sir Arthur Conan Doyle can be seen in the center of the mass. Conan Doyle, who had passed away in 1930 after years of research into the world beyond was making his comeback, returning to the earthly plane in the context in which he had long sought contact from the other side. The clairvoyant, Mary Ann Marshall, was the spirit medium for a spiritualist group in Winnipeg, Manitoba, that was extensively photographed by Dr. T.G. Hamilton. Conan Doyle had visited with the group on at least one other occasion, while still in his material form, in 1923, where he witnessed the levitation of a chair. He had also written on the subject of ectoplasm in his *History of Spiritualism*:

> From very early days Spiritualists have contended that there was some physical material basis for the phenomena. A hundred times in early Spiritual literature you will find descriptions of the semi-luminous thick vapour which oozes from the side of the mouth of a medium and is dimly visible in the gloom. They had even gone further and had observed how the vapour in turn solidifies to a plastic substance from which the various structures of the seance room are built up. More exact scientific observation could only confirm what these pioneers had stated. (225)

9. Medium Mary Ann Marshall materializes the likeness of Sir Arthur Conan Doyle in a photograph taken by Dr. T.G. Hamilton (1932) (Hamilton Family Frond Collection, University of Manitoba)

Perhaps the earliest medium to present materializations to great public
notice was Eva Carrière, or Eva C. as she was usually called. The French
medium was investigated by Charles Richet, who published accounts
of her materializations and coined the term ectoplasm to describe
the emanations from various orifices of Eva's body. Conan Doyle, who
witnessed Eva's abilities on one occasion, describes the manifestation in
the *History of Spiritualism,*

> there oozed from the medium's mouth, ears, nose, eyes, and skin this
> extraordinary gelatinous material.... You can see this streaky, viscous stuff
> hanging like icicles from the chin, dripping down on to the body, and
> forming a white apron over the front, or projecting in shapeless lumps from the orifices of the face. When touched, or when undue light came upon it, it writhed back into the body as swiftly and stealthily as the tentacles of a hidden octopus. If it was seized and pinched the medium cried aloud. It would protrude through clothes and vanish again, leaving hardly any trace upon them. With the assent of the medium, a small piece was amputated. It dissolved in the box in which it was placed as snow would have done, leaving moisture and some large cells which might have come from a fungus. The microscope also disclosed epithelial cells from the mucous membrane in which the stuff seemed to originate. (231)

❛THERE OOZED FROM THE MEDIUM'S MOUTH, EARS, NOSE, EYES, AND SKIN THIS EXTRAORDINARY GELATINOUS MATERIAL.❜

Aware that his readers might wonder what this gooey substance had to
do with the spirit world, Conan Doyle went on to describe the behavior
of the ectoplasm exuded from Eva C. and other mediums. The substance,
after leaving the body of the medium, could 'curdle' into various shapes
and forms, including human limbs and human faces. First appearing
in a two-dimensional form, these ectoplasmic blobs continue to shape
themselves until they resemble three-dimensional representations of
the human body, though sometimes in miniature. On rare occasions
something even more remarkable happens: the entity rises and separates
itself from the medium. It can then move and talk, usually claiming to
be the ghost of a deceased man or woman, and often delivers messages
for those in attendance. Thus, half a century after the Fox sisters opened
the veil to the other world and received messages through mysterious

knocks, the connection between the worlds appeared to be even firmer. Now the spirits could take on material form and speak to their audience in their own words.

Conan Doyle confessed that the nature of ectoplasm remained a mystery, though he was prepared to offer his own opinion of the mysterious substance:

> Personally, the author is of opinion that several different forms of plasm with different activities will be discovered, the whole forming a science of the future which may well be called Plasmology. He believes also that all psychic phenomena external to the medium, including clairvoyance, may be traced to this source. Thus a clairvoyant medium may well be one who emits this or some analogous substance which builds up round him or her a special atmosphere that enables the spirit to manifest to those who have the power of perception. As the aerolite passing into the atmosphere of the earth is for a moment visible between two eternities of invisibility, so it may be that the spirit passing into the psychic atmosphere of the ectoplasmic medium can for a short time indicate its presence.... The reason why some people see a ghost and some do not may be that some furnish sufficient ectoplasm for a manifestation, and some do not, while the cold chill, the trembling, the subsequent faint, may be due not merely to terror but partly to the sudden drain upon the psychic supplies. (2006, 239)

Ectoplasm, according to Conan Doyle, provides a 'firm material basis for psychical research.' When the spiritual enters the material realm it must take material form in order to more directly and clearly register with our material senses. Ectoplasm explains why some people see ghosts and some do not, and even provides an explanation for the knocks heard by the Fox sisters and others. He wrote, '[I]t may at least be stated that the usual method of their production is by the extension of a rod of ectoplasm, which may or may not be visible, and by its percussion on some solid object' (239).

Conan Doyle and many others found in ectoplasm an approach to spiritualism that seemed compatible with the scientific methods of modernity. The survivor ghosts from primitive societies could thus be made to fit better into the contemporary world, and those who reject spiritualism and the ghostly as some form of primitive superstition out of date in the scientific age could themselves be accused of failing to accept the scientific proof for and explanations of the ghostly. As Eric G. Post wrote in *Communicating with the Beyond: A Practical Handbook of Spiritualism* in 1946:

One thing must be kept in mind: spiritualistic phenomena are *supernormal*, not *supernatural*. In other words, the various occurrences are not miracles but the manifestation of forces, powers and entities which are in many cases still unexplored and not always explicable as are other natural forces that we have come to know well and accept without questioning. As our knowledge of spiritualism grows, we learn to recognize these formerly unknown forces, and the day is probably not too far off when certain spiritualistic concepts will be as readily accepted as are those of radioactivity, electronics, and plastics today. (21)

Indeed, Post's analysis of communications with the beyond reads like a technical manual. He provides a laundry list of phenomena associated with spiritual contact during a séance or other similar activities: lights, breezes, raps and other sounds, scents, table tilting, movement of objects, levitation, change of weight, elongation of the human body, touches, apports and deports, ectoplasm, spirit fingerprints, materializations, spirit photography, automatic writing, mirror writing, writing in foreign languages, automatic drawing and painting, movement of a planchette, Ouija board phenomena, slate writing, trances, xenoglossy and direct voice phenomena, to name but

10. The 'Brown Lady' of Raynham Hall, Norfolk, England (1936).

a few. Each phenomenon is carefully defined and catalogued. Then Post provides his readers with a 'how-to' guide: How to Develop Your Psychic Powers; How to Form a Private Circle and How to Conduct Private Séances, complete with table tilting, automatic writing, planchette writing, Ouija board and glass writing, trance speaking, direct-voice and trumpet speaking, and materializations.

Such a trend is emphasized even more clearly in the more recent writing of Elaine Kuzmeskus, whose introduction to the subject is actually entitled *Séance 101*. Rooted in the American spiritualist camp movement of the early twentieth century and the structured spiritualism of spiritualist churches, Kuzmeskus' approach to interactions with the spirits does indeed read like a camp training manual or seminary textbook. Spiritualism, for her, clearly comprises a body of knowledge and a system of techniques to be learned and mastered.

What does it mean when ghosts become the subjects of textbooks? Are they still scary? Do they still frighten us to the core, make us shake in our boots, cause us to wet our pants? Tylor was right: ghosts are survivors, in more ways than one. But they do not survive unchanged; they are but a shadow of what they once were. Conan Doyle was right: Swedenborg and the Fox sisters did open doorways that allowed the spirits to enter our world, our world of science and technology. Swedenborg included specters in his systematic theology, providing an explanation for visions and haunting. The Fox sisters took the strange noises that awaken us at night, the noises that cause us to look in the closets and under the beds, and systematized them, converted them into an alphabet, and the spirits from the other side spoke more clearly than ever before – but only to reveal that they too were just as uninteresting and humdrum as the average living, breathing human being. Even ectoplasm, gooey, slimy, sticky, ectoplasm, vomited from the mouth of mediums, oozing from their ears and eyes and noses, even ectoplasm was explained as the perfectly rational means of contact between our material world and the spiritual one. When photographed, ectoplasm looks even worse, like tissue or balls of cotton with glued-on faces, like sock puppets, or downscale muppets.

So ghosts do survive, but they do not always maintain their power of fright, their ability to terrorize. If we can talk to Condie through a series of raps and materializations, if she can appear before us in three dimensions composed of ectoplasm and tell us how she is doing, will she have anything interesting to say, will she continue to terrorize us? I am reminded of the old truism about horror movies that says that the more clearly you can see the monster, the less scary it is, no matter how detailed and believable the special effects may be. It is the unknown that terrorizes, the unseen that sends shivers down the spine. We don't encounter the *mysterium tremendum* by having Condie over for tea, but when we catch a fleeting glimpse of her blazing through the night. For the ghost to be holy, perhaps it must be aflame, burning like the bush in the desert, above its head tongues of fire. Perhaps its words are best heard, not around a parlor table, but at a burning altar in the deep darkness, a glowing hearth struggling to give heat on a frigid night, or a blazing campfire that casts more shadows than light.

Ghost stories seem to arise, like the phoenix, like Condie Cunningham, from fire. It seems natural to tell tales of haunts and haints while gathered around the fire, its circle of flickering light making the darkness beyond just that much darker. Around the fire we tell tales of spurned lovers bent on revenge, of lost children come face to face with the dead, of specters that walk the night seeking vengeance and redemption. Babies dropped into rolling rivers wail through the centuries from haunted bridges, ghost dogs prowl for their lost masters, the spirits of Indian braves seek eternal vengeance, jilted brides seek lost lovers to join them on the ghostly shore. The tales are told to children at summer camp. They are told by teenage boys to teenage girls parked at the outskirts of town. They are passed from one teller to another, or made up out of whole cloth as the situation demands. Their purpose, of course, is to evoke a shiver of fear, to make the heart race, the eyes peer into the darkness for any sign of movement, for the glow of eyeshine in the depths of the night.

The first volume of ghost stories by classic writer of English ghost tales, M.R. James, was *Ghost Stories of an Antiquary*, a collection of tales written to share with family and friends around Christmas fires, in those days when such tales of horror were told during the winter festival rather than at Halloween, when there were other ghosts of Christmas than those frighteners from Dickens' pen. James' purpose, he claimed, was not to present literary masterpieces, but rather stories to produce shudders in his readers. He wrote, 'If any of them succeed in causing their readers to feel pleasantly uncomfortable when walking along a solitary road at nightfall, or sitting over a dying fire in the small hours, my purpose in writing them will have been attained' (viii).

The ghostly short story, whether from the pen of M.R. James, Ambrose Bierce, Algernon Blackwood, Mark Twain, Edgar Allan Poe, Oscar Wilde, Henry James or Charles Dickens, captures the eeriness of the long-form Gothic novel and condenses it, like ectoplasm, into a form more closely resembling the ghostly folktale. It is the literary equivalent of the tales told 'round the fire.' It is also the cultural form in which the ghost has most assuredly flourished in modern times, seeding other genres such as comic books and films along the way. The pantheon of ghosts that swirl through our nights are most often the spirits of the literary imagination. Some of them, like Washington Irving's headless horsemen thundering down the roadway after Ichabod Crane or Marley's ghost, burdened with chains, rattling along the hallway, are readily identifiable characters in the cast of Western popular culture. Most, however, whirl together into a spectral cloud, like the ghosts from the Ark of the Covenant opened by Indiana Jones, indistinguishable from one another but haunting us nonetheless.

Not that all of the literary ghost tales are of the same value. Some are clearly better than others. Some have clearly become ghosts themselves, refusing to die, but walking the world beyond their appointed time, reaching through the mist to touch us still with their chilly bony hands and to call forth others of their like: a horde of imitators, of disciples, of children that greet us on page and screen. Henry James' *The Turn of the Screw* from 1898 is such a ghost story. Unsurprisingly, it too had its birth in fire. It is fire around which the characters in the opening scene are gathered: 'The story had held us, round the fire, sufficiently breathless, but except that the obvious remark that it was gruesome, as, on Christmas Eve in an old house, a strange tale certainly should be' (283). It was also fire that first brought ghosts into the world of Henry James.

His father, Henry James, Sr., also the father of the psychologist-philosopher William James, was burned by fire. As a teenager, James, Sr. suffered severe burns on one leg, resulting finally in its amputation above the knee. Bedridden for three years, his incurable pain led him to alcohol abuse and contributed to a deep depression that haunted him all of his life. As an adult he fell under the sway of Swedenborgian philosophy, especially the belief that the material world is in constant contact with the spiritual, that life is shaped by the ongoing interactions between the two realms. He came to believe that his pain and suffering were the

> ❛HE CAME TO BELIEVE THAT HIS PAIN AND SUFFERING WERE THE RESULT OF THE MEDDLING OF MALICIOUS GHOSTS AND EVIL SPIRITS.❜

result of the meddling of malicious ghosts and evil spirits. Whenever his family members, including young Henry, Jr. and William, suffered from illness or distress, James was certain that some ghostly entity was at fault.

The fire that had consumed his leg scarred his soul and traumatized his life, although surely a physical fire, was also a fire from the beyond, a fire controlled by the spirits, unholy ghosts at play.*

It is not surprising, then, that the fire that burned their father's soul would also sear the lives of Henry, Jr. and William, nor is it surprising that they would both be attracted to the ghostly, drawn to the flames like moths to a candle. William, in particular, spent much of his time, energy and professional reputation on a quest to understand the nature of spiritualist phenomena. His classic work on religion, *The Varieties of Religious Experience*, is in many ways an attempt to reject Tylor's survival theory, namely that religion – including belief in the supernatural – is but a holdover from a more primitive phase of culture, a more primitive form of thinking that is best transcended and left behind. Religion, William believed, without regard to the truth or falsity of its intellectual content, plays important roles in human life, not the least of which is what he called the 'common nucleus' of all religion, the feeling of uneasiness and its solution. William believed that this uneasiness and solution took on moral qualities in its most developed form. The uneasiness is of our own imperfection and flaws, the solution something like a unifying experience with 'a MORE of some quality.' (508) As to what the MORE might consist of, he claimed a kind of agnosticism. This MORE is, at the very least, connected to the subconscious realm of our own lives; whether or not it goes beyond that, he was unprepared to say. In much the same way, his brother Henry created his masterpiece of psychological terror by leaving the nature of the haunting in *The Turn of the Screw* unclear: as possibly just the product of the demented mind of the narrator, possibly something more.

The Turn of the Screw is the story of a young woman's descent into terror as she assumes responsibility for the care of two orphaned children at a large country estate. The children seem wonderful and well behaved, except that the older of the two, a young boy named Miles, is inexplicably expelled from his boarding school. In the course of time, the young woman begins to see spectral images of a man and a woman, apparently the ghosts of the former governess and her lover, another former employee of the estate. Slowly, the young woman learns of the illicit affair between the two and of their affection for the children, Miles and his young sister Flora.

---

* See Deborah Blum's *Ghost Hunters: William James and the Search for Scientific Proof of Life After Death* for a complete account of the James family and their relationship to the spiritualist movement.

She becomes convinced that the spectral couple have returned to lead the children down their own evil path, or to take them as their own ghostly offspring. Though the behavior of the children remains almost perfect, the young woman believes that they are a part of the plot, anxious to follow the ghosts wherever they might lead them.

Throughout the novella, James elicits fear, not through direct descriptions of anything horrible, but through the narrator's first-hand reports of her internal states, her emotions and her fears. When she observes the strange figure of a man from afar, she says,

> It was as if, while I took in – what I did take in – all the rest of the scene had been stricken with death. I can hear again, as I write, the intense hush in which the sounds of evening dropped. The rooks stopped cawing in the golden sky, and the friendly hour lost, for the minute, all its voice. But there was no other change in nature, unless indeed it were a change that I saw with a stranger sharpness. The gold was still in the sky, the clearness in the air, and the man who looked at me over the battlements was as definite as a picture in a frame. That's how I thought, with extraordinary quickness, of each person that he might have been and that he was not. We were confronted across our distance quite long enough for me to ask myself with intensity who then he was and to feel, as an effect of my inability to say, a wonder that in a few instants more became intense. (303)

On another occasion she encounters the man's specter on a stairway. She describes it this way:

> It was the dead silence of our long gaze at such close quarters that gave the whole horror, huge as it was, its only note of the unnatural. If I had met a murderer in such a place and at such an hour, we still at least would have spoken. Something would have passed, in life, between us; if nothing had passed, one of us would have moved. The moment was so prolonged that it would have taken but little more to make me doubt if even *I* were in life. I can't express what followed it save by saying that the silence itself which was indeed in a manner an attestation of my strength – became the element into which I saw the figure disappear; in which I definitely saw it turn as I might have seen the low wretch to which it had once belonged turn on receipt of an order, and pass, with my eyes on the villainous back that no hunch could have more disfigured, straight down the staircase and into the darkness in which the next bend was lost. (334–5)

Later, the young woman confesses her fears about the children to Mrs. Grose, the housekeeper. She says to her, 'No, no – there are depths, depths!

The more I go over it, the more I see in it, and the more I see in it, the more I fear. I don't know what I *don't* see – what I *don't* fear'(322).

Throughout, the reader is left perplexed as to the reality of the visions. Are they real ghosts? Has the governess uncovered the children's sinister secret? Or, is everything simply a fantasy of a disturbed mind, a mind that sees people when they are not there and looks for evil motives in the smiles of innocent children? The narrator repeatedly confesses that it is what she doesn't see that scares her, that it is strange silence, rather than loud knockings, that terrifies her. Is this a sign that she is seeing ghosts when there is nothing there or a clue to us that silence can be eerie, that absence can itself indicate presence?

Similar themes are explored in another classic ghost tale, Shirley Jackson's *The Haunting of Hill House*. In this book, a group of psychic investigators plan to spend the summer in a house notorious for its ghostly presences. The house does not disappoint. The investigators experience knockings and poundings of a sort far less polite than those heard by the Fox sisters. Messages are scrawled on walls. Rooms and wardrobes are covered in blood. Though all of the investigators experience some of the phenomena, the character of Eleanor has experiences that go beyond the others. The author raises a question over Eleanor's sanity. Do her experiences exist only in her own mind, or – an even more sinister alternative – are the phenomena the result of some strange power that she possesses? Does she somehow open the door for the spirits to enter or are the spirits themselves just reflections of her own subconscious mind, her own ghosts materialized, so to speak, within the walls of Hill House?

Like *The Turn of the Screw*, *The Haunting of Hill House* provides the possibility of a psychological interpretation of ghosts. But, because of the ambiguity that is a central part of the stories, neither one seems to offer this interpretation as a comfort to the readers. Both assume, rightly, that psychological horrors can be as terrible as real ones, that ghosts of the mind are ghosts still. Perhaps, if we can see the scientific study of spirits, like that proposed by Conan Doyle, as an attempt to find a place in the modern world for these ghostly survivors from an earlier age, then we can also see the psychologizing of ghosts in the same way. Neither approach is meant to solve the problem of ghosts, to send them away or to help belief in them pass away into the past. Rather, both represent ghosts extending their territory, haunting where they have not haunted before, in the scientific laboratory and the unconscious mind.

* * *

The Haunting of Hill House is, of course, first and foremost a haunted house story. It is not surprising, I suppose, that many tales of ghosts are tales of haunted houses, whether they be Gothic mansions, lonely cabins or un-rentable apartments. As Algernon Blackwood wrote in 1906 in his short story 'The Empty House',

> Certain houses, like certain persons, manage somehow to proclaim at once their character for evil. In the case of the latter, no particular feature need betray them; they may boast an open countenance and an ingenuous smile; and yet a little of their company leaves the unalterable conviction that there is something radically amiss with their being: that they are evil. Willy nilly, they seem to communicate an atmosphere of secret and wicked thoughts which makes those in their immediate neighbourhood shrink from them as from a thing diseased.
>
> And, perhaps, with houses the same principle is operative, and it is the aroma of evil deeds committed under a particular roof, long after the actual doers have passed away, that makes the gooseflesh come and the hair rise. Something of the original passion of the evil-doer, and of the horror felt by his victim, enters the heart of the innocent watcher, and he becomes suddenly conscious of tingling nerves, creeping skin, and a chilling of the blood. He is terror-stricken without apparent cause. (1–2)

❮IT IS THE AROMA OF EVIL DEEDS COMMITTED UNDER A PARTICULAR ROOF, LONG AFTER THE ACTUAL DOERS HAVE PASSED AWAY, THAT MAKES THE GOOSEFLESH COME AND THE HAIR RISE.❯

Likewise, Shirley Jackson described Hill House,

> No live organism can continue for long to exist sanely under conditions of absolute reality; even larks and katydids are supposed, by some, to dream. Hill House, not sane, stood by itself against its hills, holding darkness within; it stood so for eighty years and might stand for eighty more. Within, walls continued upright, bricks met neatly, floors were firm, and doors were sensibly shut; silence lay steadily against the wood and stone of Hill House, and whatever walked there, walked alone. (3)

People inhabit houses, they live in them, fight in them, love in them, suffer in them, bleed in them, die in them. It is no mystery that ghosts should haunt in them.

11. Poster for *The House on Haunted Hill* (1959) (Allied Artists).

It is the haunted house, usually a rambling Victorian mansion but sometimes, quite effectively, a middle-class house in the suburbs, that has provided the most effective location for stories of ghosts on the big screen. Both Henry James' and Shirley Jackson's short novels have been adapted for film, *The Turn of the Screw* perhaps most effectively in the 1961 film *The Innocents*. *The Haunting of Hill House* was filmed in 1963 and again in 1999, each time under the title *The Haunting*, though only the first of these captured the ambiguity of the original novel. The stories' influence goes far beyond these adaptations, however. In the case of *The Haunting of Hill House* the influence can be seen with only a quick perusal of film titles.

The House on Haunted Hill, released the same year as Jackson's novel, is a B movie classic in the genre. This low-budget movie starred Vincent Price as millionaire Frederick Loren who offers ten thousand dollars to any of his guests who survive a night in a haunted mansion without electricity and with the doors all locked to prohibit anyone's leaving. The film is

12. Poster for *The Legend of Hell House* (1973) (Twentieth Century Fox Film Corporation).

atmospheric and spooky, even though it turns out that the real danger lurking in the house on the haunted hill is found in the people, not the ghosts. This film was remade in 1999, with Geoffrey Rush in the lead role and the award raised to a million dollars. Another similarly named film, *The Legend of Hell House*, was released in 1973 and based on the earlier novel, *Hell House*, by Richard Matheson. Like *The Haunting* and *The House on Haunted Hill*, the movie is centered around a team of investigators exploring a notorious haunted house in an attempt to prove the reality of life after death. The ghosts are definitely real in this film, though their identity remains mysterious until the end.

Arguably the most effective haunted house film is Stanley Kubrick's version of Stephen King's *The Shining*. Released in 1980, the film stars Jack Nicholson and Shelley Duvall. Unlike those movies in the tradition of Shirley Jackson's novel, the haunted in this film are not paranormal explorers who know what they are getting into. Instead, Nicholson and

13. Here's Johnny!
Jack Nicholson as Jack
Torrance in *The Shining*
(1980) (Warner Bros.)

Duvall play Jack and Wendy Torrance who, along with their son Danny (played by Danny Lloyd), are hired to be caretakers of a resort hotel during the winter off-season. Life in the lonely old hotel quickly turns dreary and boring for the family, however, and spirits of former tenants begin to show themselves. Danny, who has the gift of psychic powers, or 'the shining,' is particularly attracted to the ghosts in the house. Jack, a recovering alcoholic trying to use the time at the hotel to dry out and write a novel, is slowly driven mad by the spirits. Like *The Haunting of Hill House* and *The Turn of the Screw*, the ghosts here exist somewhere between the real world and the minds of the characters.

The haunted family made another memorable appearance in 1982's *Poltergeist*, directed by Tobe Hooper, who made a name for himself with the low-budget horror classic *The Texas Chainsaw Massacre*. In the film, the Freeling family faces a haunting by a poltergeist in their suburban southern California home. The poltergeist, a type of ghost known for tossing furniture around and causing household chaos, moves furniture, breaks glass and bends silverware. At first it all appears to be harmless fun. That, of course, soon changes. A tree becomes animated and crashes through a window to abduct a child. Another child disappears into her bedroom closet. True to the haunted house storyline, the family calls in a group of experts, including parapsychologists and a spirit medium – played memorably by Zelda Rubinstein – who determine the nature of the haunting and set out to rescue the girl.

Poltergeist has always been one of my favorite haunted house movies, mostly because of its familiar domestic setting, a setting that also proved effective in 2007's *Paranormal Activity*. As long as ghosts are kept at a safe distance, in old abandoned houses or empty hotels, their ability to frighten is limited. In *Poltergeist*, the doorway to the spirit world is located in a little girl's closet, something perhaps that all children have long known to be the case. In the film, spirits communicate through television screens instead of through crystal balls, and houses in the sunny hills of southern California are no less haunted than castles on the Scottish moors.

Haunted houses are, of course, not limited to fiction, whether on the written page, the movie screen or the pages of comic books such as DC's *House of Mystery* and *House of Secrets*. Haunted houses exist in the real world, their Gothic spires and dark interiors or their ranch-house blandness housing spirits. Just like in the books and the movies, they attract investigators and researchers, parapsychologists and mediums who seek, in long musty hallways, to make contact with the spirit world.

One of the most storied haunted houses is Borley Rectory in Essex, England: a house that attracted the attention of ghost hunter Harry Price (1881–1948). Price became famous in the early twentieth century as a ghost hunter and paranormal investigator. He was something of an amateur inventor and created various devices to assist in his research, including a 'telekinetescope,' a telegraph key placed under a glass dome that, when depressed, caused a red light to glow. Thus, he reasoned, only psychic powers could cause the bulb to light. He recorded temperature changes associated with hauntings as well as other physical phenomena, thus giving his research an air of scientific rigor. Price conducted multiple investigations of Borley Rectory and at one point leased the house for a year in order to perform a round-the-clock investigation. He advertised for researchers to join him at the house and record paranormal phenomena. Deluged with applications, he selected forty individuals to take turns staying in the house. Some brought their own specially designed equipment to use in the investigation along with equipment supplied by Price. Price reported hearing strange knockings and ringing sounds in the house, observing objects move from place to place and witnessing the materializations of a Catholic medal and other small religious objects.

Other observers reported messages scrawled on the walls and glass bottles materializing in the air and then falling shatteringly to the floor. From the very beginning of his investigation, Price attracted the attention of the press. When the results of his research were published in two books, *The Most Haunted House in England* (1940) and *The End of Borley Rectory* (1946), both became bestsellers and set the standard for haunted house research and for the many ghost hunters who followed in Price's steps, as well as for the tales of Shirley Jackson and others.

In recent years paranormal investigations have again become quite popular, due in large part to the television series *Ghost Hunters* on cable's SyFy Channel and its many imitators. The ghost hunters, led by Jason Hawes and Grant Wilson, are self-described 'plumbers by day and ghost hunters by night.' Like Harry Price, they use technical equipment to investigate haunted sites and record their findings. Their organization, TAPS or The Atlantic Paranormal Society, has affiliated organizations around the world, publishes *TAPS paraMagazine*, and has a website which offers encouragement and advice to other individuals and groups wishing to participate in paranormal investigations. Like Price before them, they record rapid temperature changes, weird sounds, unusual lights and moving objects, and they report even weirder phenomena occurring just out of reach of the camera or the microphone. Like Price, their quest to quantify and categorize the ghostly phenomena, to capture it on film and make it subject to scientific investigation, is always seemingly trumped by the ability of the specter to slip through their fingers like a mist. Even in the age of digital cameras and night-vision goggles, the secret of the haunted house remains hauntingly beyond reach.

Perhaps the most common type of haunting reported is the haunting of the poltergeist, an entity whose behavior is described in ways that make it seem as if its very purpose is to befuddle the investigators, surprise the researchers and bring terror to all who enter its circle. The poltergeist is described as an energetic force known for its physical manifestations, rather than its spectral appearances. The poltergeist throws stones, stinks, moans, rings bells, knocks, speaks, materializes and dematerializes objects and makes objects sail through the air – just the sorts of phenomena ghost hunters have reported in haunted houses. Poltergeists, however, are not just ghostly practical jokers and nuisances, but something far more malicious. Poltergeists do not just terrorize by their unexpected appearances or by their strange unidentifiable sounds. Sometimes they terrorize by fire.

Psychical researcher Raymond Bayless wrote, in his classic study of the phenomena, *The Enigma of the Poltergiest* (1967),

Here we have an apparent contradiction of a favorite belief which assumes that poltergeist phenomena is harmless, and seldom, if ever, resulting in serious injury and really is rather amusing after all. This cheerful view soon assumes somber tones when the actual histories of many cases are reviewed, and a very formidable figure indeed comes into view. There is a considerable body of evidence which clearly indicates that the poltergeist can be a savage and fearful enemy, possessing grim and mysterious powers. (3–4)

Fire, according to Bayless, is one of the favorite playthings for a poltergeist. He reported that fires are generally present, in one way or another, in all major poltergeist cases. Poltergeists have been known to set furniture ablaze, to start house fires, to hurl burning peat inside a house, to place hot stones in beds to burn through the bedding, to throw burning straw and to materialize fireballs. Most gruesome of all the fiery effects attributed to the poltergeist by Bayless, however, is the phenomenon of human combustion, in which a person's body is consumed by intense fire while leaving most of their surroundings untouched. Ghosts, for Bayless, are no laughing matter. They can not only frighten, but also kill. He describes the July 1951 death of a Mrs. Reeser:

> Mrs. Reeser, a woman of one hundred and seventy pounds, had almost entirely been consumed by flames of unknown origin and the residue left consisted of her skull, fantastically shrunken in size, her left foot, and a number of seared vertebrae. . . .
>
> Evidence of the fierce flames which had destroyed Mrs. Reeser was found in the fact that the walls of her room were blackened by a greasy deposit of soot. The chair in which she had been sitting was almost totally burned, a mirror on a wall cracked by the tremendous heat of the blaze, and many other indications of the fierce fire were evident. (107)

Perhaps Condie ran screaming through Mrs. Reeser's living room, her blazing hair igniting the woman's clothes, its ghostly flame burning with the fires of hell, its ectoplasmic energies cooking, like a microwave oven, from the inside out.

Ghosts haunt.

E.B. Tylor wrote, 'The nobler tendency of advancing culture, and above all of scientific culture, is to honour the dead without grovelling before them, to profit by the past without sacrificing the present to it.' Just because something has a long pedigree in human history, he argued, does not make it necessarily a true or a good thing. Just because humans have always seen ghosts, and seeing ghosts led them to believe in gods, it does not mean that we should continue to do so today. We can honor what has gone before without blindly following the past's examples. Tylor's sentiment was a common sentiment in the heady days of the nineteenth century, when science seemed to have such a glorious and pure future and when superstition was thought soon to be a thing of the past. Ghosts and gods would quickly be forgotten, cast aside as primitive relics of primitive minds and primitive cultures. He should have known better.

Ghosts haunt.

When human beings watch their loved ones give up the ghost and breathe their last, when they lay their dead in the ground and cover them with flowers, the dead are not gone. They always return. They always will. Tylor saw this in primitive cultures and advanced, in ancient magic and modern spiritualism. Human lives mean too much for us to let them go at death. Our fathers and mothers, brothers and sisters, sons and daughters leave lasting impressions on our brains, lasting images on our corneas, lasting touches on our hearts. They always have, they always will. Tylor should have known better.

‹WHEN HUMAN LIVES END, THEY OFTEN END IN TRAGEDY, WITH DREAMS UNFULFILLED, WITH PASSIONS ENFLAMED.›

Ghosts haunt.

When human lives end, they often end in tragedy, with dreams unfulfilled, with passions enflamed. Captain Reynolds died with guilt, and so his ghost must guard the night. Mr. King died full of greed, and so his ghost must search for eternity. Condie, Condie died in the flame of youth – she burned out too quickly – and so continues to burn, flames like auburn tresses streaming behind her down the hallways of Main Hall.

Ghosts haunt.

They give us warnings of how not to live and how not to die. They give us patterns to follow and patterns to avoid. They whisper messages to us that they could not deliver in the flesh, knocking out the words that they can no longer speak.

Ghosts haunt.

When science calls them illusions, they haunt the test tubes, they sprout ectoplasmic appendages, they retreat to the dark corners of the human mind. They pass from tales told around a campfire, to stories tucked inside pulp magazines, to movie screens. They appear on television screens instead of in crystal balls. They may fade and wither under the glare of modern lights, be reduced to just another set of data in a researcher's notebook, but they are survivors. Primitive or advanced, ghosts haunt.

As long as humans stand in awe at their own mortality, at the mortality of the throngs of humans that walk and have walked this earth, as long as death remains a mystery, an unknown, then we will tremble before it. The ghost need not shout 'Boo!' to make us afraid. A human being was alive; now they are dead. This is frightening enough.

Perhaps Tylor was right. Perhaps religion did have its origins in ghostly visions and haunted dreams. But it need not be the result of some mistaken hypothesis on the part of primitives that ghostly apparitions provide evidence for the existence of some sort of 'apparitional-soul' inside every man, woman and child, a mistake that results in the elevation of the souls of some of the deceased to the status of godhood. Perhaps it is even more primitive than that, and thus even more universal.

Rudolf Otto wrote,

> The German expression *Es spukt hier* (literally, it haunts here) is also instructive. It has properly no true subject, or at least it makes no assertion as to what the *es*, the 'it', is which 'haunts'; in itself it contains no suggestion of the concrete representations of 'ghost', 'phantom', 'spectre', or 'spirit' common to popular mythology. Rather is the statement simply the pure expression of the emotion of 'eerieness' or 'uncanniness' itself. (127)

Perhaps religion has its origin in ghostly visions and haunted dreams because the ghost – the flickering remnant of the dead, the see-through shadow of those gone from our lives, the flaming phantoms of those tragically taken – in all its forms forces us to confront death as mystery, as the unknown, as the wholly other, as that before which we shudder and shake, before whose presence we wish to run and never stop, like flaming Condie running down the hall, down the stairs, down the steps, forever and forever more.

It Was a Dark and Stormy Night 2

It was a dark and stormy night; the rain fell in torrents – except at occasional intervals, when it was checked by a violent gust of wind which swept up the streets . . ., rattling along the housetops, and fiercely agitating the scanty flame of the lamps that struggled against the darkness.

Edward George Bulwer-Lytton, *Paul Clifford*

The sky is changed! – and such a change! Oh night,
And storm, and darkness, ye are wondrous strong,
Yet lovely in your strength, as is the light
Of a dark eye in woman! Far along,
From peak to peak, the rattling crags among
Leaps the live thunder! Not from one lone cloud
But every mountain now hath found a tongue,
And Jura answers, through a misty shroud,
Back to the joyous Alps who call to her aloud!

And this is in the night: – Most glorious night!
Thou wert not sent for slumber! let me be
A sharer in thy fierce and far delight, –
A portion of the tempest and of thee!
How the lit lake shines, a phosphoric sea,
And the big rain comes dancing to the earth!
And now again 'tis black, – and now, the glee
Of the loud hills shakes with its mountain mirth,
As if they did rejoice o'er a young earthquake's birth.

Lord Byron, *Child Harold's Pilgrimage*, Canto III

It was a dark and stormy night.

Edward Bulwer-Lytton opened his novel *Paul Clifford* with these words and with them sought to evoke the despair and danger of the seedier parts of nineteenth-century London. It was on the dark and stormy night in question that the novel's eponymous hero, as a child of three, lost his mother and began a life of romance, adventure, crime, punishment, sorrow and pathos worthy of a character from the pages of a Gothic romance. Indeed, *Paul Clifford* is a quintessential Gothic romance. It is neither the best nor the worst of the genre, quite popular in its day but now mostly forgotten – mostly forgotten, that is, except for the opening line. 'It was a dark and stormy night' is one of the best-known opening lines in English literature, parodied by Charles Schulz' *Peanuts* (it is the first line of Snoopy's perpetual novel-in-progress) and commemorated by a contest in its honor, a contest challenging entrants to compose the opening line of the worst imaginable novel.

This notoriety, I suppose, is more than a little unfair to Bulwer-Lytton, who, although the author of a string of forgettable novels – including *Vril: The Power of the Coming Race*,* a hollow-earth science fiction classic influential to Theosophists and Nazis alike – did leave us with such catch-phrases as 'the pen is mightier than the sword' and 'the almighty dollar.' Furthermore, 'It was a dark and stormy night,' despite all of its bad press, isn't really that bad an opening line. (Neither is *Paul Clifford* really that bad a novel. It's bad – just not *that* bad.) The line suffers mostly from its association with the excesses of Gothic fiction of which it is not the worst, just the most famous example. What the line does for the contemporary reader is to place one in a particular Gothic context. Just as surely as 'once upon a time' is a signal that we are about to begin a fairy tale, probably complete with an ending of the 'happily ever after' variety, so 'dark and stormy night' is a cue that we are about to begin a story with more sinister elements: dark forbidding castles, thunder and lightning, bats and cobwebs, death and murder, terror and all things awful. For as much as the conventions of Gothic fiction, and 'dark and stormy night' is certainly one such convention, are satirized and made fun of, they also remain powerful, continuing to evoke the terror we feel, perhaps rooted in our primeval past, at deep darkness and midnight thunderstorms, flashing lightning and howling winds, a sky without moon or stars, a night without sleep.

---

* See Gregory L. Reece, *Weird Science and Bizarre Beliefs: Mysterious Creatures, Lost Worlds and Amazing Inventions* (London, I.B.Tauris, 2008) for a discussion of Bulwer-Lytton and Vril.

Lord Byron, dilettante, poet and sex symbol, wrote hymns of praise to such darkness and fury: 'The sky is changed! – and such a change!' he wrote of the midnight tempest. His words conjure up the darkness and storm far more profoundly than Bulwer-Lytton's: 'From peak to peak, the rattling crags among/Leaps the live thunder!' It was on such a night of thunderclap and lightning flash that Byron gathered around the hearth with his friends and companions. The summer of 1816 in Geneva was uncharacteristically cold and wet. 'The year without a summer' it was called, the sun's warmth blocked by clouds of volcanic ash spewing from Mount Tambora. It was weather fitted for huddling 'round the fire with Percy Shelley and the Godwin sisters, reading ghost stories and listening to the rain and thunder late into the dark, dark night. On one dark and stormy night, Lord Byron and his companions perhaps grew bored of seeking specters in musty old books. Might not a terror of their own imaginings be more frightening still?

It was, of course, from those midnight storms of the summer of 1816 that Mary Wollstonecraft Godwin (shortly to become Mary Shelley) drew the inspiration for her tale of science gone mad with power, of the patchwork dead man rising from the grave, of lightning and energy from the sky, elemental forces bringing life where there should be none, bringing terror to her companions and to her readers for generations to come. The scene was dramatized by James Whale in his undisputed classic film, *Bride of Frankenstein* (1935). The film opens on that drawing room in Geneva, Mary and Percy and Byron listening to the howling of the wind and the crack of the thunder. With dialogue that might better suit Bulwer-Lytton than the real Lord Byron, the black-and-white Byron speaks, 'The crudest, savage exhibition of Nature at her worst without, and we three, we elegant three within.' But Byron knows that all is not elegant in the drawing room; he knows there is savagery there as well, even in Mary who shivers at the sounds of the storm, and he is not so shy that he will not confront her with the truth:

‘CAN YOU BELIEVE THAT BLAND AND LOVELY BROW CONCEIVED OF FRANKENSTEIN?’

> Frightened of thunder, fearful of the dark. And yet you have written a tale that sent my blood into icy creeps . . . Can you believe that bland and lovely brow conceived of Frankenstein, a Monster created from cadavers out of rifled graves? . . . And it was these fragile white fingers that penned the nightmare.

Yes, it was from such a lovely brow that the monstrous came. Indeed, as the audience will later learn, it is the stunning Elsa Lanchester – her Mary Shelley more beautiful on film than in real life (in this sense the opposite of Gavin Gordon's Lord Byron) – who will play the bride of the monster, the she-creature brought forth by the tempest. Mary, showing but a glimpse of the power that is within her, is puzzled by Byron's remarks. She might shiver at the storm, but she does not shiver at the horror that came from her imagination: 'I feel like telling it,' she replies. 'It is a perfect night for mystery and horror. The air itself is filled with monsters.' Then Lord Byron speaks words that send shivers down the spine. 'I'm all ears,' he says. 'While heaven blasts the night without, open up your pits of hell.'

Mary Shelley's story is, of course, the story of her novel *Frankenstein: or, The Modern Prometheus*, a tale of dismembered corpses and mad science, a tale of life from death, a tale perfect for such a dark and stormy night. But Mary was not the only one to produce a tale of horror during that summer of darkness, though hers is certainly the most famous. Those gathered around the fire with Lord Byron included Percy Shelley, Mary and her stepsister Claire Clairmont and Byron's personal physician John Polidori. They were all challenged to produce a tale of terror as dark as the storm-clouded evening. Mary's would be the most influential and the most celebrated nightmare begun that night, but another tale would see publication first and would have a lasting impact all of its own.

This tale appeared in the April 1819 issues of the periodical *New Monthly Magazine*, falsely attributed to Lord Byron. It was influenced by an unpublished and unfinished piece by Byron, and Byron was clearly the model for the title character, but the tale was actually written by Dr. Polidori. The story was *The Vampyre*, and within its pages one can find the genesis of the modern vampire, the charming aristocrat rife with sexual energy and dark allure, as well as the template for all later vampire fiction, from *Dracula* to the *Twilight* series, a template distinguished by themes of dark sexuality and of blood.

Enter Polidori's vampire, Lord Ruthven:

> It happened that in the midst of the dissipations attendant upon a London winter, there appeared at the various parties of the leaders of the town a nobleman, more remarkable for his singularities, than his rank. He gazed upon the mirth around him, as if he could not participate therein. Apparently, the light laughter of the fair only attracted his attention, that he might by a look quell it, and throw fear into those breasts where thoughtlessness reigned. Those who felt this sensation of awe, could not explain whence

it arose: some attributed it to the dead grey eye, which, fixing upon the object's face, did not seem to penetrate, and at one glance to pierce through to the inward workings of the heart; but fell upon the cheek with a leaden ray that weighed upon the skin it could not pass. His peculiarities caused him to be invited to every house; all wished to see him, and those who had been accustomed to violent excitement, and now felt the weight of ennui, were pleased at having something in their presence capable of engaging their attention. In spite of the deadly hue of his face, which never gained a warmer tint, either from the blush of modesty, or from the strong emotion of passion, though its form and outline were beautiful, many of the female hunters after notoriety attempted to win his attentions, and gain, at least, some marks of what they might term affection. (27)

Ruthven was the toast of society precisely because of his seeming lack of interest. His allure was found in his mystery, in his inscrutable nature. He aroused the passion of London's women, not because of the lavish attention and flirtation that he heaped upon them, but because of the absence of these very things. There was something dark about Lord Ruthven, something unnerving about his cold demeanor, and it was this dark frigidity that drew people to him.

Among those entranced by the mystery of Ruthven was Aubrey, a young man of just the right age to be enamored with the worldliness of Ruthven. Arranging to travel with Ruthven in order to complete his education, Aubrey discovered that the secrets of Lord Ruthven went deeper than his surface appearance. Wherever Ruthven traveled he sought out the darker corners of society, the gambling halls and barrooms, and left a path of destruction in his wake. Ruthven encouraged the success of those already walking the path of evil and darkness and he tempted the young and the innocent into dangerous waters.

[H]is eyes sparkled with more fire than that of the cat whilst dallying with the half-dead mouse. In every town, he left the formerly affluent youth, torn from the circle he adorned, cursing, in the solitude of a dungeon, the fate that had drawn him within the reach of this fiend; whilst many a father sat frantic, amidst the speaking looks of mute hungry children, without a single farthing of his late immense wealth, wherewith to buy even sufficient to satisfy their present craving. (35)

Aubrey watched as Ruthven turned seemingly worthy beggars away empty handed while he gladly shared his wealth with those who sought only wickedness.

As if this was not enough to reveal the true character of Ruthven to young Aubrey, he soon received letters from London with disturbing news. It seems that Ruthven, while rejecting the advances of the most wanton women of London society, had instead focused his attention on befouling those of pure character. Upon his departure from London it was discovered that he had seduced many innocent girls. Soon, Aubrey witnessed Ruthven's seduction of the innocent first-hand, and decided to part from his company.

While traveling alone in Greece, Aubrey became enchanted with the daughter of the innkeeper with whom he was staying. The girl, Ianthe, warned Aubrey of the vampires that haunted the region, a warning that he chose to ignore. One evening, after the sun had set, Aubrey heard a woman's scream coming from a small structure in the forest. He ran to help, but was assaulted by an unseen attacker. Frightened by the approach of others who heard the screams, Aubrey's assailant fled. Unfortunately, Aubrey had been too late to save the vampire's victim, Ianthe.

> He shut his eyes, hoping that it was but a vision arising from his disturbed imagination; but he again saw the same form, when he unclosed them, stretched by his side. There was no colour upon her cheek, not even upon her lip; yet there was a stillness about her face that seemed almost as attaching as the life that once dwelt there: – upon her neck and breast was blood, and upon her throat were the marks of teeth having opened the vein: – to this the men pointed, crying, simultaneously struck with horror, 'A Vampyre! a Vampyre!' (48)

Still not aware that Ruthven was the culprit, Aubrey joined him again briefly before their partnership was shattered by thieves who murdered the older man. Before his passing, however, Ruthven secured a vow from Aubrey that his death would not be reported to his friends and acquaintances in England. Aubrey, not understanding, nevertheless made the vow of secrecy. Before Aubrey could bury the corpse, he discovered that Ruthven had made arrangements for his servants to place the body at the top of a nearby mountain so that 'it should be exposed to the first cold ray of the moon that rose after his death' (56). When Aubrey went to find the body and prepare it for burial, he discovered that it had mysteriously disappeared.

Aubrey returned to London with his sanity in tatters. Locked away by his family, he was only released to attend his sister's wedding. Shocked to discover that she was marrying none other than Lord Ruthven, he tried to stop the ceremony, but was dragged from the room and taken back to his quarters, his rage and terror resulting in a brain hemorrhage. It did not take the end long to come.

> Aubrey's weakness increased; the effusion of blood produced symptoms of the near approach of death. He desired his sister's guardians might be called, and when the midnight hour had struck, he related composedly what the reader has perused – he died immediately after.
> The guardians hastened to protect Miss Aubrey; but when they arrived, it was too late. Lord Ruthven had disappeared, and Aubrey's sister had glutted the thirst of a VAMPYRE! (71)

Polidori's Lord Ruthven, the first modern vampire and the grandfather of so many vampires to come, thus established important features of the vampire story. The vampire rises from the dead and drinks the blood of others, elements derived from folklore and mythology. But the modern vampire is also a playboy and socialite, the toast of society, a suave seducer of women.

Filmmaker Ken Russell dramatized that dark and stormy Geneva night, and the dark and stormy nature of Byron's personality, in his 1986 film *Gothic*, a film that revels in the dark, sinister and macabre aspects of

14. Natasha Richardson as Mary Shelley, and Gabriel Byrne as Lord Byron in Ken Russell's *Gothic* (1986) (Virgin Vision).

Byron's sexuality. Natasha Richardson played a once-again too beautiful Mary Shelley alongside Gabriel Byrne's vampiric and sexually threatening Byron. Over the course of the strange night – a night haunted by the demons of opium, lust and unbridled imagination – Byron and his guests conjure up dark forces that threaten their very sanity. Their imagination, in the words of Julian Sands as Percy Shelley, gave life to 'a creature, a creation, a jigsaw of all our worst fears in flesh and blood.' The creature of the night, taking varied forms and shapes for each member of the party, is at its heart Byron himself, his seductive allure claiming not only Mary's stepsister Claire but Percy and Polidori as well. In Russell's film Shelley is a vampire, asking Mary, 'would the smooth neck of a woman be so desirable were it not for our secret wish to see upon it a trickle of blood?'

Polidori's tale of Ruthven, Russell's movie seems to say, may be truer than we imagine. Lord Byron provided the germ of the story that Polidori completed, but he did much more than that. He provided the pattern of the vampire, the handsome, exotic, mysterious man of the world, a sexual predator as much as a drinker of blood. Bela Lugosi in evening dress and cape, Gary Oldman with top hat and cane, Robert Pattinson as Edward in t-shirt and denim jacket were each in their own way playing Lord Byron when they put on the fangs for the movie cameras. Thanks to Byron, and Polidori and Ruthven, the modern vampire is a creature as at home in the drawing room as in the crypt, a creature that combines death with sexuality, the pounding heart of fear with the pounding heart of desire.

It was not always so.

The vampires that enthralled Polidori and Byron first burst forth from their crypts and into popular imagination at the beginning of the eighteenth century. Though belief in revenants, reanimated corpses that creep from the grave to wreak havoc on the living, was long a part of European folklore, it was only in the 1700s that reports of these revenants began to take on a form recognizable as the modern vampire. Indeed, during this time Europe experienced what is sometimes called a 'vampire outbreak,' when reports of undead corpses drinking the blood of the living proliferated.

French Benedictine scholar Augustine Calmet described the outbreak in his *The Phantom World* of 1746.

> In this age, a new scene presents itself to our eyes and has done for about sixty years in Hungary, Moravia, Silesia and Poland; men, it is said, who have been dead for several months, come back to earth, talk, walk,

infest villages, ill use both men and beasts, suck the blood of their near relations, destroy their health and finally cause their death; so that people can only save themselves from their dangerous visits and their hauntings, by exhuming them, impaling them, cutting off their heads, tearing out their hearts, or burning them. These are called by the name of oupires or vampires, that is to say. (vol. 2, 2)

Before this time revenants were usually without two characteristics common to the modern vampire: a body that does not suffer decomposition and a thirst for human blood. Until the early eighteenth century, folklore was plagued by troublesome corpses who refused to stay dead. Their decaying bodies walked the streets at night, spreading disease and filling the air with their foul odors. Often the corpses were exhumed and cremated, or vital organs were removed, in order to ensure that they would no longer haunt the living. The 'new scene' that Calmet described, however, was different.

They make their appearance from noon to midnight, and come and suck the blood of living men and animals in such abundance that sometimes it flows from them at the nose, and principally at the ears, and sometimes the corpse swims in its own blood oozed out in its coffin . . . This reviving being, or oupire, comes out of his grave, or a demon in his likeness, goes by night to embrace and hug violently his near relations or his friends, and sucks their blood so much as to weaken and attenuate them, and at last cause their death. This persecution does not stop at one single person; it extends to the last person of the family, if the course be not interrupted by cutting off the head or opening the heart of the ghost whose corpse is found in his coffin, yielding, flexible, swollen, and rubicund, although he may have been dead some time. (vol. 2, 52)

One of the earliest accounts of a bloodsucking vampire is the story of Peter Plogojowitz, a Serbian who died in 1725. According to the official government report, a series of deaths following closely upon Plogojowitz's burial led the public to suspect that he was a vampire. Before they died, some of the victims reported that he had come to them in their sleep. Paul Barber reproduces the reports in his excellent book *Vampires, Burial, and Death: Folklore and Reality*.

And since with such people (which they call vampires) various signs are to be seen that is, the body undecomposed, the skin, hair, beard, and nails growing - the subjects resolved unanimously to open the grave of Peter Plogojowitz and to see if such above-mentioned signs were really to be found on him. (Barber, 6)

The government official went on to describe his personal observation of
the exhumation:

> Since I could not hold these people from the resolution they had made,
> either with good words or with threats, I went to the village of Kisilova,
> taking along the Gradisk priest, and viewed the body of Peter Plogojowitz,
> just exhumed, finding, in accordance with thorough truthfulness, that first
> of all I did not detect the slightest odor that is otherwise characteristic of
> the dead, and the body, except for the nose, which was somewhat fallen
> away, was completely fresh. The hair and beard – even the nails, of which
> the old ones had fallen away – had grown on him; the old skin, which
> was somewhat whitish, had
> peeled away, and a new one
> had emerged from it. The face,
> hands, and feet and the whole
> body were so constituted,
> that they could not have been
> more complete in his lifetime.
> Not without astonishment, I
> saw some fresh blood in his
> mouth, which, according to
> the common observation, he
> had sucked from the people killed by him. In short, all the indications
> were present that such people (as remarked above) are said to have. After
> both the priest and I had seen this spectacle, while people grew more
> outraged than distressed, all the subjects, with great speed, sharpened a
> stake – in order to pierce the corpse of the deceased with it – and put
> this at his heart, whereupon, as he was pierced, not only did much blood,
> completely fresh, flow also through his ears and mouth, but still other wild
> signs (which I pass by out of high respect) took place. Finally, according
> to their usual practice, they burned the often mentioned body, in his case,
> to ashes of which I inform the most laudable Administration, and at the
> same time would like to request, obediently and humbly, that if a mistake
> was made in this matter, such is to be attributed not to me but to the
> rabble, who were beside themselves with fear. (6–7)

> **❛. . . ALL THE SUBJECTS, WITH
> GREAT SPEED, SHARPENED A
> STAKE – IN ORDER TO PIERCE
> THE CORPSE OF THE DECEASED
> WITH IT – AND PUT THIS AT HIS
> HEART . . .❜**

Perhaps an even more famous story form the time is the account of
Arnold Paole, a former Serbian soldier whose death and undeath resulted
in an official investigation and report, *Visum et Repertum*. As with Plogojowitz, Paole's death was followed by others, and reports were made that
the dead man had returned from the grave. It was recounted that Paole
himself had been troubled by a vampire and had 'eaten from the earth of

the vampire's grave and had smeared himself with the vampire's blood' in order to protect himself from the villain. Apparently, however, these measures did not work. Paul Barber provides a translation of the report.

> In order to end this evil, they dug up this Arnold Paole 40 days after his death – this on the advice of a soldier, who had been present at such events before; and they found that he was quite complete and undecayed, and that fresh blood had flowed from his eyes, nose, mouth, and ears; that the shirt, the covering, and the coffin were completely bloody; that the old nails on his hands and feet, along with the skin, had fallen off, and that new ones had grown; and since they saw from this that he was a true vampire, they drove a stake through his heart, according to their custom, whereby he gave an audible groan and bled copiously, Thereupon they burned the body the same day to ashes and threw these into the grave. These people say further that all those who were tormented and killed by the vampire must themselves become vampires. (Barber, 16)

In order to stop the spread of the contagion, the bodies of Paole's four victims were also exhumed and destroyed in the same way.

This was not a sufficient remedy, however: the report states that some five years later a series of deaths in the village seemed to indicate that there was, once again, a vampire among them. It was suspected that since Paole was known to have attacked cattle as well as people, and since the meat from the cattle was subsequently eaten by villagers, the disease might have been spread in that way. When those who had eaten the tainted meat passed away, they returned as vampires themselves. Once again graves were opened and bodies exhumed and examined. These people were also found to exhibit signs of vampirism, namely an undecayed state and large amounts of apparently fresh blood.

From these accounts and many others from the period a picture of the vampire arises that is quite different from the Hollywood version. This undead creature, though less decayed than might have been expected, did show some signs of decomposition. Plogojowitz, for example, was missing part of his nose. Others had sloughed off their old skin and replaced it with new. Some accounts held that vampires would chew on their own flesh until they discovered a way out of their graves, sometimes reducing their hands to stumps. Instead of the pale complexion of Bela Lugosi, vampires were often described as ruddy, their color a sign that they had been drinking blood. Likewise, instead of thin wraith-like creatures, they were often bloated, filled with blood, like ticks about to burst. Some accounts of vampires describe them as beings without bones, nothing more than blood-filled sacks, walking under the power of the devil. When their graves were opened, they did not lie in stately repose but were covered in blood that flowed from their eyes and ears and nose, soaking the ground around them and exploding from them when their bodies were punctured by their slayers.

Polidori's Vampyre brought fear to his victims. It was a fear that festered in drawing rooms and parlors: a fear of moral debauchery, of ethical collapse, of sexuality free of society's strictures. Lord Byron was the perfect prototype. The vampires of folklore, however, brought a more primitive terror. The vampire preyed upon the fear of darkness at a time when darkness was deep, when a cloud-filled stormy sky could hide the hand in front of the face and when strangers could creep unseen to your bedside. The vampire preyed upon the fear of disease at a time when disease was even more devastating than it is today. It was dread of a disease that could strike a community unannounced and kill without mercy. The vampire of folklore preyed upon the fear of death at a time when death was

‹THE VAMPIRE PREYED UPON THE FEAR OF DARKNESS AT A TIME WHEN DARKNESS WAS DEEP, WHEN A CLOUD-FILLED STORMY SKY COULD HIDE THE HAND IN FRONT OF THE FACE AND WHEN STRANGERS COULD CREEP UNSEEN TO YOUR BEDSIDE.›

up close and personal. Today the bodies of our loved ones are embalmed, made up to look as good as in life, buried in comfort, placed deep in the ground surrounded by steel or concrete. But in the days of the vampire decay was plain to see. Shallow graves and scavengers brought the corpse to the surface, brought the smell to the nose, the horror to the eyes. People could see what happened to their loved ones after they died. They could watch them decay like rotting meat.

The stories of Plogojowitz and Paole, along with other tales of blood-sucking vampires, caught the attention of polite – and as it turned out, not so polite – society. The foreign and exotic quality of the tales struck a chord with the romantic imagination of Western Europe and soon inspired the birth of the literary vampire, a creature sexualized from its beginning. As early as 1748, German Heinrich August Ossenfelder's *Der Vampir* stalked a maiden who had rejected him because of her obedience to her mother's piety.

And as softly thou art sleeping
To thee shall I come creeping
And thy life's blood drain away.
And so shalt thou be trembling
For thus shall I be kissing
And death's threshold thou' it be crossing
With fear, in my cold arms.
And last shall I thee question
Compared to such instruction
What are a mother's charms?

In 1797, Goethe's *The Bride of Corinth* also featured a vampire as a protagonist, this time a woman who returned from the grave to seek her lover.

From my grave to wander I am forc'd,
Still to seek The God's long-sever'd link,
Still to love the bridegroom I have lost,
And the life-blood of his heart to drink.

In 1813, Lord Byron himself published the epic *The Giaour*, in which a Christian soldier slain in Muslim Turkey was cursed to return as a vampire.

But first, on earth as Vampire sent,
Thy corpse shall from its tomb be rent:
Then ghastly haunt thy native place,
And suck the blood of all thy race;
There from thy daughter, sister, wife,
At midnight drain the stream of life;
Yet loathe the banquet which perforce
Must feed thy livid living corpse.

Lord Byron, of course, had more influence on the literary vampire through the work of Polidori, where he himself became the model for the bloodsucking fiend. After the publication of *The Vampyre*, vampires were everywhere: not quite a dime a dozen, but close.

Probably written by a number of authors over the course of its run, but often attributed to Thomas Preskett Prest, in 1845 *Varney the Vampire; or The Feast of Blood* appeared as a London 'penny dreadful,' a cheaply printed and cheaply priced serialized publication. The adventures of Varney continued for more than a hundred weekly chapters over the next two years. Varney's tale began with his assault upon Flora Bannerworth, on a dark and stormy night.

> A tall figure is standing on the ledge immediately outside the long window. It is its finger-nails upon the glass that produces the sound so like the hail, now that the hail has ceased. Intense fear paralysed the limbs of the beautiful girl. That one shriek is all she can utter – with hand clasped, a face of marble, a heart beating so wildly in her bosom, that each moment it seems as if it would break its confines, eyes distended and fixed upon the window, she waits, froze with horror. The pattering and clattering of the nails continue. No word is spoken, and now she fancies she can trace the darker form of that figure against the window, and she can see the long arms moving to and fro, feeling for some mode of entrance. What strange light is that which now gradually creeps up into the air? Red and terrible – brighter and brighter it grows. The lightning has set fire to a mill, and the reflection of the rapidly consuming building falls upon that long window. There can be no mistake. The figure is there, still feeling for an entrance, and clattering against the glass with its long nails, that appear as if the growth of many years had been untouched. She tries to scream again but a choking sensation comes over her, and she cannot. It is too dreadful – she tries to move – each limb seems weighted down by tons of lead – she can but in a hoarse faint whisper cry, – 'Help – help – help – help!' (8)

When the creature entered the room, his appearance was less that of Lord Ruthven than that of Arnold Paole.

> The figure turns half round, and the light falls upon its face. It is perfectly white – perfectly bloodless. The eyes look like polished tin; the lips are drawn back, and the principal feature next to those dreadful eyes is the teeth – the fearful looking teeth – projecting like those of some wild animal, hideously, glaringly white, and fang-like. It approaches the bed with a strange, gliding movement. It clashes together the long nails that literally appear to hang from the finger ends. No sound comes from its lips. (9)

The assault on the girl came quickly.

> With a sudden rush that could not be foreseen – with a strange howling cry that was enough to awaken terror in every breast, the figure seized the long tresses of her hair, and twining them round his bony hands he held her to the bed. Then she screamed – Heaven granted her then power to scream. Shriek followed shriek in rapid succession. The bed-clothes fell

in a heap by the side of the bed – she was dragged by her long silken hair completely on to it again. Her beautifully rounded limbs quivered with the agony of her soul. The glassy, horrible eyes of the figure ran over that angelic form with a hideous satisfaction – horrible profanation. He drags her head to the bed's edge. He forces it back by the long hair still entwined in his grasp. With a plunge he seizes her neck in his fang-like teeth – a gush of blood, and a hideous sucking noise follows. *The girl has swooned, and the Vampire is at his hideous repast!* (10)

Varney's tale went rapidly downhill from there. Since a decline in sales for one issue would have brought about the end of the series, the tale was written so that it could always be concluded quickly, resulting in a jarring narrative, with frequent crises and dénouements. The story, however, was popular among its target audience, the urban working class, and did introduce some elements to the vampire mythos that would outlive it. *Varney*, for example, emphasized the vampire's fangs, its ability to hypnotize its victims, and its supernatural strength. Most importantly, it gradually transformed Varney into a sympathetic character, a victim of circumstance who is horrified by his curse and longs to be free of it.

Much more polished and literary, not to mention succinct, was J. Sheridan Le Fanu's *Carmilla*, a novella published in 1872. This time the vampire was a young woman named Carmilla who took up residence with the young Laura while her mother traveled. Laura, who narrates the story, was glad to have company in the lonely castle she shared with her father. Carmilla, as she describes her, sounds nothing like the vampires of folklore.

Her complexion was rich and brilliant; her features were small and beautifully formed; her eyes large, dark, and lustrous; her hair was quite wonderful, I never saw hair so magnificently thick and long when it was down about her shoulders; I have often placed my hands under it, and laughed with wonder at its weight. It was exquisitely fine and soft, and in colour a rich very dark brown, with something of gold. I loved to let it down, tumbling with its own weight, as, in her room, she lay back in her chair talking in her sweet low voice, I used to fold and braid it, and spread it out and play with it. (32)

Much to Laura's dismay Carmilla would share very little of her history, other than the fact that she came from an old and noble family. When pressed for information, Carmilla drew Laura into her embrace to soothe her hurt feelings.

She used to place her pretty arms about my neck, draw me to her, and laying her cheek to mine, murmur with her lips near my ear, 'Dearest, your little heart is wounded; think me not cruel because I obey the irresistible law of my strength and weakness; if your dear heart is wounded, my wild heart bleeds with yours. In the rapture of my enormous humiliation I live in your warm life, and you shall die – die, sweetly die – into mine. I cannot help it; as I draw near to you, you, in your turn, will draw near to others, and learn the rapture of that cruelty, which yet is love; so, for a while, seek to know no more of me and mine, but trust me with all your loving spirit.'

And when she had spoken such a rhapsody, she would press me more closely in her trembling embrace, and her lips in soft kisses gently glow upon my cheek.

Her agitations and her language were unintelligible to me.

From these foolish embraces, which were not of very frequent occurrence, I must allow, I used to wish to extricate myself; but my energies seemed to fail me. Her murmured words sounded like a lullaby in my ear, and soothed my resistance into a trance, from which I only seemed to recover myself when she withdrew her arms. (34)

Laura found herself both attracted to her strange visitor and repulsed by her, though over time their sensual attraction seemed to grow.

Sometimes after an hour of apathy, my strange and beautiful companion would take my hand and hold it with a fond pressure, renewed again and again; blushing softly, gazing in my face with languid and burning eyes, and breathing so fast; that her dress rose and fell with the tumultuous respiration. It was like the ardour of a lover; it embarrassed me; it was hateful and yet overpowering; and with gloating eyes she drew me to her, and her hot lips travelled along my cheek in kisses; and she would whisper, almost in sobs, 'You are mine, you shall be mine, you and I are one forever.' Then she has thrown herself back in her chair, with her small hands over her eyes, leaving me trembling. (35)

> **❝IT WAS LIKE THE ARDOUR OF A LOVER; IT EMBARRASSED ME; IT WAS HATEFUL AND YET OVERPOWERING; AND WITH GLOATING EYES SHE DREW ME TO HER . . .❞**

Soon, Laura began to receive forebodings of her companion's true nature. Local peasant girls began to die unexpectedly. A peddler stopped at the castle to sell charms to protect against vampires and offered, as a dentist, to remove the protruding canines that he noticed upon Carmilla's lips. Finally, Laura herself began to have dreams of Carmilla's nocturnal visits to her bed.

> Sometimes there came a sensation as if a hand was drawn softly along my cheek and neck. Sometimes it was as if warm lips kissed me, and longer and more lovingly as they reached my throat, but there the caress fixed itself. My heart beat: faster, my breathing rose and fell rapidly and full drawn; a sobbing, that rose into a sense of strangulation, and turned into a dreadful convulsion, in which my senses me and I became unconscious. (63)

Following the onset of these dreams, Laura began to suffer from a strange illness characterized by weakness and fatigue. Her doctor, noticing marks upon her neck, diagnosed vampirism as the cause of her illness and gradually thereafter the mystery was revealed.

Carmilla, it was discovered, was in reality the Countess Mircalla, long dead and buried near the ruins of her ancestral home. Upon opening the grave, the body of Carmilla was found, her 150-year-old corpse as wonderfully preserved as if life was still within her. Medical examiners determined that the body possessed faint respiration and heartbeat. The limbs remained flexible. The body floated in seven inches of blood. Evidence in hand, the vampire was destroyed.

> The body, therefore, in accordance with the ancient practice, was raised, and a sharp stake driven through the heart of the vampire, who uttered a piercing shriek at the moment, in all respects such as might escape from a living person in the last agony. Then the head was struck off, and a torrent of blood flowed from the severed neck. The body and head were next placed on a pile of wood, and reduced to ashes, which were thrown upon the river and borne away, and that territory has never since been plagued by the visits of a vampire. (115)

Concluding her tale, Laura described some features of vampirism. The vampire must renew itself with daily slumber in its grave and with the consumption of blood. The blood lust is not without its peculiarities, however. While in most cases the vampire attacks its victims, 'overpowers with violence, and strangles and exhausts often at a single feast,' in other instances the vampire approaches the kill with subtlety. The vampire, it seems, is prone to become obsessed with certain of its victims, an obsession resembling the passion of love.

In pursuit of these it will exercise inexhaustible patience and stratagem, for access to a particular object may be obstructed in a hundred ways. It will never desist until it has satiated its passion, and drained the very life of its coveted victim. But it will, in these cases, husband and protract its murderous enjoyment with the refinement of an epicure, and heighten it by the gradual approaches of an artful courtship. In these cases it seems to yearn for something like sympathy and consent. (117)

Carmilla was a monster, a bloodsucking undead fiend. But she was driven by the same desires that can corrupt the living: the desire for love and acceptance, the desire for understanding.

Twenty-five years after the publication of *Carmilla* the most famous vampire of all was unleashed upon the world in the undisputed classic vampire tale, Bram Stoker's *Dracula*. By this time the basic elements of today's vampire were in place, needing only the elaboration and development that a modern novel could provide. Bram Stoker borrowed freely from those elements, as well as from folklore and history, in order to produce a tale that has resisted aging and decay as well as any vampire could.

In addition to the literary influences from Dracula's vampiric precursors, Stoker also drew heavily from Eastern European folklore, including E. Gerard's 1885 essay on Transylvanian superstitions. Gerard's Transylvania provided the perfect location for a vampire tale – far enough away to seem exotic to English readers and 'uncivilized' enough to make the existence of some ancient evil plausible. Gerard wrote as the introduction to her essay,

Transylvania might well be termed the land of superstition, for nowhere else does this curious crooked plant of delusion flourish as persistently and in such bewildering variety. It would almost seem as though the whole species of demons, pixies, witches, and hobgoblins, driven from the rest of Europe by the wand of science, had taken refuse within the mountain rampart, well aware that here they would find secure lurking-places, whence they might defy their persecutors yet awhile. (130)

Indeed, the geography itself was perfect for the horror tale.

The scenery . . . is peculiarly adapted to serve as background to all sorts of supernatural beings and monsters. There are innumerable caverns, whose mysterious depths seem made to harbor whole legions of evil spirits: forest glades fit only for fairy folk on moonlight nights, solitary lakes which instinctively call up visions of water sprites; golden treasures lying hidden in mountain chasms. (130)

Gerard described the prevalence of the devil in Transylvania, evident from place names: Gregynia Drakuluj (Devil's Garden), Gania Drakuluj (Devil's Mountain) and Yadu Drakuluj (Devil's Abyss), for example. She also described one of the most fearsome of Transylvanian monsters, the *nosferatu* or vampire. According to Gerard,

> every person killed by a *nosferatu* becomes likewise a vampire after death, and will continue to suck the blood of other innocent people till the spirit has been exorcised, either by opening the grave of the person suspected and driving a stake through the corpse, or firing a pistol shot into the coffin. In very obstinate cases it is further recommended to cut off the head and replace it in the coffin with the mouth filled with garlic, or to extract the heart and burn it, strewing the ashes over the grave. (142)

Stoker also found in Transylvanian history the perfect identity for his vampire, the fifteenth-century Romanian prince, Vlad Tepes or Vlad the Impaler. Vlad famously led armies against the Ottoman Turks and impaled his enemies on stakes. Vlad's father was a member of the Order of the Dragon and thus called Vlad Dracul, meaning 'Vlad the Dragon' or 'Vlad the Devil.' Thus, his son the Impaler was known as Vlad Dracula, 'the son of the Dragon' or 'the son of the Devil.' In Stoker's hands, Vlad Tepes became Count Dracula.

Jonathan Harker describes the Count as he appeared in his Transylvanian castle:

> His face was a strong – a very strong – aquiline, with high bridge of the thin nose and peculiarly arched nostrils; with lofty domed forehead, and hair growing scantily round the temples but profusely elsewhere. His eyebrows were very massive, almost meeting over the nose, and with bushy hair that seemed to curl in its own profusion. The mouth, so far as I could see it under the heavy moustache, was fixed and rather cruel looking, with peculiarly sharp white teeth; these protruded over the lips, whose remarkable ruddiness showed astonishing vitality in a man of his years. For the rest, his ears were pale, and at the tops extremely pointed; his chin was broad and strong, and the cheeks firm though thin. The general effect was one of extraordinary pallor.
>
> Hitherto I had noticed the backs of his hands as they lay on his knees in the firelight, and they seemed rather white and fine; but seeing then now

15. Vlad Tepes, Dracula, as depicted in a sixteenth-century painting.

close to me, I could not but notice that they were rather coarse – broad, with squat fingers. Strange to say, there were hairs in the centre of the palm. The nails were long and fine, and cut to a sharp point. As the count leaned over me and his hands touched me, I could not repress a shudder. It may have been that his breath was rank, but a horrible feeling of nausea came over me, which, do what I would, I could not conceal. (18–19)

Dracula, a complex work of fiction, has of course been the subject of various interpretative theories. Some have seen the novel as a parable of good versus evil, a contemporary version of St. George and the Dragon. Others react to the novel's psycho-sexual themes, blood drinking symbolizing an intimacy not yet allowed in the Victorian novel. Still others see the character of Dracula as a metaphor for the waves of Eastern Europeans sweeping into England at the end of the nineteenth century, bringing their superstitions and diseases with them. For some it is simply a Gothic romance married to a rousing adventure story, complete with spooky castles and crypts as well as courageous men on horseback chasing a villain through the countryside. It is probably the case, as with all great novels, that there are multiple approaches to this text, each providing an entrée into the author's intent, the cultural setting in which it was produced, or the impact it has had on culture. It cannot be forgotten, however, that *Dracula* is, first and foremost, a horror story. It may provide social commentary or sexual innuendo but it also provides plenty of goosebumps and scares. Like Harker, when we meet Dracula and his minions in the pages of this book, we 'cannot repress a shudder.'

We shudder as Harker rides through the Transylvanian countryside to meet Dracula's servant at Borgo Pass, when the snarling wolves encircle his carriage, when the door to the ancient castle grates from disuse as it swings open, when Dracula remarks of the howling wolves, 'Listen to them – the children of the night. What music they make!', when Harker's careless use of a razor causes the Count to leap at his throat like some demon from hell, when Dracula climbs down the outer wall of the castle like a giant spider-thing, when the baby's mews come from the sack that Dracula presents to his vampiric brides, when those brides seek to make Harker their own, and when Harker realizes that the castle is a prison and he a prisoner. All these shudders appear in the first act alone, when Harker visits the Count in his home country. Equally terrifying scenes follow in London as the monster stalks Lucy and Mina, turning Lucy into one of his blood-drinking disciples, when the Host burns Mina's forehead, when the insane Renfield gobbles the flies and the spiders and the birds, and shouts those hideous words: 'The blood is the life! The blood is the life!'

Dracula also terrifies because in its pages the modern vampire stands fully formed. Rooted in the vampire tales of Eastern Europe, he is nevertheless much more. Dracula is an ancient warrior, stalking the world a half-millennium after his birth. He possesses lands and wealth and servants among the dead and the living. He transforms into the bat and the wolf, drinks the blood of the living and methodically plans an assault on London – and from there, the world. Though without the Byronic charm until tuxedoed Bela Lugosi portrayed the character on stage and then the screen as a resident of opera houses and drawing rooms, Stoker's Dracula was nevertheless a horrifyingly modern fiend with the modern world as his intended victim. In Stoker's book, of course, Mina is saved and Dracula's plans are foiled by his enemies. In the real world his conquest was complete.

In 1922, F.W. Murnau's unauthorized film version of *Dracula*, *Nosferatu: A Symphony of Horror*, appeared with Max Schreck as the evil Count Orlok.

16. Max Schreck as Count Orlok in *Nosferatu: A Symphony of Horror* (1922).

Orlok, unlike Stoker's Dracula, was depicted as a horrifying creature, with pointed ears, clawed hands and large rodent-like teeth. The movie followed the plot of the novel closely enough that Stoker's widow was able to sue successfully for copyright infringement. The film remains frightening, even by today's standards, with its expressionist scenery and lighting adding to the sense of the weird.

It is the performance of Bela Lugosi as Stoker's Count that set the standard for all portrayals of vampires to come, however. Originating his interpretation of the character on stage, he brought Dracula to life on film as directed by Tod Browning. His exotic accent and looks for the first time brought Lord Ruthven and Count Dracula together into the epitome of the modern vampire. Though clunky at times, especially toward the end, the film opens with scenes of the Count in his Transylvanian home that are eerie, the music-less soundtrack and painted backdrops adding to the mystique rather than hampering it. When Lugosi's Dracula says to Renfield, 'I never drink . . . wine,' I always shudder.

After Browning's and Lugosi's *Dracula*, the Count, and vampires in general, were everywhere. *Dracula's Daughter* premiered in 1936. Lon Chaney Jr. and John Carradine tried out the role of the famous Count in the 1940s. Lugosi himself reprised the role of the Count in 1948's *Abbott and Costello Meet Frankenstein* – this time playing it for laughs and embracing what had by then become a stereotyped characterization.

The horror element was revived in 1958 with Hammer Studio's *Dracula*, in which Christopher Lee played the lead. This was followed

17. Christopher Lee and
Melissa Stribling in a
publicity shot for *Dracula*
(1958) (Hammer Films).

by a rapid succession of sequels. In 1979 John Badham directed Frank
Langella in what was billed as a remake of the Browning/Lugosi film.
Countless other versions have followed, including Francis Ford Coppolla's
stylized *Bram Stoker's Dracula*, starring Gary Oldman, which, as the name
indicates, remains somewhat truer to the tone of the book than do many
other adaptations, albeit with a romantic element straight out of 1932's
The Mummy.

Of course, the character of Dracula is certainly not the only vampire
to be portrayed in film. While most Hollywood vampires are portrayed as
good-looking debonair fiends intent on preying on innocent young women
before feasting on their blood, some filmmakers have embraced the more
monstrous versions of the creature. In the 1979 miniseries *'Salem's Lot*,
based on the Stephen King novel by the same name, the vampires look
less like the suave Lugosi and more like the creepy Max Schreck's Count
Orlok. The vampires in the comic book and film *30 Days of Night* appear
even more like zombies or the pre-vampiric revenants of folklore.

Most fictional vampires stay rather close to the Dracula/Ruthven standard, however, though not without some elaborations and changes. Anne

18. Gary Oldman in *Bram Stoker's Dracula* (1992) (Sony Pictures).

Rice's 1976 novel, *Interview with the Vampire*, has probably done the most to update and further sexualize the undead. In this novel, and its many sequels, readers are introduced to the vampire known as Lestat. Lestat's story is filled with romance and pathos fit for a soap opera (indeed, Rice was undoubtedly influenced by the 1960s television soap opera *Dark Shadows* and its vampire star Barnabas). In that sense Lestat is a modern, post-Dracula version of Varney. Rice's greatest contribution to the genre, however, is her description of Lestat's social circle. Lestat is not a solitary vampire stalking the lonely night. Neither is he a vampire lord, like Dracula, ruling his vampire hordes. Lestat is a social being, surrounded by other vampires in a secret society, other vampires whom he at times hates and at other times loves – a family with whom he fights and from whom he draws his support. The reasons Rice's vampires prey on blood are complex. Sometimes it is for food, sometimes for pleasure and sometimes because they are lonely. They transform humans into vampires in order to create more of their kind, in order to find children and parents and lovers for themselves.

The influence of Rice's vampire society/vampire soap opera can be seen in much of the film and fiction that followed, including 1987's *Lost Boys*

19. Jonathan Frid as Barnabas Collins, and Grayson Hall as Julia in the ABC Television series *Dark Shadows*.

and 2003's *Underworld* and its sequels, although in this latter case the setting is a centuries-old war between the vampire society and a werewolf clan. The Ruthven-meets-Dracula-meets-Varney themes are also prevalent in Stephenie Meyer's *Twilight* novels and their movie adaptations, as well as television's *The Vampire Diaries*, *Being Human* and *True Blood*. In all of these cases the vampires, like Varney, are humanized and sympathetic and, like Dracula and Ruthven, are cool and sexy. In many ways these factors serve to limit the horror elements that are traditionally found in vampire tales. The vampire's struggle against the urge to feed is treated as akin to a teenager's struggle to resist sexual temptation. As portrayed, vampires are a misunderstood minority in need of acceptance and love, not stakes through the heart.

Not that these themes are universal in contemporary vampire film and fiction. As a matter of fact, characters such as Blade and Buffy the Vampire Slayer – both of which are the subject of comic book, television and theatrical treatments – struggle against the evil vampiric hordes, intent on spreading their evil to the world. These stories of brave adventurers engaged in an epic struggle with the evil undead hark back to Stoker's novel, its third act an adventure piece with a team of heroes hot on the trail of the villain Dracula, a storyline masterfully revived in the 1970s by Marvel Comics in the magazine *The Tomb of Dracula*, especially as scripted by Marv Wolfman and illustrated by Gene Colan. In *The Tomb of Dracula*, a charismatic, evil and yet sympathetic vampire lord battles against the descendants of his old enemies, Harker and Van Helsing, and against his own human descendant, Frank Drake. The series introduced Blade as an important character and provided the template for the Blade films as well as the Buffy series, not to mention the portrayal of America's sixteenth president in Seth Grahame-Smith's novel, *Abraham Lincoln: Vampire Hunter.*

Dracula's assault on Western culture has not been limited to the adult world. Vampires are even more pervasive than that. Children learn to count under the guidance of *Sesame Street's* Count Von Count and enjoy breakfast cereal endorsed by Count Chocula. Bunnicula, the vampire rabbit, appears in a series of popular children's books, and Olivia discovers that her twin sister Ivy is a vampire in Sienna Mercer's *My Sister the Vampire* series of books. In *Dick and Jane and Vampires* by Laura Marchesani and Tommy Hunt, 'When innocent Dick and Jane meet a creepy, cape-wearing vampire, the unexpected happens: he becomes their friend!' These juvenile vampires are harmless, hardly frightening at all. But of course, we might say that about the vampire in general. Their tales might give us goose-bumps, might make us lock our bedroom windows tight, but they are nothing to fear. They are, after all, the product of the Gothic imagination, born in the human mind on some dark and stormy night. They are fictions, figments of our imagination, fanciful folklore transformed into a literary stereotype. There is no reason to be afraid. They aren't real.

20. A Count Chocula clothing patch premium from the General Mills cereal.

21. Cover illustration for *Dick and Jane and Vampires* by Laura Marchessani and illustrated by Tommy Hunt (2010) (Grossett and Dunlop).

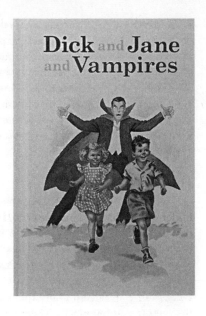

* * *

Dion Fortune, an early twentieth-century occultist, believed in the reality of vampires, not the eighteenth-century folkloric fiend – the boneless bag of blood shambling from its grave in search of sustenance – and not the Byronic predator of Victorian drawing rooms, but something just as sinister, just as deadly. Fortune's suspicions about the existence of such creatures arose while working with psychiatric patients as a student. Some patients, she noticed, were more exhausting to work with than others. She observed in *Psychic Self-Defense*, 'It was not that they were troublesome, but simply that they "took it out" of us, and left us feeling like limp rags at the end of a treatment' (43). The students' observations were reinforced by the nurses who administered electrical treatments to the same patients. They learned that 'the same patients equally "took it out of" the electrical machines and that they could absorb the most surprising voltages without turning a hair' (43).

Fortune also noticed similar features evident in relationships character-ized by what she called 'morbid attachments.' These relationships, between mother and daughter, mother and son, man and woman, were marked by the existence of an extremely dominant partner and a weaker, dependent partner. The weaker of the pair always showed characteristic symptoms: a sensitive temperament, pale complexion, slight build, weakness and sug-gestibility. Fortune explained these phenomena in terms of telepathy and the magnetic aura of the human body.

> Knowing what we do of telepathy and the magnetic aura, it appears to me not unreasonable to suppose that in some way which we do not as yet fully understand, the negative partner of such a rapport is 'shorting' on to the positive partner. There is a leakage of vitality going on, and the dominant partner is more or less consciously lapping it up, if not actually sucking it out. (44)

Often this draining of energies takes place unintentionally, without the knowledge of the dominant partner. Fortune called this 'psychic parasitism.' In other instances, however, the dominant person is more than a parasite and knows exactly what they are doing. This intentional assault on another's energy is what Fortune called 'psychic vampirism.'

Such beings are not unheard of in folklore, Fortune observed. She notes, for example, that in the Philippines there is a belief in a being called a Berberlang. These creatures are human ghouls that must occasionally eat human flesh. When hungry they hide in the grass and enter a trance, thus liberating their astral bodies, which can fly to the homes of their victims and devour their entrails.

> The Berberlangs may be heard coming, as they make a moaning noise, which is loud at a distance and dies away to a feeble moan as they approach. When they are near you, the sound of their wings may be heard, and the flashing lights of their eyes can be seen dancing like fire-flies in the dark. (45)

Fortune theorized that psychic vampires begin as individuals who, for some reason or another, need an inordinate supply of energy to survive. Perhaps beginning as parasites, they may become aware of their condition and learn techniques to control their astral bodies. Upon the death of their bodies, these vampires can remain alive in their astral forms and continue to prey upon the living. Their victims, if brought to death by the loss of energy due to this predation, may themselves become astral vampires in turn.

Fortune related a story of such an incident in which a young man was wasting away and showing all the signs of being victimized by a vampire. The boy was exposed to the menace through frequent visits with his cousin who had returned from the war in France suffering from 'shell-shock.' The cousin had been sent home from the front after he was caught in the act of necrophilia. According to the adept Fortune identified as 'Z', who personally examined the case,

> [S]ome Eastern European troops had been brought to the Western Front, and among those were individuals with the traditional knowledge of Black Magic for which South-Eastern Europe has always enjoyed a sinister reputation among occultists. These men, getting killed, knew how to avoid going to the Second Death, that is to say, the disintegration of the Astral Body, and maintained themselves in the etheric double by vampirising the wounded. Now vampirism is contagious; the person who is vampirised, being depleted of vitality, is a psychic vacuum, himself absorbing from anyone he comes across in order to refill his depleted resources of vitality. He soon learns by experience the tricks of a vampire without realizing their significance, and before he knows where he is, he is a full blown vampire himself, vampirising others. The earthbound soul of a vampire sometimes attaches itself permanently to one individual if it succeeds in making a functioning vampire of him, systematically drawing its etheric nutriment from him, for, since he in his turn is resupplying himself from others, he will not die from exhaustion as victims of vampires do in the ordinary way. (48)

In this particular case it was theorized that the cousin was not the primary vampire but was himself the victim of an astral vampire. It was possible that both the cousin and his astral master were feeding on the young man in question.

Contemporary occultist Konstantinos claims that surveys indicate that one out of five people experience an attack from a psychic vampire at some point in their lives, though these are not usually fatal. Like Fortune, he believes that psychic vampires exist both as living humans who can project their astral bodies, and as pure astral forms who remain alive by feeding off the energy of others. In *Vampires: The Occult Truth* he wrote, 'These are the darkest creatures. Although they start out as humans, upon their mortal deaths, intentional psychic vampires can become monsters in every sense of the word. Like vampires of fiction, intentional psychic vampires also go through a transformation that grants them eternal "life"' (143).

Konstantinos believes that most assaults by psychic vampires happen at night with the victim helpless in bed. The entity enters the room just as the prey is beginning to drift off to sleep. Because the energy transfer requires astral contact, the creature will usually come to rest on the chest of the target, resulting in a kind of paralysis. If by chance the victim awakens at this point he or she is likely to feel a heavy weight on their chest and be unable to move their arms or legs. They may sense the presence of another intelligence or even catch a fleeting glimpse of a shadowy, amorphous creature. In such instances the experience can be quite terrifying. The victim may have the overwhelming urge to scream but be unable to make a sound. The vampire may actually prefer that the victim have this level of awareness because the excitement may make the energy transfer easier.

I, for one, have had just such experiences as this, caught between sleep and wakefulness, between dream and reality. I have felt a weight on my chest. I have been paralyzed, unable to move a muscle. I have wanted to scream, needed to scream, to jar myself awake as well as to call for help, to plead for help. I have wanted to scream and been unable to, squeaking out a feeble cry, my chest too heavy to provide enough air to inflate my lungs, vibrate my vocal cords or open my mouth. Perhaps it was just a night terror, just some funny thing that happens when the night is dark, not dark and stormy, but dark and quiet, silent, foreboding. Or perhaps I am the one in five. Perhaps in the darkness there are predators lurking unseen, ghostly things, smoky things, the undead, the vaporous soul that is all that is left of a human being, the rest melted away, rotted away, revealing the dark and evil center.

Konstantinos writes, 'They might not turn into bats, they might not live forever, and they might not even drink blood, but as we've seen, there just might be such beings as vampires' (172).

It was a dark and stormy night.

I sidestepped puddles on the sidewalk and clung close to the old buildings to avoid the rain. Thunder rolled along the Mississippi River. Long after midnight in New Orleans, Louisiana, I prowled the streets looking for a vampire bar. Its name was innocuous and it was just far enough outside the French Quarter not to attract many tourists. I was told about the bar by vampires in an internet chat room. Most of the time, it was just a bar, albeit one with a Goth clientele, but on this night of the week, in the early hours after midnight, it was where the vampires came to share drinks and stories.

I found the place after a while. The bouncer at the door was dressed in black leather and wore a long black cape. He looked at me suspiciously. I was sure that I did not look like the typical patron. As a matter of fact I was certain that I looked like just the sort of tourist this kind of place would most like to avoid. Inside was dark and understated. Above and behind the bar were projected moving images, a movie that seemed to be ignored by the patrons. In the movie, a nude woman was strapped to a chair and blood was being drained from her veins into clear tubes and bottles. Her lips moved but there was no scream, the sound turned down in favor of the throbbing music that filled the bar. I found a stool at the bar and ordered a drink. The people were what I expected: twenty-somethings dressed in black, their hair dyed to match, piercings and tattoos in abundance.

After a bit I noticed that the people at the bar were moving into a backroom that was separated from the main hall by a curtain of beads. I followed. In this room was a small stage with seating along the walls. On the stage a young couple acted out some S&M fantasy. She was on all fours, dressed in an all-white cat-suit. He was shirtless and wielding a whip. The performance was tame. There was no blood or nudity, just a kind of gentle play-acting. After a few minutes they left the stage and were replaced by a young woman in black. She sat on a stool and read a love poem. Unlike the first couple, she was greeted by a round of polite applause.

As the crowd moved back toward the bar, I was approached by a woman in black, with long auburn hair. 'Do you know what this is?' she said.

I wasn't sure what she meant and must have looked puzzled because she asked her question again, this time with the answer implied. 'You do know this is a fetish bar, don't you?'

I smiled, looked around the room, shrugged my shoulders and said, 'Well, yeah.'

'What are you looking for?' she asked as she motioned for me to join her at a table.

'I'm looking for vampires.'

I could hear the thunder rumble over the sound of the loud music. The lights flickered just once.

> **'"WHAT ARE YOU LOOKING FOR?" SHE ASKED AS SHE MOTIONED FOR ME TO JOIN HER AT A TABLE. "I'M LOOKING FOR VAMPIRES."'**

Looking for real vampires, as it turns out, is not as difficult as it might at first seem. Influenced by Anne Rice's vampire novels as well as such role-playing games as *Vampire: The Masquerade*, and connected through, at first, independently published 'zines and newsletters and then later the internet, real vampire communities, both real world and online, flourished from the 1990s. According to Joseph Laycock, whose book *Vampires Today:*

The Truth about Modern Vampires is based on extensive access to Atlanta's Vampire Alliance,

> A real vampire is first and foremost a self-designated label. This separates real vampires from the creatures of myth and folklore as well as from various criminals who have been labeled as vampires by the media. . . . Other than being self-designated, there is currently no universal definition of a 'real vampire.' Some drink blood to sustain their health and some do not. Some describe a sensitivity to sunlight while others enjoy the beach. Many compare vampirism to a medical condition with tangible health needs while others dissent. For some, vampirism is a religion or a spiritual path while others ascribe no religious meaning to it. (viii)

Laycock distinguishes between 'lifestyle vampires,' who choose to emulate vampires of literature and film, and 'real vampires,' who are persons with a biological or spiritual need to feed on the energies of others. *Lifestyle vampires* often dress in black and wear colored contact lenses and prosthetic fangs. They dress and act like vampires by choice. *Real vampires*, on the other hand, have an actual need to feed. They may participate in the lifestyle vampire milieu or they may not.

The community of real vampires is far from monolithic. At the most basic level it is usually divided into psychic and sanguinarian Vampires. *Psychic vampires* are often described as similar, if not identical, to those vampires described by Dion Fortune. They feed off of the energy of others. Fortune's approach, however, was the approach of an outsider. For her the vampire was something to be feared and protected against. As one might expect, the vampires themselves offer a very different viewpoint on their nature and existence and on their perceived threat to others.

Michelle Belanger, self-described psychic vampire, writes in *The Psychic Vampire Codex*,

> A thriving community of self-aware psychic vampires exists hidden beneath our mainstream culture. Many of these people refer to themselves as 'vampyres,' using the alternate spelling to differentiate themselves from the vampires of folklore and myth. This vampire subculture is rich and diverse, and its members have the most reliable information about their experiences. Unfortunately, their voices are rarely heard. (5)

Belanger, among others, has been working in recent years to remedy this situation.

According to Belanger, psychic vampires are humans who feed on the energy of other humans. The reason vampires must feed is an open question in the vampire community. Some believe that a religious or spiritual sickness has reduced their own stores of energy, others that a higher spiritual metabolism requires more energy than can be generated on their own, others that vampires lack a strong connection to the universal sources of energy, and still others that their need for excess energy is the result of a genetic mutation. Belanger writes,

> Among psychic vampires, it is agreed that their nature is defined by need. While all beings exchange energy with their environment, there is a certain equilibrium that is nevertheless maintained. The draw of an ordinary person is constant and low level, barely noticeable to him- or herself or anyone else. Furthermore, ordinary people give as well as take energy, and there is rarely a huge disparity between the amount given off and the amount taken in.
>
> Psychic vampires require enough energy that they must take significant amounts of it in. The drain this generates is very noticeable, and there is a distinct disparity between energy intake and outflow. The powerful draw possessed by most psychic vampires has inspired some magickal workers to describe them as energetic 'black holes.' (8)

According to Belanger's *The Psychic Vampire Codex*, vampires feed on three levels. Ambient feeding does not take energy from individuals but rather absorbs the energy from large crowds or strong emotions. Surface feeding does take energy from individuals but only 'skims the surface of their energy bodies' (89). Contact feeding is a form of surface feeding that is characterized by physical contact. Finally,

> Deep feeding is the most profound level, reaching into the energy that lies at a person's very core. This style of feeding forges a connection between both partners that can linger not just one lifetime but many. The connection can inspire an empathic and often even a telepathic bond. For this reason, it is an exceptionally intimate style of feeding, and it should only be done with the full knowledge and consent of the person being fed from. (90)

Psychic vampires tend to form communities around websites and internet chat rooms with real world contacts made through annual festivals and conventions. Sci-fi and horror conventions will often feature special sections devoted to the vampire community. In some larger cities, including New York, Atlanta and London, there are organized vampire associations. Organization often follows patterns set by the Anne Rice novels or role-playing games. Some communities are organized as houses, some as orders, some as courts and some as churches. Belanger's own House Kheperu is further organized by castes consisting of priests, warriors and counselors.

Many vampire communities have been influenced by the Black Veil, a code of vampire ethics originally written by Father Sebastian Todd in the 1990s. The Black Veil offers guidance on a variety of issues related to vampire life. For example the Veil encourages vampires to be cautious in revealing their nature to others and recognize that their actions will reflect on the rest of the vampire community. Vampires are encouraged to respect the diversity of opinions concerning the nature of vampirism, to respect their elders and to seek to participate in the life of the vampire community. The Veil, as reproduced by Belanger in *The Psychic Vampire Codex*, instructs vampires, 'Do not allow your darkness to consume you. You are more than just your hunger, and you can exercise conscious control. Do not be reckless. Always act with a mind toward safety. Never feed because you think this makes you powerful; feed because that is what you must do' (266). In regards to donors, the Veil says,

> Feeding should occur between consenting adults. Allow donors to make an informed decision before they give themselves to you. Do not take rapaciously from others, but seek to have an exchange that is pleasant and beneficial for all.
> Respect the life that you feed upon and do not abuse those who provide for you. (267)

Belanger's community and others with a more metaphysical approach take part in rituals that mimic those of mainstream religion. For example, in *The Vampire Ritual Book*, rites are offered for celebration of annual holy days such as the Night of Transformation, the Night of Immortal Stars, the Night of Double Power, and the Festival of Radiant Light. Rites of passage are also available for use by vampire communities, including initiation ceremonies, marriages, naming of infants and burial services.

One rite, called the Promising of a Donor, blesses the union between a vampire and his or her donor. In this ceremony, the donor promises, among other things, 'to give of myself . . . so that my life may strengthen his life, and my soul may strengthen his soul' and 'to be mindful of his hunger, so that when he is in need, I am there to provide.' The vampire promises 'to care for . . . and to cherish the gift she provides for me, so that she never feels I have taken her for granted,' and 'to protect (my donor) and to never demand more than she can safely give; for her life is as my life and her soul is as my soul' (122–7).

Donors for psychic vampires are, of course, contributors of energy for their vampire partners. Despite the folkloric and fictional accounts of vampires, no blood is exchanged in these relationships. This, however, is not the case for all types of real vampires. While psychic vampires are a bloodless lot, *sanguinarian vampires* are a different story. According to Lady CG, a self-described sanguinarian vampire, in her book *Practical Vampyrism for Modern Vampyres*, written with Barbara Clarke, 'there is a species of hominid on this planet that has a dietary requirement for blood' (8).

For 'sangs' – the shortened form of sanguinarian – the need to consume blood is a central feature of life. Without consuming blood they suffer from sickness, unstable emotions, apathy and an insatiable appetite. Lady CG advises anyone suffering from these symptoms to look into the possibility of vampirism as the cause. Such people should see a physician to rule out other problems and if the condition persists, eat lots of rare steak for a month. On this diet, vampires will usually begin to feel much better. Their cravings should go away. Then, 'Once you KNOW you are a vampire, you should definitely study bloodletting, get a blood test and if you are over the age of 18, start on the endless search for a lifetime worth of donors, or a great sympathetic butcher in your neighborhood' (15). Butchers are the perfect source for beef blood, and Lady CG suggests mixing it with wine.

In addition to the need for blood, sanguinarian vampires are also likely to possess several other distinguishing characteristics. They are usually gifted with charm and the ability to be highly persuasive to other people; they are talented in energy manipulation or magick and they have the skill of empathy, the ability to read other people's emotions and determine whether people are potential friends or foes. Vampires have greater than average strength and increased night vision. Lady CG says she possesses the ability to summon other vampires. She also claims to be able to change her perception of time, an ability she calls 'blinking':

So, let's say I have a too large yard to rake (just as a mundane example). Let's assume, for a moment, that I have 2 hours of raking, and an appointment, I can't miss, in an hour. I take my rake and start in one corner of the yard, as I would always do. I start to work at a moderate, but rhythmic pace. Now, it's not a necessary step, but I find it helps me if I focus myself using a rhyme of some sort. For example:

This is my need
My need for speed
As I go . . .
TIME SLOW!
. . . FOCUS on your task at hand, in minute detail.

Feel power flow through your body, and SEE your hands or legs or whatever you're using to accomplish your task, flying at an amazing speed.

Feel the seconds stretch . . . every second is a minute or longer.

Concentrate . . .

Check the time when your task is ¼ done . . .

Adjust your rhyme to suit the amount of time you have left, if necessary. (149–50)

Lady CG offers advice for living the vampire lifestyle. She provides information concerning how to acquire beef blood, how to raise the subject of vampirism with potential donors and how to develop safe bloodletting practices. She recommends Otherkin, especially weres, as potential donors, as well as cutters and blood fetishists. For bloodletting itself, she offers very practical advice:

* Although it's all about feeding, your safety and your donor's safety are your number one priorities! If you or your donor is ever uncomfortable, STOP immediately.

* Sterile equipment, gauze, and an antibiotic gel are your BEST FRIENDS! Clean cuts and lancet pokes before and after you cut or poke. Bandage IMMEDIATELY!

* Shallow cuts in unobvious places are safest and usually most comfortable for your donor. Never cut 'across grain' when cutting a muscle.

* Exacto knives, while readily available are NOT the tools of choice! The edges are often rough and can lead to scarring and the cut can be VERY painful and slow to heal. They are unsafe as a method of extracting blood and better left for their intended purpose . . . as a household or industrial TOOL! (58–9)

Lady CG's need for blood is fairly limited, thankfully. She, and most sangs, are satisfied with just a few drops of human blood every seven to ten days, or a couple of very rare steaks in the same period. The latter, while a fine substitute when human blood is not available, is not a permanent replacement. Sanguinarian vampires need the energy and power that comes from other human beings, and the most direct way to receive that energy is through the consumption of blood.

Psychic vampires and their sanguinarian cousins mostly seem to get along with one another, with psychic vampires suspecting that their sang brothers and sisters are too influenced by vampire mythology and popular culture and not in tune with their spiritual side, and sangs being suspicious that the psychic vamps are kidding themselves and not yet at peace with the reality of what they are. Sometimes, however, the disagreements are fierce, with each accusing the other of misrepresenting the vampiric reality. Most vampire chat rooms or real world organizations tend to attract members of one group or another, with the two groups mingling freely at festivals and night clubs.

The woman across the table from me told me her name was Raven, not her real name I should understand, but her online and club identity. Everyone has one, I was told. 'If you're looking for vampires, then you've come to the right place,' she said. 'There are vampires all over this bar.'

I looked around the room again. Black leather, piercings, long coats. 'Real vampires?' I asked. 'Not just posers?'

'I suppose it's a little of both.' Raven was a large woman, with a deep masculine voice. She lit a cigarette. 'So what are you really looking for? Are you some kind of vampire bait? Because most of us here frown on grazing, it poisons the blood supply, if you know what I mean.'

I didn't know what she meant and she could tell.

'If you're looking for some vampire encounter it's probably not going to happen. You don't have the look. You should probably find another bar.'

'No. It's nothing like that. I'm writing a book.'

'Yeah? Can't wait to read it.'

I didn't think she was serious.

The images above the bar changed. Now Bela Lugosi was on screen, but not as Dracula. It was Tod Browning's *Mark of the Vampire* with Lugosi as Count Mora. The film was notorious in its day for supposed incestuous themes involving the Count and his daughter, Luna. It was a remake of Browning's *London After Midnight*, a silent film starring Lon Chaney. Its black-and-white flickering images for some reason spooked me more than those I had seen before, where the vampirism seemed sterile, surgical, modern.

Raven began to talk. She told me about how vampires are stereotyped, how people don't understand them. She told me how one must build up a trusting relationship with a vampire before they will share their secret with you. You can't just walk into a bar and start talking with a stranger. You should first make contacts on the internet, get to really know people, earn their trust.

I ordered us both another round of drinks. The thunder continued to roll down the river. More people came into the bar. Raven kept talking.

She had been awakened to her sang nature for the past six months, but had only had blood once and didn't enjoy it. It was hard for her to find a donor, a term that she didn't really like, anyway. It had to be the right person. (Don't get your hopes up, her eyes told me. I didn't.) She likes girls, which she thinks makes it harder. She offered advice on how to sell my book to vampires and on the best places to eat cheap in the city. She told me how much things had changed since Hurricane Katrina slammed ashore, washing away lives and livelihoods.

She was bluffing. I could tell. She seemed as uncomfortable and out of place as I did in this vampire bar in the French Quarter on a dark and stormy night. Maybe that was why she sought me out, because I looked uncomfortable too.

I could see in the other room that someone was back onstage, this time with musical instruments. It looked like a band was going to start playing. Raven kept looking between me and the other room. I could tell that I was losing her. It was time to go. I offered to buy her another beer before I left, but hers was only half gone. I drank down the last drops from my glass, rattled the ice around a bit, then walked out into the dark and stormy night.

When the rains came and soaked the ground, the shallow graves would turn to mud. The bodies, buoyant and bloated with gases, would rise, push through the wet ground, grope for the moonlight. The shrouds of the dead would be no longer white, but stained with the earth, stained with blood. When the storm ceased, yet before the sun rose, the wolves and dogs would find them, rip them, feast on their rottenness. In the morning, after the dark and stormy night, there would be terror. The bodies of loved ones, once buried, now unearthed, scattered around, tumble bumble, here and there.

In the cold of winter, when the nights were longer and darker than ever, the people would huddle together inside their windswept homes. Face to face, disease would spread. Unsanitary conditions bred death. Rats and fleas, likewise driven inside by the cold and the dark, brought sickness too. And when the sick finally died, they would not stay dead, they would crawl and scratch their way out of the ground, spread their contagion, feast on the blood of the living until their bodies were bloated, ready to burst.

Rudolf Otto wrote, 'The dead man, in point of fact, exercises a spell upon the mind only when, and only because, he is felt as a thing of horror and "shudder"' (119). He conjectured that our reactions to the dead are two-fold: there is 'disgust at the corpse's putrefaction, stench, revoltingness' (119); there is also the feeling of our own personal mortality that the sight of a corpse can engender. Prior to these reactions, however, and sometimes obscured by them, is the reaction to the numinous, the shudder, the dread,

> **❛THE DEAD MAN, IN POINT OF FACT, EXERCISES A SPELL UPON THE MIND ONLY WHEN, AND ONLY BECAUSE, HE IS FELT AS A THING OF HORROR AND "SHUDDER."❜**

the awe at the wholly other that is revealed in the presence of the absence of life. The vampire elicits this shudder, this dreadful awe, by revealing this absence of presence. The vampire is the living dead.

If ghosts are the last flicker of human souls, the last glimmer of that better half of human nature, then vampires are what's left of the other half after disease and death and decay have had their turn. They are the horrible, stinking remains of the body, the corpse that walks, the parasite that maintains its own tenuous hold upon reality by drinking deeply from the rich red blood of the living. They shambled forth from the grave at the end of the Dark Ages, made their way to London and Hollywood, and they prey upon us still.

Oh, along the way they became more civilized. They had to if they were going to survive in the modern world. They became rich and powerful on the backs of their servants and slaves. They grew handsome and beautiful and seduced our young. They became playmates for our children. They corrupted our morals as well as our bodies.

In time, we learned to preserve our corpses so that they would not decay so quickly. We embalm them and make them up to look good as new. They smile in their coffins surrounded by flowers and we no longer smell their stink or see their decay. Their caskets are made of steel and sealed in vaults buried six feet deep. You would think that we would have shed these fears of bodily decay, but fear is resilient; horror is persistent. So, with the real terror locked underground, we find other things to fear. With antibiotics and immunizations we push death further and further away. We can pretend it isn't coming and not be bothered by it when it arrives.

So, our vampires become specters, evil clouds of mischief that sit on our chests at night and drink our energy, the very energy we need to work our jobs and go to the gym and extend our lives. But we replenish it with energy drinks and Starbucks and go on our way. Lifestyle vampires proliferate, obsessed with the cool image portrayed on screen, by the allure of the darkness, an allure that only sets in when it becomes so dark that you can no longer see the rotting corpse waiting to take you in its arms.

Rising up in these last days like Lugosi from his crypt, 'real vampires' come out of their coffins and closets and confess to the world what they are by telling us what they are not. They are not the undead. They are not Peter Plogojowitz. They are not Lord Ruthven or Count Orlok or Count Dracula. They do not turn to bats or wither at sunrise or control the wolf and the rat. Many of them don't even drink blood. They take energy, just enough, so that no one is harmed. Those that do drink blood prick holes in the skin and lap it like a vampire bat or mosquito. They don't bite through flesh with their canines and drink the blood deeply and long, leaving nothing but a pale and withered corpse where once stood a living breathing man or woman. If they are not Plogojowitz or Dracula, if they don't kill in order to live, then why take this name, why live this lifestyle?

Is it because of the power of the vampire, the power of the legend and the lore? The vampire is not a victim to death. The vampire is not a slave to culture. The vampire pushes the dirt away and strides forth into the night. The vampire controls the minds of the weak. The vampire plays by its own rules, like Lord Ruthven and Lord Byron; it rejects the morality of the masses in favor of something more.

But the vampire is dead. It is death that grants his power, death that gives him strength, death that he serves, and it is for death that he recruits an army, killing to quench his thirst and to fill his belly, but also to draw others into the grave that they too might rise again. Be they psychic or sang, 'real vampires' are, thankfully, all about life, life from the sharing of energy, life from the sharing of blood. But it is death that the vampire of folklore and fiction hides in his fashionable clothes and good manners. Over time the vampires, like society, have gotten better at hiding the dark end, the rotting destruction of our flesh and bones. Hidden or not, it is there to see if we will only look. A bit of his nose has fallen off. Something has chewed at the end of her fingers. The smell of death lingers on her clothes.

And it lingers on mine. And it lingers on yours.

We are all 'real vampires' in this sense. We all must constantly seek for sources of life, sources of energy, sources of hope. We must create relationships in order to live, relationships with people willing to give and willing to receive. And, like vampires, as quickly as the sun rises, we can turn to dust. Like vampires, without these things crucial for life, we will rot, slough off our skin, drop a bit of our nose, bloat with gases of decay, float in a pool of our own blood. As it turns out, we are all Peter Plogojowitz trying our damnedest to be Lord Byron, or at least Bela Lugosi. As it turns out, every night is dark and stormy.

Oh Grandmother, What Big Teeth You Have!

Even a man who is pure in heart
and says his prayers by night,
may become a wolf when the wolfbane blooms
and the autumn moon is bright.

from *The Wolf Man*

A huntsman was just passing by. He thought it strange that the old woman was snoring so loudly, so he decided to take a look. He stepped inside, and in the bed there lay the wolf that he had been hunting for such a long time. 'He has eaten the grandmother, but perhaps she still can be saved. I won't shoot him,' thought the huntsman. So he took a pair of scissors and cut open his belly. He had cut only a few strokes when he saw the red cap shining through. He cut a little more, and the girl jumped out and cried, 'Oh, I was so frightened! It was so dark inside the wolf's body!'

Jacob and Wilhelm Grimm, *Little Red Cap*

I always imagine her with her hood pulled down over her eyes, one hand clutching the cloth tightly at her throat, head bent, startled by every snapping twig, every cry of a bird. But this incorporates too much of my own fears and insecurities into the picture. The girl, Little Red, is an innocent, like Adam and Eve in the garden, and her innocence protects her from fear. She walks down the woodland path to her grandma's house without a worry in the world, chasing every butterfly, smelling every rose. It is this innocence that is almost her undoing.

22. Little Red Riding Hood by Gustave
Dore (1863).

The story of Little Red Riding Hood is, I suppose, one of those historical tales for children that L. Frank Baum reacted against: a tale with a
moral lesson to teach and a disagreeable incident to drive the lesson home.
In their retelling of the story the Brothers Grimm made the moral explicit
and ensured that their heroine had thoroughly learned it. At tale's end
Little Red thinks to herself, 'As long as I live, I will never leave the path
and run off into the woods by myself if mother tells me not to.'

Unfortunately, this is the wrong lesson. It wasn't going off the beaten
track that got Little Red into trouble. She met the wolf on the path, on
the main road, in broad daylight, and left the path at the wolf's suggestion
simply to gather wildflowers for her grandma. Leaving the path only cost
the girl a little time. Little Red wasn't assaulted because she went where
she wasn't supposed to go, or because she took a wrong turn and ended
up in the wrong neighborhood or wandered down a dark alley at night.
No, the wolf struck from the safety of her grandmother's house, from the
safety of her grandmother's bed. It was her naivety that put her in danger.
She didn't know what we wizened adults have come to understand: it is
usually someone you know, usually someone in the family.

Perrault's version of the tale got closer to the truth, perhaps, by making
the moral lesson a sexual one. Before the wolf ate Little Red he first enticed
her to undress and crawl into bed with him. Alas, poor Little Red was not
around to learn the lesson at the end, so Perrault had to state it for her.

From this short story we discern
What conduct all young people ought to learn.
But above all, young, growing misses fair,
Whose orient rosy blooms begin t'appear:
Who, beauties in the fragrant spring of age,
With pretty airs young hearts are apt t'engage.
Ill do they listen to all sorts of tongues,
Since some inching and lure like Syrens's songs.
No wonder therefort 'tis, if over-power'd,
So many of them has the Wolf devour'd.
The Wolf, I say, for Wolves too sure there are
Of every sort, and every character.
Some of them mild and gentle-humour'd be,
Of noise and gall, and rancour wholly free;
Who tame, familiar, full of complaisance
Ogle and leer, languish, cajole and glance;
With luring tongues, and language wond'rous sweet,
Follow young ladies as they walk the street.
Ev'n to their very houses, nay, bedside,
And, artful, tho' their true designs they hide,
Yet, ah! these simpering Wolves! Who does not see
Most dangerous of Wolves indeed they be? (26)

Some wolves, Perrault knew, approach you on the street and in your grandma's parlor. Some wolves masquerade as family friends, respectable gentlemen, kindly grandmothers.

There are other bits of this tale that don't just serve to promote a moral lesson, however. There are other things that are going on here, things more gruesome and eerie. They lead the reader to suspect that Perrault and the Grimms were themselves engaged in a bit of modernizing, precursors to Baum in the attempt to soften fairy tales for children. There is the woodcutter, for example, who arrives at grandma's house to find the door open and the wolf sleeping in her bed. Thinking that the beast may have swallowed the old woman whole, he carefully sliced the thing's belly open and was surprised to pull both grandma and the little girl from inside the animal's skin. It is a happy ending for all, even though the avenue to that happiness reeks of terror. What must it have been like inside that creature's skin, trapped in the utter darkness, Little Red and grandma crammed in there together, like babes returned to the womb? But the Grimms pass over those details; as far as Little Red is concerned, she is just happy to be free because it was so dark inside the wolf's body. Grandma is soon nourished back to health by the good food brought by her loving granddaughter. The woodcutter claims the wolf skin as his own.

And then there is the French tale of 'The Grandmother' recorded by Paul DeLarue, a tale in which the horror is compounded and the moral lesson hard to find. In this tale a little girl, who is neither named nor distinguished by her red cap, was asked by her mother to take bread and milk to her grandmother. The little girl followed the path until she came to the crossroads, the most public of places, where all kinds of people – and devils – can be met. There the little girl met a werewolf, not an ordinary wolf but a creature part human, part beast, a creature wholly outside the human realm of experience. The werewolf wanted to know where she was going and which path she was taking. The girl told the beast and then they both went on their way. The werewolf raced ahead to the grandmother's house, where he killed and ate the old woman, placing some of her flesh in the pantry and some of her blood in a bottle on a shelf.

When the little girl arrived with her presents the werewolf called to her from the grandmother's bed and told her to put the milk and bread in the pantry and to make herself a snack. There is plenty of sausage and wine, she was told, enough for a delicious meal. So the little girl celebrated the dark Eucharist, ate the flesh and drank the blood. Then, her appetite sated, her thirst quenched, she followed the commands of the voice from the bed, took off all of her clothes, and climbed under the covers with the monster. Then, the familiar refrain, the call and response liturgy so familiar to every child, though in this version tinged with a bit more of the bizarre, a bit more of the uncanny:

> Oh, Grandmother, how hairy you are!
> *It's to keep me warmer, my child.*
>
> Oh, Grandmother, what long nails you have!
> *It's to scratch me better, my child!*
>
> Oh, Grandmother, what big shoulders you have!
> *All the better to carry kindling from the woods, my child!*
>
> Oh, Grandmother, what big ears that you have!
> *All the better to hear with, my child!*
>
> Oh, Grandmother, what big teeth you have!
> *All the better to eat you with, my child!* (232)

In this version of the tale, the little girl realized the danger she was in and came to her senses in time. Pretending that she had to go to the bathroom, the little girl ran away home. The werewolf chased after her, but was unable to stop her before she made it to safety. Of course, the conclusion is not all good. There is no 'happily ever after.' The little girl has broken the taboo: she has eaten human flesh, she has committed the terrible sin. Soon, she will notice the hair growing on her palms, her nails growing long, her shoulders widening, her ears stretching, her nose elongating, her mouth longing to taste the forbidden fruit once again. Sometimes dead is better. She has saved her life, but lost her soul.

Some souls are lost, and some are sold for a price.

In December 1521, Pierre Burgot – known as 'Gros Pierre' to the masses – and Michel Verdun were tried in Poligny, France. They were charged with the bloodthirsty murder of men, women and children as well as with the eating of human flesh. At the trial, Pierre confessed that nearly two decades before, while tending an unruly and widely scattered flock of sheep during a violent thunderstorm, he had been approached by three men in black riding on black horses. One of the men asked Pierre why he looked so forlorn. When Pierre told him about his missing sheep, the man, called Moyset, made a tantalizing offer. If Pierre would serve him as lord and master, all of his sheep would be returned safely.

What else could he do, caught in a horrific storm, afraid that his sheep would be lost forever? Like the good shepherd, he left the ninety and nine to seek those who were lost, risked his own safety in a desperate quest for his flock, lay down his life for his sheep. The shepherd faced the loss of his livelihood, the ruin of his finances, faced poverty and starvation at the hands of unpredictable nature, that most primitive source of human terror that overtakes us huddling in corners as thunder crashes around us, watching the rivers rise, the levées break, the waters overflow, washing away homes and lives, the past and the future. No wonder he so willingly sold his soul to the devil riding the black horse. On the spot, Pierre consented, renouncing God and all things holy. He knelt and kissed the man's black, cold and lifeless hand.

In time, Pierre was called to attend a warlock sabbat where he met Michel. Michel anointed Pierre with an ointment that had been given him by the demon Moyset and by Michel's own demon familiar. To Pierre's horror, the ungent caused him to experience a fabulous transformation. His body became hairy and his hands and feet became like paws. Pierre was transformed into a wolf!

As wolves, Pierre and Michel attacked and murdered a seven-year-old boy. On another hunt they fell upon a woman who was in her garden gathering peas – someone's grandmother, no doubt. They killed and ate the flesh of a four-year-old girl, leaving only one arm untouched. No mention is made of the color of her bonnet. Intoxicated by the taste of warm blood, the pair slew many others, their killing sprees accompanied by other acts of debauchery and evil. They confessed to having intercourse with she-wolves, something they claimed to enjoy more than lovemaking with women. As wolves, the two terrorized the surrounding area for months until Michel was caught in the act. Shot by a witness, Michel, in the form of a wolf, left a trail of blood to his hut. The authorities followed the trail, only to find Michel in human form, along with his wife, who was bathing his bleeding wound.

❮INTOXICATED BY THE TASTE OF WARM BLOOD, THE PAIR SLEW MANY OTHERS, THEIR KILLING SPREES ACCOMPANIED BY OTHER ACTS OF DEBAUCHERY AND EVIL.❯

This tale, recounted by Montague Summers in his *The Werewolf in Lore and Legend,* is one of the most horrifying and gruesome of the tales of men changed to wolves to be found in folklore and legend. An old woman slaughtered; a small boy mutilated; a four-year-old girl killed and eaten, the only evidence of her existence the hollow in her parents' lives and a neglected arm left behind, perhaps because the murderers were chased away before they were able to finish their meal by a woodcutter with a sharpened axe or perhaps just left behind because the beasts had grown full and content, having reached their limit, the arm like the last drumstick in a bucket of chicken when you push back from the table. The community was left to wonder who the next victim would be, listening for the howl of wolves in the distance, for that horrible sound of scratching at the door.

Was this fear a novelty, brought on by a demonic presence or was this a fear that gripped the people throughout their lives? Surely there had before been wolves brave enough and hungry enough to attack the weakest, the youngest, the oldest; nature, red in tooth and claw, creeping its way into their lives, devouring their most precious things, ending their dreams. But this was not like that. This was much more horrible, for the trail of blood led not to a wounded wolf, but to a wounded man. The terror was not stalking them from outside their camp, but from within.

The other, loathsome and terrible, was one of their own. Neither the demon with the skeletal hand nor the sabbat magic make this fact any more horrible than it already is. The werewolf is one of us, the terrible forces of nature contained in human flesh; the wolf, not in sheep's clothing, but in man's skin, in human flesh, met at the crossroads and in the public square. Perhaps this is why centuries-old tales still catch our attention, still hold us by the throat.

Many such tales were collected by Sabine Baring-Gould (1834–1924). This Victorian Renaissance man collected folksongs, wrote bestselling novels, analyzed medieval and occult folklore and penned the famous hymn 'Onward, Christian Soldiers.' Other than this particular contribution to church life, his most famous and lasting work is his *The Book of Were-Wolves* from 1865. In this book, Baring-Gould examined werewolf folklore from a rationalist perspective and sought to distill the legends into something suitable for analysis. Professing skepticism as to the physical reality of the werewolf phenomenon, he devoted a great deal of space in the book to discussing the horrible deeds of ordinary human beings, including cannibalism, grave desecration and murder, suggesting that perhaps it was deeds such as these that inspired the supernatural tales of the werewolf. He described his task as reconstructing the werewolf in the same way as a paleontologist might put flesh on the bones of a long extinct dinosaur.

> [J]ust as the paleontologist has constructed the labyrinthodon out of its foot-prints in marl, and one splinter of bone, so may this monograph be complete and accurate, although I have no chained were-wolf before me which I may sketch and describe from the life. The traces left are indeed numerous enough, and though perhaps like the dodo or the dinormis, the werewolf may have become extinct in our age, yet he has left his stamp on classic antiquity, he has trodden deep in Northern snows, has ridden rough-shod over the medievals, and has howled amongst Oriental sepulchers. He belonged to a bad breed, and we are quite content to be freed from him and his kindred, the vampire and the ghoul. Yet who knows! We may be a little too hasty in concluding that he is extinct. He may still prowl in Abyssinian forests, range still over Asiatic steppes, and be found howling dismally in some padded room of a Hanwell or a Bedlam. (5–6)

Unlike the paleontologist, Baring-Gould did not excavate physical remains, but folktales and stories from the past.

From Olaus Magnus, in his *Historia de Gentibus Septentrionalibus* from 1555, Baring-Gould related a tale centered on the medieval celebration of Christmas.

On the feast of the Nativity of Christ, at night, such a multitude of wolves
transformed from men gather together in a certain spot, arranged among
themselves, and then spread to rage with wondrous ferocity against
human beings, and those animals which are not wild, that the natives
of these regions suffer more detriment from these, than they do from
true and natural wolves; for when a human habitation has been detected
by them isolated in the woods, they besiege it with atrocity, striving to
break in the doors, and in the event of their doing so, they devour all the
human beings, and every animal which is found within. They burst into
the beer-cellars, and there they empty the tuns of beer or mead, and pile
up the empty casks one above another in the middle of the cellar, thus
showing their difference from natural and genuine wolves. . . . Between
Lithuania, Livonia, and Courland are the walls of a certain old ruined
castle. At this spot congregate thousands, on a fixed occasion, and try
their agility in jumping. Those who are unable to bound over the wall,
as is often the case with the fattest, are fallen upon with scourges by the
captains and slain. (53–4)

Likewise, he related a story from John of Nuremberg in which a priest
traveling in a foreign country became lost in the woods. Drawn to a campfire, the priest discovered not a man, but a wolf, seated over it. The wolf
spoke to the priest in a language that he could understand and explained
that he was of the 'Ossyrian race' and as such both he and his wife were
cursed to spend seven years in wolf form. If they were still alive at the end
of this period they would resume human form and return to their former
lives. Unfortunately, the wolf's wife was mortally ill. Would the priest
agree to visit with her and offer her the last rites? After witnessing how the
wolf used his paws as hands, the priest believed the wolf's tale and agreed.
Upon offering the last rites to the she-wolf, the priest watched in amaze-
ment as she peeled off her wolf skin, from head to navel, and revealed the
old woman underneath, the holy rites revealing the true humanity of the
creature in her final moments, freeing her in the way the woodcutter's axe
freed the grandma (59–60).

Baring-Gould not only excavated werewolf tales from humanity's
superstitious past, but noted that in 'the south of France' many in his day
still believed that certain men were transformed into wolves. He reports
that it was believed that bastards were especially prone to being werewolves
and should be watched more carefully than men of a better pedigree. It
was also believed, he noted, that a werewolf in human form would often
have unusually broad hands, short fingers and hairy palms. It was held that
during the full moon these men were overcome with a desire to run. They

would rise from their beds, jump out of windows and plunge into fountains. Following this nighttime bath, their unholy baptism, they would rise from the water covered with fur and walking on four feet. The werewolves raided fields and villages, attacking livestock and humans. Near dawn, the creatures returned to their fountains, where they resume human form and then go home to their beds (105–6).

The French werewolves, known as *loup-garou*, were in some cases thought to transform themselves into wolf form by dressing in a skin given to them by the devil. At night, as they prowled, they were pursued by the devil, who scourged them at the foot of any cross they should happen to pass. The only way to free such werewolves from this accursed state was to stab them three times in the forehead with a knife. Others believed that the werewolf was the revived corpse of a damned person who had freed himself from the grave in an attempt to escape torment.

> The first stage in the process consists in his devouring the cerecloth which enveloped his face; then his moans and muffled howls ring from the tomb, through the gloom of night, the earth of the grave begins to heave, and at last, with a scream, surrounded by a phosphorescent glare, and exhaling a fetid odor, he bursts away as a wolf. (107–8)

This creature that haunted our ancestors was a monstrous beast, the product of cannibalism, some dread deal with the devil or of some ancient curse. Christmas Eve drunken revelries became murderous rampages by those who took the dark form of the wolf. Donning some horrible animal skin, mortals took part in an unholy baptism, then ran wild in animal orgies, devouring human flesh.

Taking place against the background of ancient and medieval religion, these stories are not, as Otto might have said, just degraded fancies meant to evoke the pale shadow of numinous dread. No, these tales were surely purveyors of the real thing, of the shuddering awe that is at the heart of religion. Pierre became the beast by swearing a black oath against God. The devil was in the heart of the wolves, torturing them when they came too close to the cross. While for modern readers these tales may seem nothing but superstitious legends substituting easy thrills for real terrors, surely this was not so in an age when the cross had real power, when the devil was real and when human life seemed to be in the hands of fate alone.

Likewise, these stories are far more than simple moral tales. They show human beings face to face with the other, with the great and terrible, and this other is not a distant nature, feared only when one wanders off the beaten path. The other is not just the howling wolves, precursors to the domesticated hounds that became ever present at the side of their human masters. The werewolf dwells among us. We follow his bloody trail to our very door. While modern society may laugh at those who still believe that werewolves, real honest-to-god werewolves, prowl the dark woods and the urban ghettoes, while folklore and legend may seem quaint, we have other ways of telling ourselves these tales, other ways of revealing the wholly other in our midst.

In 1881, Robert Louis Stevenson's *Treasure Island* was serialized in *Young Folks* magazine, the adventures of young Jim Hawkins and the pirate Long John Silver sparking the literary success of its author. The tale of pirates and buried treasure has come to be regarded as one of the classics of children's literature and as Stevenson's most important contribution to the genre – contributions that also included *Kidnapped* and *A Child's Garden of Verses*. In 1886, Stevenson published the novella, *Strange Case of Dr. Jekyll and Mr. Hyde*. In time, it too became a story for children. It did not begin that way.

Purportedly inspired – like Mary Shelley's *Frankenstein* before it – by a nightmare, the story of Jekyll and Hyde is one of the most influential horror tales ever written. Its theme, of the duality that lies at the heart of human nature, of the evil that lurks in the hearts of even the kindest and best of us, of the atavistic beast lurking beneath our civilized facades, is in many ways the central horror paradigm of the modern age. Good and evil are blurred. Right and wrong are confused. Within each of us, the unknown other hides, waiting for a chance to come to the surface.

Jekyll's alter-ego Hyde is a diminutive, broken, corrupt monster, a monster who trampled a child under his feet without thought of morals or Christian kindness. Stevenson's narrator, Utterson, found him so far beyond the parameters of civilized humanity that he could not make out what it was about him that made him so loathsome.

> There is something wrong with his appearance; something displeasing, something down-right detestable. I never saw a man I so disliked, and yet I scarce know why. He must be deformed somewhere; he gives a strong feeling of deformity, although I couldn't specify the point. He's an extraordinary looking man, and yet I really can name nothing out of the way. (12)

Hyde is an ambiguous evil, an unknown other, beyond categorization because he is beyond the morality of civilized humanity.

23. Poster for *Dr. Jekyll and Mr. Hyde* (1931) (Paramount Pictures).

Finding immediate success, the story of Henry Jekyll and his transformations into the vile Mr. Hyde was soon adapted for the stage and, in time, the screen. In these adaptations the mystery that sustains the narrative of the book, the unknown identity of Hyde, was cast aside. The trick was revealed from the beginning. Jekyll and Hyde were of the same essence, of the same flesh and blood. Instead of the startling revelation this provided for early readers of the story, this premise came to provide the foundation for the drama's narrative. In Stevenson's narrative Jekyll expressed the pain and ecstasy of this transformation.

> The most racking pangs succeeded: a grinding in the bones, deadly nausea, and a horror of the spirit that cannot be exceeded at the hour of birth or death. Then these agonies began swiftly to subside, and I came to myself as if out of a great sickness. There was something strange in my sensations, something indescribably new and, from its very novelty, incredibly sweet. I felt younger, lighter, happier in body; within I was conscious of a heady recklessness, a current of disordered sensual images running like a millrace in my fancy, a solution of the bonds of obligation, an unknown but not an innocent freedom of the soul. I knew myself, at the first breath of this new life, to be more wicked, tenfold more wicked, sold a slave to my original evil; and the thought, in that moment, braced and delighted me like wine. (111)

Time and again, on stage and screen, the handsome and kind Jekyll became the monstrous Hyde. The leading man was transformed before our very eyes into the loathsome villain. The werewolf would never be the same.

The influence of *Jekyll and Hyde* on the shape of the werewolf is clearly seen in the way that werewolves were depicted by Hollywood following the release of 1932's film version of the tale starring Frederic March in the title role(s). With its astonishing-for-the-day transformation scenes and makeup, it was only natural that movie werewolves would follow suit. In full Mr. Hyde makeup, March even looked more like a wolf-man than like Stevenson's version of the character. Soon thereafter, in 1935's *The Werewolf of London*, Henry Hull played Dr. Wilfred Glendon, a researcher who was attacked by a Tibetan werewolf and subsequently cursed with nightly transformations into a wolf-man, rather than a wolf proper. This werewolf maintained so much humanity that he dressed in hat and coat before going out on his nighttime murdering sprees. Though the character became progressively more animalistic with each transformation, he maintained his human nature – he continued to be portrayed by a man in makeup. And so we see a truth that was there all along. The terror of the wolf-man is not just the terror of nature, it is the terror of human nature.

The influence of *Jekyll and Hyde* is also seen in 1941's more successful and influential werewolf movie, *The Wolf Man*. Starring Lon Chaney, Jr., son of the famous 'Man of a Thousand Faces,' *The Wolf Man* tells the story of American Larry Talbot, who was bitten by a gypsy werewolf

24. Poster for *Werewolf of London* (1935) (Universal Pictures).

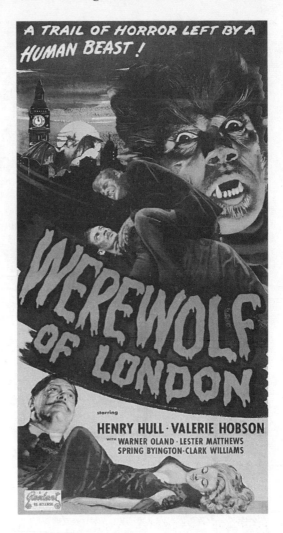

while visiting his estranged father in Wales. The werewolf, played by Bela 'Dracula' Lugosi, thus infected Larry Talbot with the curse. Larry's transformations came during the nights of the full moon, when he became a hairy wolf-man who terrorized the countryside.

Chaney's Talbot was an everyman, a gentle, slightly slow-witted American, struggling to find his place in the world. Unlike Lugosi's exotic Dracula or Karloff's lumbering monstrosity, Chaney could be you or

25. Lon Chaney, Jr. and Evelyn Ankers in *The Wolf Man* (1941) (Universal Pictures).

me. If he could be a wolf-man, then anyone could. Chaney appeared in several sequels which teamed the Wolf Man with other famous Universal monsters, notably Frankenstein's Monster and Dracula, including 1943's *Frankenstein Meets the Wolfman*, 1944's *House of Frankenstein*, 1945's *House of Dracula* and 1948's *Abbot and Costello Meet Frankenstein*. Though reduced to a joke over time, his would forever after be the iconic werewolf of Western pop culture: a tortured soul transformed by the light of the full moon into a bipedal, half wolf/half man.

In 1957, to choose one film among many, Michael Landon starred as a young werewolf, perhaps epitomizing America's growing concern that the youth of the day were out of control, in *I Was a Teenage Werewolf*, a role that was more overtly played for laughs by Michael J. Fox in 1985's *Teen Wolf*.

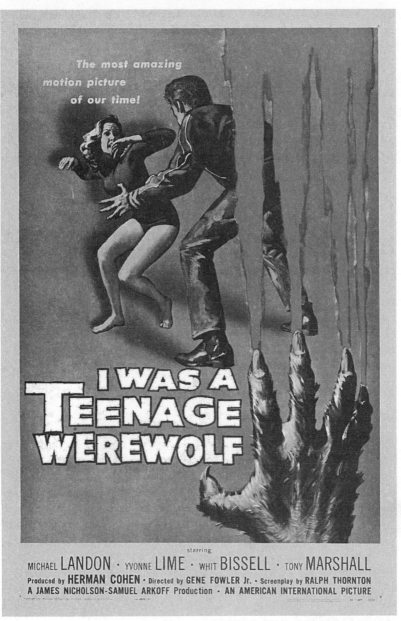

26. Poster for *I Was a Teenage Werewolf* (1957) (American International Pictures).

Movies were not the only place where wolf-men raised their hirsute heads. In 1972, Marvel Comics introduced *Werewolf by Night*, the unfortunately named Jack Russell, who upon turning eighteen inherited the family curse and transformed under the light of the full moon into a humanoid wolf-man. Likewise in Marvel's *Spider-Man* comics an updated version of the werewolf story was told. John Jameson, astronaut son of *Daily Bugle* publisher J. Jonah Jameson, found the mystical Godstone while exploring the moon and was subsequently transformed into Man-Wolf, a grey wolf-man in a yellow and green space suit. In the 1970s, General Mills' Fruit Brute Cereal – though not as big a seller as their Frankenberry and Count Chocula – had as its mascot a wolf-man style werewolf dressed in rainbow-colored overalls. As silly as some of these incarnations were, and some of them were very, very silly, the wolf-man endured.

If the haunting tales of werewolves found in folklore and fairy tales had served to bring the monstrous close at hand, to bring the threats and alienness of nature onto the path, down to the crossroads, into the bedroom, Mr. Hyde and the Wolf Man brought it to where it had really been lurking all along: in our hearts, under our skin. Little Red had better watch out for strangers. Yes, and she had better watch out for friends and grandmas too. And if she looks closely enough into her own little red beating heart she'll learn that there is plenty that is monstrous, plenty that is fearful living there. When we read about the agonizingly wonderful transformation to the evil Mr. Hyde in Jekyll's own words we

27. A reminder to 'Turn It Off' from General Mills' cereal mascot Fruit Brute.

28. Oliver Reed in *The Curse of the Werewolf* (1961) (Hammer Films).

might as well be listening to our own inner voice. When we watch the transformation of Jekyll to Hyde or Talbot to Wolf Man on late-night television we might be looking in a mirror.

Strange Case of Dr. Jekyll and Mr. Hyde is not the only work of fiction important for an understanding of modern werewolves, of course. Published in 1933 – the same year as Montague Summer's book on werewolves and hot on the heels of the Frederic March version of *Jekyll and Hyde* – Guy Endore's *The Werewolf of Paris* should perhaps be regarded as the classic novel of the werewolf genre. Though it served as the inspiration for Hammer Studio's *Curse of the Werewolf* (1961), albeit with Oliver Reed as a wolf-man rather than as the more traditional werewolf depicted in the novel, it is now mostly forgotten. Nevertheless, *The Werewolf of Paris* set the standard for 'realistic' depictions of werewolves, and its influence can be seen in the long history of violent and highly sexualized werewolf films and novels that followed.

The book is the story of Bertrand Caillet, fathered by a priest whose family was cursed for its past evil deeds. Born on Christmas Eve, with bushy eyebrows and hairy palms, young Bertrand began having nightmares at an early age, dreams of running through the fields in the form of a wolf. When local farmers started losing livestock it did not take long for the blame to be placed on a werewolf. When a wolf was shot with a bullet made from a melted silver crucifix, Bertrand's guardian found that the young boy had a mysterious wound in the same spot. Locking Bertrand in his room was not enough to stop him from his assaults on innocents, however. Endore describes one of Bertrand's transformations when the reality of his dream life first struck home. The passage could have been written as a scene in a modern horror film.

> He knew when an attack was coming on. During the day he would have no appetite. It was particularly the thought of bread and butter that nauseated him. In the evening he would feel tense and both tired and sleepless. Then he would arrange his window and lock his door, and having taken his precautions, he would lie down. Frequently he would wake in the morning, in bed, with no recollection of what had happened at night. Only a wretched stiffness in his neck, a lassitude in his limbs, that could come from nothing but miles of running, scratches on his hands, and feet, and an acrid taste in his mouth argued that he had spent the night elsewhere. On one such occasion, however, full conviction awaited him when he rose. Under his bed he caught a flash of white. It was a human forearm! A man's. The fingers were clutched tightly into a fist. Hair, as if torn from a fur coat, protruded from the interstices between the fingers. (95)*

Bertrand was fated to a life of evil. He murdered and devoured his best friend, desecrated graves and consumed their contents and had an incestuous encounter with his mother. Escaping to Paris, Bertrand prowled the streets, claiming victims and terrorizing the public. It was only when he fell in love with a woman with whom he shared a sado-masochistic relationship that he could briefly tame the beast.

> Suppressing a moment's hesitation, he bent over her body . . . The blood welled up, ruby-red. He put his mouth to it at once and drank greedily. His lips made ugly, sucking noises, as he strove to extract all the blood he could. Her fingers played with his hair, meanwhile. 'Poor little baby,' she murmured. Her mind reeled, filled with unsubstantial pictures, with

---

* Quotations for this hard-to-find book are taken from an electronic version of the text found at http://vb-tech.co.za/ebooks/Endore%20Guy%20-%20 The%20Werewolf%20of%20Paris%20-%20HO.pdf.

broken threads of unconnected thoughts. Now they were locked in each other's arms again. Sleep separated them at last. They lay exhausted, their limbs still entangled, the sweat of their embraces drying in the night breeze. The candle burned unheeded, until the flame expired in a mass of molten wax. In the morning, when daylight woke them up, he was a different person. He looked with horror upon his deeds. With his finger tips he touched her wounds and wept. 'I'm killing you,' he moaned. 'What a fate!' He slapped his brow with the palm of his hand, that hairy palm. (129)

His life, of course, ended tragically. Bertrand was buried, and when the corpse was later exhumed, a startling discovery was made.

The body . . . was not found in the coffin, instead, that of a dog, which despite 8 years in the ground was still incompletely destroyed. The fleshy parts and the furry hide are found mingled in a fatty mass of indistinguishable composition. A nauseous odor spreads from the body. (164)

If *Jekyll and Hyde* humanized the werewolf and brought the uncanny home to roost, *The Werewolf of Paris* revealed the fierce and brutal nature of the beast. More graphically violent and sexual than anything allowed by the Hollywood of the day, Endore's novel prepared the werewolf for the post-Holocaust, post-Hiroshima, post-Manson future. Bertrand ripped at the soft flesh of his victims' throats, lapped up the warm flowing blood and gnawed human flesh from human bones. He killed without mercy then wallowed in his inextinguishable grief. He ripped the flesh of his lover, clawed at her back, suckled the flow of her blood. He enticed Little Red into his bed, tortured her in the night, then wept over her scars in the morning.

Like Dr. Jekyll and like Larry Talbot, Bertrand remained a sympathetic character. Endore's werewolf is the monster of folklore, but the monster of folklore humanized and sexualized. Like a soldier returning from war, Bertrand had committed terrible acts of violence, he had acted with immoral promiscuity, but he remained heroic, welcomed back into the arms of his lover. In *The Werewolf of Paris* we see for perhaps the first time a werewolf in all its violent and amoral ferocity and in all its strange allure.

The allure of the beast is one of the themes found in a third, critically important werewolf novel, Jack Williamson's *Darker Than You Think*. In this 1940 novel, Will Barbee is a newspaper reporter who stumbled upon a dark and sinister conspiracy. While covering the story of Dr. Lamarck Mondrick's return from an archeological expedition to the Gobi Desert

– a return that was marked by Mondrick's murder – Barbee discovered Mondrick's secret: in the ancient past *homo sapiens* had struggled against another advanced species called *homo lycanthropus*. Fighting the ravages of the Ice Age, *homo lycanthropus* evolved abilities that made it a threat to its human cousins: abilities such as telepathy, clairvoyance and prophecy in addition to something even more sinister.

> Almost every primitive people is still obsessed with the fear of the *loup-garou*, in one guise or another – of a human-seeming being who can take the shape of the most ferocious animal of the locality to prey upon men. Those witch people, in Dr. Mondrick's opinion, learned to leave their bodies hibernating in their caves while they went out across the ice fields – as wolves or bears or tigers – to hunt human game. (220)

In Williamson's book, these witch-people were the horrible monsters of ancient folklore and legend, the werewolves, ogres and demons that haunted humanity's history. In time, however, *homo sapiens* had found the strength to resist the assaults of the enemy. Domesticated dogs became their protectors and weapons of silver allowed them to fight back. In time, the monsters were forced into hiding, impelled to disappear into forests and caves or to hide among humans, keeping their horrible secret while contaminating the human bloodline with their own sinister genes.

Most frightening of all, as Barbee learned, was the fact that werewolf blood flowed in the veins of many present-day humans. Sometimes the traits became dominant, resulting in psychic abilities or homicidal mania. In recent days, he also learned, the throwback hybrids had begun to gather into secret clans and organizations, breeding themselves purer and purer, waiting for their prophesied leader, the Child of Night, to lead them in an assault on humanity, a reclamation of their rightful place. Hiding in plain sight as normal members of society, the werewolves were constructing sinister plots to regain supremacy once more, transforming themselves by night into wolves, tigers and winged pterosaurs, dragons from the ancient past. Barbee's terror at this revelation was soon overwhelmed by his growing awareness of his own abilities and his own place in the secret society. Torn at first between his human sense of morality and the powerful and uncanny call of the darkness, he finally made his choice, gave up his humanity and embraced the otherness that was within him.

Many films, such as *The Howling* (1981) and *Underworld* (2003), as well as the influential role-playing game *Werewolf: The Apocalypse* were clearly influenced by *Darker Than You Think* and turned on the idea, not

29. Belinda Balaski in *The Howling* (1981) (Sony Pictures).

of solitary individuals struggling against the curse of the werewolf, like Dr. Jekyll, Larry Talbot and Bertrand Caillet, but of a werewolf culture, a society of shapeshifters hidden from the eyes of mainstream culture. In *Werewolf: The Apocalypse* the werewolves, or Garou, are beings created by Gaia, the spirit of the earth, to fight on the side of good against the forces of destruction, the Wyrm, and against the oncoming apocalypse. In *The Howling*, based on the novel of the same name by Gary Brandner, the werewolves are members of the Colony, an exclusive resort community. In Neil Marshall's *Dog Soldiers*, the werewolves live together as a human family when they are not terrorizing the Scottish highlands as a vicious pack of lupine monsters. Jekyll may have found some pleasure in his transformation into the deformed Hyde but he struggled to be free of the curse. Bertrand's werewolf was sexy and enticing, but Bertrand's orgies of pleasure were followed by sorrow, guilt and shame. However, in *Darker Than You Think* and its progeny, to be a werewolf is not to be a cursed loner, plagued by the monster within, but to be a member of an exclusive club, a member of a people distinguished by their connection to the different within themselves.

30. Still from *Dog Soldiers* (2002) (Kismet Entertainment Group).

* * *

The sound began down deep in his chest, rose to a growl in his throat, and then forced its way between his lips as a snarl. The coarse silver hair on his neck bristled. His ears, covered with the same silver fur, twitched. There was a burst of air from his nostrils, a snort of warning and territorial claim. The muscles in his arm began to twitch. His head snapped quickly to the left, then to the right. Thrown back against my seat by a sudden change in direction and speed, I instinctively clutched at the door handle of the mini-van, my eyes darting between the oncoming traffic and the hairy form in the driver's seat. His reactions to the traffic were quick and aggressive – canine reactions, lupine reactions. For just a moment I was terrorized, speeding down the highway with a werewolf at the wheel.

I found Wolf VanZandt online, an elder statesman among the digital werewolf community, and was amazed to discover that he lived only an hour from me. A couple of email enquiries, a brief phone call, and I was on my way to lunch with him. Wolf appears to be in his mid- to late fifties and works for a charitable organization, testing disabled adults and children for job placements. He lives in an apartment in the historic business district of Selma, Alabama, near the Alabama River and just steps away from the Edmund Pettus Bridge, that epicenter of both bestial cruelty and human nobility in the civil rights protests on Bloody Sunday, March 7, 1965. Nearby, Edgar Cayce, the sleeping prophet, once operated a photography studio and dreamed of long-lost Atlantis, torn apart by the enmity between the Sons of the Law of One, who followed the path of righteousness, and the Sons of Belial, who followed a decidedly darker path.

I had lunch with Wolf at a local 'meat and three' restaurant. Unlike Warren Zevon's London werewolf, we didn't have beef chow mein or pina coladas (and Wolf's unruly fur was far from 'perfect'), but instead ordered meat loaf, tomato pie, and iced tea. Throughout the meal Wolf was uncomfortable in the straight-backed chair, which offered no place for his (invisible) tail. Other than that he seemed completely at ease in his own skin, more than happy to talk to me about his wolf-nature and the werewolf community of which he is a part.

Werewolves, Wolf explained, are by their nature mostly solitary creatures, joining packs only occasionally for woodland gatherings known as 'howls.' Wolf is one of the elder weres in an annual gathering known as the Southeastern or SEHowl, billed as one of the largest and longest-running howls in the country. Mostly, however, the werewolf community is found online, in chat rooms such as the Werewolf Café (werewolfcafe. com) and the Werelist (werelist.net). Online, Wolf often plays the role of an expert, or at least as someone who has been around for a while, knows a lot of other werepeople and is not afraid to state his mind and share his personal experiences.

Wolf traces the origins of modern werewolves to the late twentieth century, when

> some people began realizing, as children, that there was something different about them. They lived life more intentionally, paid more attention to what was going on around them, were more empathic, and felt as though they did not quite fit in with the people around them. On the other hand, they identified very well with various nonhuman animals – often to the point of conceptualizing themselves as nonhuman.*

These individuals should not be thought of dysfunctional misfits, however. According to Wolf,

---

* This, and the following quotes from Wolf are from thetheriantimeline.com.

On the average, they got along well with their families, they had friends, they succeeded in school, many worked for themselves, many worked for others, and they were happy and well adjusted. But they were unique, as far as they knew, and they kept their differences a secret.

Then, in the early 1990s, with the birth of the internet, this diverse group of individuals began to find each other. An online group, alt.horror. werewolves, founded as a forum for fans of werewolf movies, soon became a forum for the discussion of members' personal lives and experiences. As Wolf puts it, 'The Weres had found each other.'

The Otherkin community that grew from those first tentative conversations is a diverse and individualistic group, prowling at night in internet chat rooms devoted to theoretical discussions of the nature of the beast. Otherkin usually work from their own experiences to create definitions and categories to explain their common experiences. One member of the community, the author and self-identified therian Lupa, has provided an overview of the Otherkin community and illustrates the diversity of experiences and opinions within the community. According to Lupa's *A Field Guide to Otherkin*, the definition for Otherkin is:

> a person who believes that, through either a nonphysical or (much more rarely) physical means, s/he is not entirely human. This means that anyone who relates internally to a nonhuman species either through soul, mind, body, or energetic resonance, or who believes s/he hosts such a being in hir [sic] body / mind. (26)

Lupa goes on to further define a sub-group within the community of Otherkin, therianthropes or therians: 'These are people who identify as Earth-based animals in some respect. The species represented tend to be wolves, big cats and other more impressive animals but I've seen horse, rabbit, deer and even dinosaur, earwig and kiwi therians' (25). 'Therian' is for Lupa the modern-day name for werewolves and shapeshifters, the creature whose essence is both human and animal. Unlike the werewolves from folklore, however, therians are not a threat to livestock or humans, but live mostly normal lives as part of the human community.

Lupa reports that, true to their name, shapeshifters do shift forms, but this shifting mostly takes place on the nonphysical level, 'though mild changes to the physiology and senses are occasionally reported' (126). According to Lupa and other writers, this shifting takes on myriad forms. These include *mental shifting*, in which an individual reverts mentally to their animal form; the individual begins to feel and act like the animal, including howling or whining like a wolf. *Bi-location shifting* takes place when an individual's inner animal is projected into the external world, allowing the person to move about in animal form. In *dream shifting*, the individual becomes their inner animal

> *(BI-LOCATION SHIFTING TAKES PLACE WHEN AN INDIVIDUAL'S INNER ANIMAL IS PROJECTED INTO THE EXTERNAL WORLD.)*

in a dream state; sometimes this corresponds with bi-location shifting. *Phantom shifting* describes the experience in which the individual can see or feel their animal limbs. They may experience a tail or feel the fur on their body. Usually, others cannot sense the changes. For some, this state is semi-permanent, meaning they almost always feel the presence of their tail, and so on. Lupa writes:

> In Otherkin, phantom limbs often consist of body parts that were present in their Other selves, but not in the human body. Wings, tails, and other nonhuman appendages are common, as are variations on body shape, such as wolf ears on the nonphysical form of a lupine theriathhrope . . . While for the most part phantom limbs have a nonphysical existence, there are the rare claims of them affecting physical reality. Occasionally a phantom limb may react to a physical obstacle in the same way that a flesh and blood limb would. (43)

Journey shifting takes place when the individual takes part in a Shamanic journey in the form of their inner animal. In *aura shifting* the person's auric field is transformed into that of their inner animal. Finally *physical shifting* is, unsurprisingly, the most controversial of the shifting types. Some people deny that it happens at all, while others argue that it can occur on rare occasions, with greater or lesser levels of completeness.

Wolf confessed to me that he had experienced, on rare occasions, something that might be considered a physical shift, though he stressed that this should not be understood as a transformation on the order of the change from human to wolf or even on the order of the change from Jekyll to Hyde. He described it as a period of more intense identification with his animal nature, even more intense that his usual heightened senses and phantom tail. He emphasized that this was far from the normal experience and was perhaps only an intense form of phantom shifting. As he described it, a far more common experience for him might be categorized as dream bi-location shifting: an experience in which his animal form takes on a more substantial, though still not necessarily physical, form while he dreams. Wolf argues that there is evidence of this sort of experience to be found in ancient werewolf legends. He also thinks that it might offer a solution to some of the mysteries surrounding the modern werewolf experience.

Though always careful to emphasize that his theories are his alone and that he does not speak for the therian community as a whole, Wolf does not hesitate in sharing his own personal understanding of the modern werewolf phenomenon. He believes, for example, that present-day therians are genetically linked to the European werewolf community of the Middle Ages and that population and environmental pressures may have resulted in the reawakening of this long-hidden hereditary strain.

Wolf writes,

> Before the Werewolf Trials of the later Middle Ages when thousands of mentally ill or simply despised people were tortured to death by the Inquisition for being 'werewolves', there really were people known as 'werewolves'. Far from being insane, they were respected in their communities. They even had a special position in the church – they were called the Dogs of God and Saint Peter's Wolves.*

Wolf finds evidence for the existence of these holy werewolves in some of the ancient legends themselves, but especially in the records of the Inquisition regarding the 1692 trial of the Livonian werewolf Thiess as recorded by Carlo Ginzburg in his *The Night Battles: Witchcraft and Agrarian Cults in the Sixteenth and Seventeenth Centuries*.

According to Ginzburg, Thiess confessed freely to the charge of being a werewolf. He also claimed that he once suffered a broken nose during a battle with a peasant named Skeistan, who happened to have been deceased at the time. Skeistan was a witch and had risen from his grave, along with other witches, to carry seed grain into hell in order to curse the community's crops. Thiess, as a werewolf, had battled to stop this travesty and had been hit in the face with a broomstick by the witch. Thiess also claimed that such battles took place three times each year, on the night of St. Lucia before Christmas, at Pentecost and on the night of St. John. On these nights, 'The werewolves proceeded on foot, in the form of wolves, to a place "beyond the sea": hell. There they battled the devil and

---

*   From thetheriantimeline.com.

witches, striking them with long iron rods, and pursuing them like dogs. Werewolves, Thiess exclaimed, "cannot tolerate the devil'" (29).

When the judges demanded to know why Thiess and the others would transform themselves into dogs and journey to hell, he explained that they went in order to bring back from hell those things that had been taken there by the witches: livestock, grain and other agricultural products. To fail in their task would mean a lean year for the harvest and hunger for the people.

The judges in this account seemed quite shaken by this strange testimony. They apparently had great difficulty in understanding werewolves as being on the side of God and opposed to the devil. Thiess kept insisting, however, that

> werewolves were anything but the servants of the devil. The devil was their enemy to the point that they, just like dogs – because werewolves were indeed the hounds of God – pursued him, tracked him down, and scourged him with whips of iron. They did all of this for the sake of mankind: without their good work the devil would carry off the fruits of the earth and everyone would be deprived as consequence. (29)

Ginzburg argues that the judges' understanding of werewolves as servants of the devil notorious for destroying livestock was incompatible with what seems to be an older concept of werewolves as servants of God. Thiess, he argues, represents an earlier understanding of werewolves in which the dogs of God battle witches and devils in defense of a bountiful harvest. In addition to the evidence of Thiess' advanced years, and the assumption that he acquired his beliefs about werewolves at an early age, Ginzburg also notes a mid-sixteenth-century tale of a young man of Riga who fell to the ground during a banquet. One of the witnesses recognized the man as a werewolf. When he revived, the young man related that he had left his body to battle a witch that had been flying around in the shape of a red-hot butterfly. 'This *was* an ancient belief, then. But . . . under pressure from the judges, the original positive qualities of the werewolves began gradually to fade away and become corrupted into the execrable image of the man-wolf, ravager of the livestock' (31–2).

Wolf VanZandt believes that the ancient dogs of God, the hounds of St. Peter, are once again on the move, called for what purpose he is not yet sure. Modern therians may be the new hounds of God, when their struggling consciousness finally comes to shake off the false histories that they have been taught. Hundreds of years of false consciousness must fade away for the werewolf to once again hear the call to battle with the forces of evil. All the horrible tales of old were told from confused or sinister motives, but the truth remains, hidden even in the ancient legends and tales. The wholly other within the werewolf breast is the presence of the divine.

The wolf stands outside the camp and howls. The wolf sniffs around the edges of the circle of light cast by the fire. Its paws pad silently, but we know it is there. It is nature incarnate, with ears to hear the sounds of its prey, eyes to see in the darkness, mouth filled with gleaming white teeth, sharp so as to bite through the neck of its victims.

The wolf takes many forms. It comes with rolling earth and crashing wave. It comes with the dry heat of a rainless summer. It comes slithering on the ground, bounding from a tree, crawling up our pants legs. It comes with a howling wind, huffing and puffing and blowing our houses down. The fear of the wolf is surely the fear of nature, the fear of the uncontrollable elements that are arrayed against us, the unseen force, the unexpected flash of lightning. It is the primal Other. Beyond morality, beyond culture, beyond law.

Sometimes it sleeps in the camp, sits with us around the fire, kills with hands and not claws, guns and not fangs. Sometimes the wild uncontrollable thing is in the person with whom we share a pot of coffee, the person with whom we share a bed. The unexpected comes from the house next door. Who would have guessed? He looked so normal, was a good neighbor, how did we not know? Hence the werewolf, the human-beast, the man with red eyes and sharp canines who kills and destroys with the unpredictability of nature, with the suddenness of a storm. The beast is among us. We hide from it, but the world, the natural world, is never far from our door. We seek to control it, but it cannot be tamed.

❛It is at once both the wolf in sheep's clothing, waiting to spring on us unawares, and the hound with the beating heart of the wolf, longing to run wild in the night.❜

But if the werewolf can represent the shuddering fear that we feel when faced with the wildness of nature, it can also represent freedom from the stifling domesticity of our civilization. It is at once both the wolf in sheep's clothing, waiting to spring on us unawares, and the hound with the beating heart of the wolf, longing to run wild in the night, to howl at the moon, to shake loose the collar and break free from the cage. For some the werewolf is a sign of carnage, of natural evil breathing down our necks. For others, it is the symbol of freedom, not a tool of the devil, but a hound of God.

Maybe Wolf VanZandt would say, before Little Red Riding Hood, before Little Red Cap, before the tale of the grandmother, maybe there was an older, truer tale. Maybe before the wolf was profaned before generations of children, maybe the wolf – the werewolf – was the hero. Perhaps Little Red and the grandmother were not such innocents after all. Perhaps it was they who did the work of the devil. Perhaps Little Red left the path to seek out the secret ingredients of some witch's boiling potion, some brew to curse the ground and kill the crops. The werewolf, then, was forced to enact a cunning scheme. He must kill the grandmother first and dress in her clothes, thereby taking on her power. Then he must lie in wait for the arrival of Little Red, the most powerful of the two witches, so that he can catch her by surprise, swallow her whole before she knows what bit her. Perhaps that ancient liturgy should be read the other way round, as a threat, not from the devil in the shape of a wolf, but to the devil in the shape of innocence.

O Grandmother, what big teeth you have.
All the better to eat you with, my child.

This Little Piggy 4

And the unclean spirits went out, and entered into the swine; and the herd (they were about two thousand) ran violently down a steep place into the sea, and were choked in the sea.

Mark 5:13

What would you do if a herd of filthy pigs came into your parlor and began to make themselves at home? Would you invite such a thing? Would you pay no attention to them in the hope they would soon leave of their own accord? Would you try to clean up their mess as fast as they made it? You would do none of these things. You would drive them out as quickly and unceremoniously as possible! And that is to be our attitude toward demon spirits. As soon as they are discovered they are to be driven out.

Frank and Ida Mae Hammond, *Pigs in the Parlor*

This little piggy went to Hades,
This little piggy stayed home,
This little piggy ate raw and steaming human flesh,
This little piggy violated virgins,
And this little piggy clambered over a heap of dead bodies
to get to the top.

Neil Gaiman and Terry Pratchett, *Good Omens*

Stories of demons are told in Sunday school by white-haired ladies in floral dresses, and in sanctuaries bathed in the kaleidoscope light of stained glass by gentlemen in white and black robes. Thus demons are given an imprimatur lacked by other creatures of the night. They cannot so easily be relegated to folklore and superstition or transformed into lovable mascots for breakfast cereals. Their existence is attested to by scripture and endorsed by Jesus. They are fallen angels, the servants of Satan. They are pure evil, the darkest of the dark, the denizens of hell. As much as the sophisticated and rational might like them to go away, they will not. They possess us now as they always have, since the days of Jesus, since Jesus called them by name and cast them into swine.

The Gospel according to Mark tells of Jesus' meeting with a wild and ferocious man, untamable, who shattered the chains that were meant to keep him safe and meant to keep him away from the desolate hills and the tombs of the dead, where he cried and slashed his flesh with stones. Possessed by an unclean spirit, he made his home among the graves – a dead soul among dead souls – his only companions rare and solitary mourners and farmers from the hills with their stinking, squealing swine.

Jesus, seeing the man's tattered clothes and his matted hair, smelling the stink of the dead on him, looked into his eyes and recognized the torment that was there, saw the unclean thing that was within, the dirty creature in his soul that was even more foul than the dirty creature he was on the surface. Jesus spoke with authority and ordered the demon to come out of his victim, to come out and set the man's spirit free.

From the man's mouth came words that were not his own: the voice of a demon. 'Jesus,' it pleaded, 'son of the most high God, do not torment me!'

Jesus, perhaps seeking to find the secret to the demon's power, asked his name.

'My name is Legion, for we are many.'

Legion, a name loaded with meaning for early readers of this account from the Gospel, a name that brought to mind images of the Roman infantry and the empire whose will it enforced, images of political and economic domination, of tax levies and military conscriptions, of tumbling temple walls and bloody crosses. But Jesus, the exorcist, does not step back when he hears the name. He does not cower. Instead it is Legion that falters, Legion that begs Jesus not to send them out naked, but to cast them into a herd of swine.

The swine themselves were unclean creatures, loathed by the Jews but kept to please the Roman masters. A pig had been sacrificed upon the altar of the temple of God in Jerusalem by Antiochus Epiphanes, an unholy event known to the prophet Daniel as 'the abomination of desolation,' and the animal had thereafter been associated with outside invaders, be they Greek or Roman. Pigs were forbidden by God, yet allowed to roam these hills and defile the tombs of the saints. Where else should the demon known as Legion be sent, but into the swine? The herd of swine fled, squealing and grunting, away from the man of God, the exorcist with power over them. They fled into the sea, choking and drowning, leaving nothing behind to show their presence. The exorcist cast out the demons, and the demons fled.

Since the days of Jesus, belief in demons has come and gone; likewise, belief in the possession of human bodies by these spirits of darkness. At times, Western society has seen demons hiding in every dark corner, responsible for all human temptations. They have been blamed for mental illness, for moral shortcomings and for the sundry natural evils that plague humanity. The Middle Ages was a time when demons were especially common, present in the lives of peasants and kings, sinners and saints. Demons of envy, sloth, lust and greed cavorted with their peers to make the life of human beings difficult and miserable. But, as the Dark Ages passed, as knowledge increased and diseases were cured, demons went into hiding and dropped from human consciousness. The modern age offered scientific explanations where supernatural ones had once prevailed.

In the twentieth century, and at the dawning of the twenty-first, many have wondered that Western society is still not free of these enemies of humanity, these dark deceivers. The Middle Ages, when demons were at their worst, was a time of pestilence and disease. Our age is a time of medical wonders. The Middle Ages was a time of ignorance and superstition. Our age is a time of knowledge and information. There is no reason that we too should be possessed by devils and demons, by the leathery-winged creatures of nightmares and mythology. Surely, when Jesus cast out demons he was only curing mental illness falsely named, a cure best performed today with psychotherapy and psychotropic drugs. Surely the exorcism of Legion is a fable, a political tale meant to show the power of God over kingdoms of the world, the demon merely a metaphor for the Roman occupation of Judea. Surely we know better today. We, of all people, of all ages, should be free from the need for the exorcist, for the demon slayer.

Yet, two thousand years after Jesus healed the man of his mental illness, two thousand years after insurrection against the Roman overlords was dramatized by casting the demon named Legion into a drowning herd of swine, two thousand years after the exorcist Jesus cast the demon out, another exorcist stood at the front of a tent, open Bible held over his head in one hand, a microphone in the other. He spoke with authority, with forceful certainty.

* * *

'The devil and his demons prowl like roaring lions, like wolves among the sheep. They are here among us tonight. I sense their presence.'

Voices from behind me shouted, 'Amen!' and, 'Yes, Jesus!'

'But the Bible says that if we resist the devil he will flee from us. The Bible says that believers shall be given the power to cast out demons in Jesus' name. Do you believe it?'

'Yes, Jesus!'

'Tonight, I claim that authority. Tonight, I claim that promise. Jesus, tonight I stand before these people in your name. I call the demons of hell to stand before your judgment. I call them forth to be cast out like the swine they are.'

The exorcist paced the floor like a caged lion. The Bible, still held aloft, its soft leather cover and thin leaves exaggerating every movement he made, looked like a thing alive. His shouts then faded into whispers.

'I call on every man, woman or child in this place to bow your heads now before Almighty God. Look deep into your hearts, deep into your souls. Look to the place where you are broken, the place where you hurt the most, the place where you keep the fear and the pain balled up and tamped down. Think back on the wickedness that you have committed and that has been committed against you. Think back to the time you played with that Ouija board, to that horror movie that gave glory to the devil, to that moment of anger when you cursed the Lord's holy name, to that sexual sin, that perversion that you battle every night. Look deep into your heart until you find that point of shame.'

Behind me someone began to speak in tongues. The syllables poured out of her mouth, disconnected from all meaning.

'Thank you, Jesus!' someone shouted from across the room.

I looked up and watched the exorcist. He looked back over his shoulder and gave a command to one of his lieutenants. A woman stepped from the shadows behind him and went into the crowd. Now she spoke in tongues as well, her voice matching the cadence of the other. Are they talking to one another, I wondered, speaking soul to soul, sharing intimate details too pure for common language?

Now there were sounds coming from all around me, mumbled syllables of glossolalia, shouts of joy, sobbing voices at the point of breaking, growls and grunts and squeals. The lieutenants were all over the room, listening to confessions, speaking prayers, trying in vain to hold the trembling and jerking bodies, to contain the wild flailing limbs.

The exorcist, having stirred the pot, now watched it come to a boil.

*   *   *

Demons began to stir in the late twentieth century thanks to William Peter Blatty's novel, *The Exorcist* and William Friedkin's blockbuster adaptation of the book for the big screen. The cultural event that was *The Exorcist* burst on the scene with Blatty's novel in 1971 and reached a fever pitch two years later as the world watched Linda Blair, as Regan MacNeil, succumb to dark demonic forces. Demons, formerly most effectively depicted by filmmakers in 1957's *Night of the Demon* (*Curse of the Demon* in its U.S. release), were now truly terrifying. The world watched in horror as the angelic-faced little girl was transformed into a living force of evil who spat bile and profanities at priests and defiled herself with a crucifix. Opening the day after Christmas, the film became a cultural phenomenon, and exorcism – previously regarded as a primitive and archaic custom believed in only by those among the most superstitious or fundamentalist segments of the population – was suddenly the hot topic for conversations at cocktail parties, in college classrooms and in Sunday schools.

Not that exorcisms were entirely unheard of in the Western world prior to Linda Blair's head-turning performance as a twelve-year-old girl possessed by an ancient spirit. As a matter of fact, Blatty himself was inspired by reports of a real-life exorcism performed in the United States in 1949. The story was first brought to public attention in an August 10, 1949 article in the *Washington Post* which detailed an account of a thirteen-year-old boy from a Washington, D.C., suburb who had been taken to St. Louis for a Catholic exorcism. The boy's family reported strange noises from his bedroom, the violent shaking of his bed while he slept, and objects jumping off of tables when he entered a room. During the exorcism, the

31. Max Von Sydow, Jason Miller and Linda Blair in *The Exorcist* (1973) (Warner Bros.).

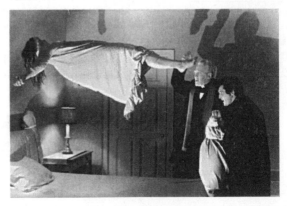

boy reportedly spoke in Latin – a language that was unfamiliar to him – threw violent tantrums and hurled blasphemous curses at the priests. It was this story that piqued the interest of Georgetown University English major Blatty, and inspired him to write his famous novel. Discovering more details of the case in a diary kept by one of the priests involved in the exorcism, Blatty's tale is a graphic and sensationalized version of this real-life exorcism.

In turn, the 1949 exorcism has striking parallels with an even earlier American exorcism from the 1920s, the account of which was very influential in conservative Catholic circles in the mid-twentieth century. The events surrounding this demonic possession were recorded by the Reverend Celestine Kapsner in the 1935 pamphlet *Begone Satan!* Kapsner's account, based on the testimony of the Reverend Joseph Steiger, a witness to the 1928 exorcism performed in Earling, Iowa, has been reproduced and read by generations of conservative Catholics and, as much as any other publication prior to *The Exorcist*, served to bring demonic possession and exorcism into the consciousness of modern society.

Steiger became involved in the exorcism through his friend, Father Theophilus Riesinger, who asked Steiger for permission to perform the solemn ceremony at a local Franciscan convent in his parish. Riesinger described the possessed woman to Steiger as a pious and well-respected member of her community who received the sacraments regularly in her youth. After her fourteenth birthday, however, she reported that some unseen force kept her away from the church and from the sacraments. Despite her great desire to enter the house of worship, her wishes were thwarted by forces she did not understand. She reported that sinister inner voices suggested wicked thoughts to her. She had to fight against impulses to shatter the font of holy water in her church, to attack her spiritual advisor and to 'tear down the very house of God.' Neither doctors nor psychiatrists could find any cause for these strange feelings of animosity toward all things holy.

Under examination by priests, the demonic nature of her condition came to the fore. The woman showed evidence of understanding languages she had never heard or read, particularly Latin. Whenever priests would offer blessings in Latin, she would become enraged and foam at the mouth. Objects sprinkled with holy water, even when she was unaware of it, would cause her great anxiety. It seemed that the rite of exorcism was the only course available.

The possessed woman continued to demonstrate these bizarre behaviors after she arrived at the convent. As Kapsner described it:

The well-meaning Sister in the kitchen had sprinkled holy water over the food on the tray before she carried the supper to the woman. The devil, however, would not be tricked. The possessed woman was aware at once of the presence of the blessed food and became terribly enraged about it. She purred like a cat, and it was absolutely impossible to make her eat. The blessed food was taken back to the kitchen to be exchanged for unblessed food; otherwise the soup bowls and the plates might have been crashed through the window. It was not possible to trick her with any blessed or consecrated article; the very presence of it would bring about such intense sufferings in her as though her very body were encased in glowing coal.*

As the exorcism began, with Steiger assisting, the woman was placed on a bed, her sleeves and dress bound tightly. The strongest of the nuns were chosen to assist in case of attempted violence against the exorcist. As the prayers began in earnest the woman lapsed into unconsciousness, a state in which she remained throughout the ritual. Her lack of consciousness, however, did not prevent her from responding dramatically to the service. Kapsner describes a scene straight out of 2010's *The Last Exorcism*.

Father Theophilus had hardly begun the formula of exorcism in the name of the Blessed Trinity, in the name of the Father, the Son, and the Holy Ghost, in the name of the Crucified Savior, when a hair-raising scene occurred. With lightning speed the possessed dislodged herself from her bed and from the hands of her guards; and her body, carried through the air, landed high above the door of the room and clung to the wall with a tenacious grip. All present were struck with a trembling fear. Father Theophilus alone kept his peace.

With great effort, the woman was pulled from the wall and returned to her bed. This time she was held down more tightly by the nuns. Again, Kapsner describes the scene:

The exorcism was resumed. The prayers of the Church were continued. Suddenly a loud shrill voice rent the air. The noise in the room sounded as though it were far off, somewhere in a desert. Satan howled as though he had been struck over the head with a club. Like a pack of wild beasts suddenly let loose, the terrifying noises sounded aloud as they came out of the mouth of the possessed woman. Those present were struck with a terrible fear that penetrated the very marrow of their bones.

---

* This and following quotations from *Begone Satan!* are taken from the online edition located at www.ewtn.com/library/NEWAGE/BEGONESA.HTM.

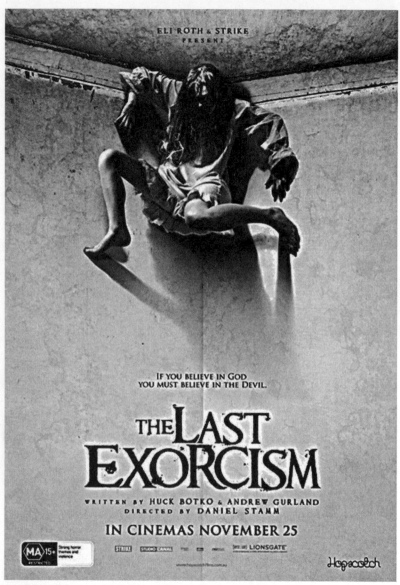

32. Poster for *The Last Exorcism* (2010) (Lionsgate).

The exorcist ordered the demon to be quiet, but the howls continued. Soon, people throughout the neighborhood heard the screams and came running to the convent to investigate, suspecting torture or murder. One witness reportedly said, 'Not even a pig stabbed with a butcher knife yells with such shrieking howls as these.' Soon, news of the exorcism spread throughout the parish.

With crowds gathering outside, the exorcism continued. From the mouth of the woman now came torrents of vomit, as well as the foul and disgusting sounds.

Outpourings that would fill a pitcher, yes, even a pail, full of the most obnoxious stench were most unnatural. These came in quantities that were, humanly speaking, impossible to lodge in a normal being. At that [time] the poor creature had eaten scarcely anything for weeks, so that there had been reason to fear she would not survive. At one time the emission was a bowl full of matter resembling vomited macaroni. At another time an even greater measure, having the appearance of sliced and chewed tobacco leaves, was emitted. From ten to twenty times a day this wretched creature was forced to vomit though she had taken at the most only a teaspoonful of water or milk by way of food.

A wide variety of different voices issued from the woman's mouth, some sounding human, but others sounding bestial or completely unnatural. Some of the sounds were described as clearly beyond the abilities of a human throat to utter.

This ugly bellowing and howling took place every day and at times it lasted for hours. At other times it sounded as though a horde of lions and hyenas were let loose, then again as the mewing of cats, the bellowing of cattle and the barking of dogs. A complete uproar of different animal noises would also resound. This was at first so taxing on the nerves of those present that the twelve nuns were forced to take turns at assisting in order to save themselves and to have the necessary strength to continue facing the siege.

During the exorcism ritual Riesinger spoke to the woman in German and Latin. Even though she had no knowledge of these languages, she replied in kind. When, on occasion, the priest made slight errors of pronunciation or grammar, the woman would rudely interrupt and correct him. Through these conversations with the woman it became clear to the exorcist that she was possessed by multiple spirits, some human and some demonic. The demon Beelzebub seemed to be the strongest force, but the spirit of the woman's deceased father, Jacob, was also quite powerful, as was the spirit of Judas Iscariot, the betrayer of Jesus. In time, the spirit of Jacob confessed that he had often tried to force his daughter to commit incest with him. When she resisted, he had cursed his daughter and wished for devils to enter her body to entice her to all sorts of wicked actions. It was this curse, when she was fourteen years old, that had brought on her possession.

During the performance of the ritual, the possessed underwent severe physical transformations.

> the woman's face became so distorted that no one could recognize her features. Then, too, her whole body became so horribly disfigured that the regular contour of her body vanished. Her pale, deathlike and emaciated head, often assuming the size of an inverted water pitcher, became as red as glowing embers. Her eyes protruded out of their sockets, her lips swelled up to proportions equaling the size of hands, and her thin emaciated body was bloated to such enormous size that the pastor and some of the Sisters drew back out of fright, thinking that the woman would be torn to pieces and burst asunder. At times her abdominal region and extremities became as hard as iron and stone. In such instances the weight of her body pressed into the iron bedstead so that the iron rods of the bed bent to the floor.

The exorcism lasted for twenty-three days, from morning to night, and pushed Riesinger and the other participants almost to the breaking point. Finally, on December 23, 1928, there was a break in the demonic hold over the woman.

> [W]ith a sudden jerk of lightning speed the possessed woman broke from the grip of her protectors and stood erect before them. Only her heels were touching the bed. At first sight it appeared as if she were to be hurled up to the ceiling. 'Pull her down! Pull her down' called the pastor while Father Th. blessed her with the relic of the Cross, saying: 'Depart, ye fiends of hell! Begone, Satan, the Lion of Juda reigns!'
>
> At that very moment the stiffness of the woman's body gave way and she fell upon the bed. Then a piercing sound filled the room causing all to tremble vehemently. Voices saying, 'Beelzebub, Judas, Jacob, Mina,' could be heard. And this was repeated over and over until they faded far away into the distance.

Whether or not Blatty was aware of the exorcism from 1928 is unclear, though it is hard to imagine how he could not have been. Nevertheless, it is apparent that the features of exorcism popularized by *The Exorcist* were not created out of whole cloth, but were established in the modern popular religious imagination, at least of conservative Catholics, as early as the 1930s. In Kapsner's account we see elements that would resurface in 1949 and again in the early 1970's. The possessed understands Latin, reacts violently to holy water and other sacred objects, climbs walls like Spider-Man, levitates, disgorges disgusting fluids, undergoes physical contortions, swears and blasphemes and utters foul and animalistic-sounding noises. Everything good and beautiful seems to be taken away, leaving in its place a debased humanity. In some ways, this makes the demon-possessed more terrible than the werewolf. In the latter case, the human is reduced to the state of an animal. In the case of demonic possession, the human is reduced to a state lower than that of the beast, reduced to a corruption of all that is good, reduced to a fiend of blasphemous nature. While it may be true that Blatty's book, and its cinematic adaptation, introduced these themes to the general public, to the masses, it is not true that *The Exorcist* is the source of these themes. That source resides deeper in our culture, deeper in our religion, deeper in our psyches, deeper in the darkness of our lives.

Those who blame *The Exorcist* for the 1976 death of Annaliese Michel, coming just two years after the German release of the film, should keep this in mind. Her death, following sixty-seven rites of exorcism performed in her native Germany, resulted in the trial and conviction of her parents and two priests for negligent manslaughter. While the heroic depiction of the exorcist-priests in *The Exorcist* film and the publicity and interest aroused by its release could certainly have contributed to the fateful outcome of Michel's story, that story, like demonic possession itself, has deeper sources.

Raised in a strict Catholic Bavarian community that was opposed to the liberal reforms of Vatican II, Michel was surely raised in a context in which demons were a part of life. Michel was herself even more extreme in her devotion than were others in her community, sleeping on the floor in the cold of winter to atone for the sins of others. In 1969, according to the courts, Michel suffered her first epileptic seizure and in just a few short years was seeing the faces of demons in the people and things around her. She shredded her clothing, crawled around on all fours, barked like a dog, ate bugs and drank her own urine. In 1975 she requested an exorcism.

Over half of the exorcism sessions, performed by the Revs. Ernst Alt and Arnold Renz, were recorded on tape – many of which are today available on the internet. Eric Hansen, in a review of 2005's *The Exorcism of Emily Rose*, a film based on the 1976 exorcism, for the *Washington Post*, wrote that 'Michel's recorded voice can still send shivers up your spine. It is the voice of a demon, growling, barking, inhuman – and surprisingly like the voice of Linda Blair in "The Exorcist."'* Considering the popularity of *The Exorcist*, one wonders why Hansen is surprised. There is, after all, no reason to suspect that Michel was unfamiliar with the movie or that something at the core of the *zeitgeist* of the mid-1970s would not have influenced the course of her possession. Michel did not die at the hands of her would-be redeemers, at least not directly. She died of self-imposed starvation, believing that her death might atone for the sins of her lost generation and of the faithless priests who adhered to the edicts of Vatican II.

When Malachi Martin published *Hostage to the Devil* in 1976, he had at least two things in common with Annaliese Michel, whose exorcism and death took place that very year. Like Michel, the former Jesuit and bestselling novelist approached exorcism and demonic possession from a position no doubt influenced by *The Exorcist*. Likewise, and perhaps more significantly, he shared Michel's concerns about the modernization of the Catholic Church and what he saw as the growing faithlessness of its clergy.† *Hostage to the Devil*, like *Begone Satan!* and the book and film versions of *The Exorcist*, proved to be critically important in keeping belief in demonic possession alive in the modern world. Along with *The Exorcist*, it helped to introduce exorcism to a large and diverse audience beyond the confines of the Catholic Church.

Martin's book begins with what he calls 'A Brief Handbook of Exorcism,' in which he elaborates on the principles and practices associated with the possession of and deliverance from evil spirits. According to Martin, the process should begin with examinations by medical doctors and psychiatrists who must first rule out any physical or psychological causes for the candidate's behavior. When all other explanations are exhausted, Church authorities make the final judgment as to whether or not they believe the person is possessed.

The Church examiners, according to Martin's account, must look for several indications of true possession.

---

* Eric T. Hansen, 'What in God's Name? A New Film Examines a 1976 Exorcism, Asking What Possessed Those Involved,' *Washington Post*, September 4, 2005.

† Although Michael W. Cuneo, in his excellent *American Exorcism: Expelling Demons in the Land of Plenty*, questions Martin's conservative credentials, Cuneo does also admit that protests at the liberalization of the Church are usually included in Martin's own accounts of why he left his religious order (15).

[A] peculiar revulsion to symbols and truths of religion is always and without exception a mark of the possessed person. In the verification of a case of possession by Church authorities, this 'symptom' of revulsion is triangulated with other physical phenomena frequently associated with possession – the inexplicable stench; freezing temperature; telepathic powers about purely religious and moral matters; a peculiarly unlined or completely smooth or stretched skin, an unusual distortion of the face, or other physical and behavioral trans-formations; 'possessed gravity' (the possessed person becomes physically immovable, or those around the possessed are weighted down with a suffocating pressure); levitation (the possessed rises and floats off the ground, chair, or bed; there is no physically traceable support); violent smashing of furniture, constant opening and slamming of doors, tearing of fabric in the vicinity of the possessed, without a hand laid on them; and so on. (13)

> **'... THE INEXPLICABLE STENCH; FREEZING TEMPERATURE; TELEPATHIC POWERS ABOUT PURELY RELIGIOUS AND MORAL MATTERS ...'**

The exorcism itself usually follows a pattern of six stages identified by Martin as: presence, pretense, breakpoint, voice, clash and finally expulsion. The *presence* of an alien force is felt at the beginning of the exorcism and throughout by everyone in the room. Though an unmistakable something, the presence is intangible, seeming to be nowhere and everywhere, both singular and plural.

Invisible and intangible, the *Presence* claws at the humanness of those gathered in the room. You can exercise logic and expel any mental image of it. You can say to yourself: 'I am only imagining this. Careful! Don't panic!' And there may be a momentary relief. But then, after a time lag of bare seconds, the *Presence* returns as an inaudible hiss in the brain, as a wordless threat to the self you are. (18)

According to Martin, at the earliest stages of the exorcism, this presence seeks to hide behind the personality of the possessed in what he calls the *pretense*. The demon may remain silent or speak in the voice of the victim. Possession is denied, seemingly by the possessed themselves, but this is merely a clever camouflage. The focus of the exorcist during these early stages must be upon breaking this charade and exposing the demon for what it really is. As this *breakpoint* nears, the exorcist may become confused as the demon fights back: 'His ears seem to *smell* foul words. His eyes seem to *hear* offensive sounds and obscene screams. His nose seems to *taste* a high-decibel cacophony . . . Panic – the fear of being dissolved into insanity – runs in quick jabs through everyone there. All present experience this increasingly violent and confusing assault' (19–20).

Finally, if the exorcist remains strong during this assault, the demon will reveal itself. At this breakpoint the spirit will speak of the possessed in the third person. A sure sign that the breakpoint stage has been reached is the appearance of the *voice*.

> The *Voice* is an inordinately disturbing and humanly distressing babel. The first few syllables seem to be those of some word pronounced slowly and thickly – somewhat like a tape recording played at subnormal speed. You are just straining to pick up the word and a layer of cold fear has already gripped you – you know this sound is alien. But your concentration is shattered and frustrated by an immediate gamut of echoes, of tiny, prickly voices echoing each syllable, screaming it, whispering it, laughing it, sneering it, groaning it, following it. . . If the exorcism is to proceed, the *Voice* must be silenced. (20)

To silence the voice, Martin insisted that the exorcist must engage the sprit in a *clash*: a battle of wills between the demon and the exorcist. The exorcist begins by forcing the demon to identify itself and then invokes divine authority to force the demon to leave its host. During this stage, both the possessed and the exorcist may experience severe and violent assaults on their persons. The possessed may undergo bodily contortions and physical disfigurement. The exorcist may have it even worse.

> He is attacked by a stench so powerful that many exorcists start vomiting uncontrollably. He is made to bear physical pain, and he feels anguish over his very soul. He is made to know he is touching the completely unclean, the totally unhuman.
>
> All sense may suddenly seem nonsense. Hopelessness is confirmed as the only hope. Death and cruelty and contempt are normal. Anything comely or beautiful is an illusion. Nothing, it seems, was ever right in the world of man. He is in an atmosphere more bizarre than Bedlam. (23)

Finally, if the exorcist's willpower is strong enough, the demonic presence may be ordered to leave the possessed. Martin called this stage the *expulsion*. Everyone in the room will sense the absence of the evil presence. Minds will clear. Joy will return. The possessed may be physically tired and exhausted, but will feel a sense of peace and relief. Sometimes voices will be heard receding into the distance. Sometimes there will be a sudden quiet. In some cases the victim will remember the exorcism. Sometimes they will not.

Martin illustrated these stages by relating five contemporary exorcisms, exorcisms that he claimed were but a sampling of the large number of demonic possessions and exorcisms of which he was personally aware. Martin claimed to base the case histories on extensive interviews with the principals involved and on audio recordings of the exorcisms themselves. If anyone doubted that the events portrayed in *The Exorcist* could be true, doubted that such exorcisms could take place in the modern day, Martin claimed to offer proof that demonic possession is real and that exorcisms occur more frequently than anyone would have ever suspected.*

Perhaps the most haunting account of demonic possession among Martin's collection is the account of a demon named 'Uncle Ponto.' The case of Uncle Ponto differs somewhat from the norm, Martin tells us, because Uncle Ponto is a special class of demon, known as a familiar spirit. The victim of such a demonic presence does not demonstrate the characteristics of a normal possession and the individual's personality is not subsumed under that of the demon. The familiar spirit rather seeks to become a constant companion to the victim. The relationship can become so intimate that the familiar knows every thought and feeling that the victim has. The victim loses all privacy. His life is an open book to his companion, who can often be both seen and heard by the possessed.

Martin describes how Uncle Ponto appeared to his victim, Jamsie:

A glance in the rearview mirror was enough: Uncle Ponto was on the back seat, that same uncouth smirk on his face that always enraged Jamsie.

'I told you before,' Jamsie shouted violently into the mirror, 'that is a dirty smile. A pig's smile! A foul, swinish smile.'

. . . Jamsie could see the squarish head ending in what was almost a point, the narrow forehead with the tiny zigzag eyebrows slanting upward, the large, bulbous eyes with the whites so reddened that you could hardly distinguish them from the deeply pink irises. And Ponto's nose and mouth and chin – what there was of chin - had always reminded Jamsie of a long, thin pencil stuck in a very ungainly Idaho potato.

Ponto's face looked as if it had been put together in the dark by several people working at cross-purposes, with each part coming from a different face. No one part really matched another part. Even his face color, a

---

* For the question of whether or not Martin's accounts are reliable see Michael W. Cuneo, *American Exorcism: Expelling Demons in the Land of Plenty.*

brownish-black, clashed with his sparse blond hair, which sat like a cheap
toupee on top of that peculiar pointed head.

. . . Ponto's was a caricature of a human face . . . At times it did not
look human at all. It was something else for which Jamsie had no name –
neither animal nor human nor even a nightmare face born in bad dreams
or shown in the Chamber of Horrors. (250)

Ponto stood about four feet, six inches tall, though Jamsie described a
sense of overwhelming size that inexplicably accompanied him.

Jamsie learned to anticipate Ponto's appearances because of a strange
odor that usually preceded him (and lingered an hour or so after he
had gone). He would appear in all sorts of unexpected locations, in the
backseat of the car, sitting on the living room radiator, inside an elevator,
swinging from a highway overpass, in restaurants and at the radio station
where Jamsie worked. Ponto would place money on a counter to pay for
Jamsie's meals, turn faucets on, turn car engines off and on, and switch the
automobile headlights from low to high beam.

Over time, Uncle Ponto began to be jealous of Jamsie's relationship
with women and finally began to try and persuade Jamsie that the two of
them should get married.

Taking this as just a part of Ponto's usual nonsensical prattle – of which
there was always quite a lot in those days – Jamsie thought Ponto would
prattle on to something else if he kept quiet. But Ponto was serious, and
he said so.

'Jamsie! I'm serious. Let's get married.'

Goose pimples started on Jamsie's arms and legs. For the first time
Jamsie began to be seriously afraid of Ponto. (281)

This terrifying thought pushed Jamsie toward suicide and finally
convinced him to seek help from a priest friend and to participate in the
exorcism which freed him from Ponto's influence.

The other possessions described by Martin follow the more familiar
path established by *Begone Satan!* and dramatized in *The Exorcist*, namely
the possession of an individual by an evil spirit who gradually assumes
control over the victim's body. As such his book offers little that is
different from what was seen in earlier accounts of exorcisms or what was
dramatized in *The Exorcist*. The importance of Martin's book, however, is in
its insistence that possessions and exorcisms were taking place in modern-
day America and in larger numbers than anyone had ever imagined. Of
course, as with the stories of Jesus, the modern critic is tempted to look

upon Martin's stories as either misinterpretations of mental illness or as politico-theological morality tales. Indeed, Jamsie's account of Uncle Ponto certainly sounds like the testimony of someone suffering from paranoid schizophrenia. Likewise, it is clear that Martin emphasizes elements of the stories that illustrate a particular theological position. The possessed are guilty of moral and sexual confusion, of dabbling in the occult and of falling under the sway of liberal theologians such as Teilhard de Chardin – trespasses that leave them open to demonic influence and possession.

Of course, Malachi Martin would most likely have seen this kind of rationalist interpretation as just the sort of modern faithlessness that opens the door for demonic influence. It should not be surprising, one might say, that the last quarter of the twentieth century saw such a demonic outbreak. The rejection by modernity of the reality of evil demonic forces is the very thing that increases their presence and their power.

‹It should not be surprising, one might say, that the last quarter of the twentieth century saw such a demonic outbreak.›

Demons are at home among the faithless, within the souls of infidels and unbelievers, in the tombs of the dead and within unbelieving swine. Like Father Karras in *The Exorcist*, we must first overcome our skepticism, our disbelief, before we can confront the evil that is all around us. We must overcome our modern blindness in order to see the swinish smiles on the face of the demons riding in the backseats of our cars and lurking outside our living room windows.

Early in 1976, the same year in which Annaliese Michel's brief life came to an end and Malachi Martin told the world about Uncle Ponto, the Lutz family fled from their home in Amityville, New York. Within little more than a year Jay Anson's book based on their experiences, *The Amityville Horror* (a subsequent movie adaptation followed in 1979 and again in 2005) hit the bestseller lists. The Lutzes' home, it was claimed, was possessed by an evil spirit, a demonic force, something more frightening than a simple ghost or the disembodied spiritual remains of an unhappy former tenant.

The Lutzes purchased the house, knowing of its violent history. Just a year earlier, the house had been the scene of a horrifying murder. Ronald DeFeo had used a high-powered rifle to murder his parents, two brothers and two sisters while they slept. Because of the crime, the house was now in the Lutzes' price range and they saw no reason to suspect that there was anything wrong with the house itself.

It did not take long for the Lutzes to change their minds. From the moment they moved into the house they were overwhelmed by weird phenomena. Strange knockings were heard. George Lutz suffered terrible mood swings. Black stains appeared in their toilet bowls. A window in one room of the house was repeatedly found covered with hundreds of flies. An inexplicable wind blew the front door off its hinges and warped the door frame. Windows were thrown open in the middle of the night. Cash disappeared. A ceramic lion seemed to move itself around their living room. A hidden room was discovered in the basement, its walls painted a blood red.

Most frightening of all was daughter Missy's insistence that her invisible playmate, Jodie the pig, was real, a fact that was confirmed for the Lutzes in one particularly eerie encounter.

Kathy turned off the chandelier and looked around to take her husband's hand in the darkness. She screamed.

Kathy was looking past George's shoulder at the living room windows. Staring back at her were a pair of unblinking red eyes!

At his wife's scream, George whirled around. He also saw the little beady eyes staring directly into his. He jumped for the light switch, and the eyes disappeared in the shining reflection in the glass pane.

'Hey!' George shouted. He burst through the front door into the snow outside.

The windows of the living room faced the front of the house. It didn't take George more than a second or two to get there. But there was nothing at the windows.

'Kathy!' he shouted. 'Get my flashlight!' George strained his eyes to see the back of the house in the direction of Amityville River.

Kathy came out of the house with his light and his parka. Standing beneath the window where they had seen the eyes, they searched the fresh, unbroken snow. Then the yellow beam of the flashlight picked up a line of footprints, extending clear around the corner of the house.

No man or woman had made those tracks. The prints had been left by cloven hooves – like those of an enormous pig. (148–9)

The Lutzes, understandably, abandoned their home to its demons. Others, however, were drawn to the house in an attempt to explain the evil phenomena reported by its owners. Among the psychics and mediums who tried to find the supernatural cause for the family's experiences were

Ed and Lorraine Warren. Following their investigation of the Lutzes and their home, they attested to the reality of an evil force within the house. Lorraine describes herself as a clairvoyant, able to detect and interact with spiritual presences. Ed, on the other hand, preferred the term 'demonologist' and claimed to be an expert on demonic infestations. Their story was most famously told in Gerald Brittle's 1980 book *The Demonologist: The Extraordinary Career of Ed and Lorraine Warren.*

Demonic infestations, unlike hauntings, are – according to the Warrens – associated with the presence of inhuman spirits.

> A preternatural entity, the inhuman spirit is considered to be possessed of a negative, diabolical intelligence fixed in a perpetual rage against both man and God.
>
> What the sprit is, what it can do, and what its existence ultimately portends is the work and concern of the demonologist. (5)

The Warrens believed that demonic infestations, unlike hauntings – which often center around a particular location, such as the place of death of an unhappy spirit – tend to be brought about by the actions of the living. The Warrens described this as the *Law of Attraction*. People who do negative or unnatural things tend to attract negative spirits or demons, regardless of the location. A demonic presence may be also attracted through more direct means, as Regan McNeil attracted the demon in *The Exorcist*, by using a Ouija board; the Warrens called this the *Law of Invitation*.

> 'By the Law of Invitation,' Ed continues, 'it's ask-and-ye-shall-get. An individual can deliberately summon the demonic through a ritual or via some channel of sincere communication. This is an open, voluntary gesture involving ceremonial magic, incantations, séances, use of the Ouija board, or secret profane rituals where an individual *voluntarily* invites a demonic presence to himself.' (100)

Once present in a house or object, however, the demonic influence can remain, regardless of the human presence. Thus the Lutzes could have inherited the demon when they purchased their home. Their house was infested through no fault of their own.

For the Warrens, demonic infestation was actually a stage in the process of total possession. The strategy of demons during the infestation stage is to generate fear through strange phenomena. A more intense stage of infestation was identified by the Warrens as oppression. *Demonic oppression* is marked by an intense onslaught of phenomena, as the Lutzes witnessed before they left their Amityville home. It may also include a psychological attack upon the victims, with the goal of complete possession. According to Ed Warren, 'When possession occurs, the inhuman spirit no longer attacks you, it *becomes* you, so to speak. Seizing the body of the person and imposing its will over that of the human spirit is the ultimate goal of the demonic spirit'(Brittle, 164). The Warrens, themselves Catholic, believed that full-blown possession usually required a priest exorcist in order to release the victim from the demonic forces.

Ed and Lorraine Warren garnered quite a bit of publicity related to their involvement with the Amityville case. Though they never again worked on a case that achieved such notoriety, the Warrens nevertheless continued to bring demonic possession and exorcism before the public through television appearances and media events. If Blatty brought exorcism to the attention of the general public and Martin convinced many readers that demonic possession was a real and current phenomenon, then the Warrens were among the first to take demonic possession on the road and to the media. Their 'man and woman on the street' personalities helped to make demonology and exorcism accessible. Demons, the Warrens claimed, were even more common than Martin had suggested and were responsible for haunting phenomena as well as classical possessions. Furthermore, the Warrens demonstrated that you did not have to be a Catholic priest in order to be a demon buster. Demons, according to the Warrens, are a pervasive threat to modern life, but they can be defeated by heroic individuals with a little knowledge and a bit of clairvoyance. If Ed and Lorraine Warren can be demonologists and demon hunters, then so can we all. As it turns out, we don't even have to be Catholic.

> **‹DEMONS, ACCORDING TO THE WARRENS, ARE A PERVASIVE THREAT TO MODERN LIFE, BUT THEY CAN BE DEFEATED BY HEROIC INDIVIDUALS WITH A LITTLE KNOWLEDGE AND A BIT OF CLAIRVOYANCE.›**

Two rows behind me a large woman was on her knees sobbing and moaning. A man who must have been her husband knelt beside her. Two other men stood over her, both praying loudly. One of them placed his Bible against her forehead. She reacted violently, jerking her head backward as if in pain, and began to hiss like a snake. Her husband brushed the hair from her forehead and whispered something into her ear.

The exorcist stood silently, alone at the front. The Bible was now on a table, the microphone at his side. His eyes were closed and his lips were moving as if he was saying a prayer. Something that looked like anger flashed in his eyes and he shouted into the microphone:

'In the name of the Lord Jesus Christ I command you to be silent!'

In the space of a heartbeat the room grew still.

'The Bible says that all things should be done decently and in order!'

'Yes, Lord.'

'The Bible says that those who speak in tongues should wait on an interpreter.'

'Yes!'

He exhaled loudly into the microphone, then pinched his brow as if frustrated or fighting a headache.

'This sister over here,' he said, pointing to the woman on her knees behind me. 'Bring this sister to me. The Lord has chosen her for deliverance.'

The woman struggled to her feet with the help of her husband and the other two men. Whispers of affirmation could be heard from among the crowd.

The exorcist wasted no time. 'Sister,' he said, 'do you come here seeking deliverance from a demon?'

She nodded her head slowly.

'Are you a believer in Jesus Christ? Have you been washed in the blood?'

Again she nodded.

'Then this demon has no right to your body. This demon is a trespasser and must be made to go. Are you ready to be set free?'

'Yes!' she shouted and threw herself backward. She slumped against her husband and one of the other men rushed over to give his support to her limp body.

The exorcist placed his Bible flat against her forehead and shouted into the microphone. 'Demon, I command you to appear. I demand to speak with you.'

The woman struggled and moaned as if she was in pain, then, still supported by the two men, she spoke. 'What do you want?' she asked.

'Tell me your name.'

The woman was silent. She tried to free herself from the men who were holding her up.

'Demon, you are subject to our Lord Jesus Christ and I am his messenger. You must obey me. What is your name?'

The woman mumbled something that I did not understand. What she said seemed significant to the exorcist, however. He stepped back from the woman and gave the audience a knowing look.

'This woman is possessed by a spirit of voodoo,' he said. He then asked her husband if his wife had ever visited Haiti. He shook his head.

'Is it possible that her ancestors came from Haiti?' the exorcist asked.

'I suppose it's possible,' her husband replied.

'Demon!' the exorcist shouted. 'Are you a spirit of voodoo?'

The woman nodded her head.

'How long have you been with this woman?'

'Since before she was born.'

The exorcist again gave the crowd a knowing look. He said, 'This spirit is a generational spirit. It has been in this woman's family for generations, entering in, no doubt, when her family participated in demonic voodoo rituals. It has plagued this poor woman all of her life. It is time for it to go!'

The crowd erupted into applause. People shouted 'Amen!' and 'Praise God!'

The exorcist motioned for the audience to quiet down, then he approached the woman's husband. 'Are you her husband?' he asked.

'Yes, yes I am.'

'And you know that the Bible says that the husband is the head of the wife and that her body is subject to your authority?'

The man nodded.

'Then you have the authority to cast out this demon. The generational curse that was put upon her family is no longer valid because you have authority over your wife. The demon cannot stay if you command it to go. Will you do that?'

'Yes, yes I will.'

The exorcist motioned for the woman's husband to join him and for another man to take his place by the woman's side.

'Repeat after me,' the exorcist told the husband. 'As this woman's husband in the eyes of God and man . . . I am given authority over her by Christ . . . As Christ is the head of the Church . . . so I am the head of my wife . . . You have no right to reside within her . . . and I cast you out . . . I cast you out . . . I CAST YOU OUT!'

The woman screamed and thrashed, then slumped to the floor. After just a moment she crawled to her knees. Both arms were held above her head and she began to shout, 'Hallelujah! Hallelujah! I'm free! I'm free!'

The crowd erupted in shouts of 'Amen!' and 'Praise the Lord!'

The demon was gone, without levitation, without vomit, without Latin, without spinning heads or defiled crucifixes. I was disappointed. I was also, deep down inside, relieved.

Casting out demons is one of the 'gifts of the spirit,' along with healing and speaking in tongues, celebrated by the charismatic movement and has been a part of charismatic worship since the dawn of the twentieth century. It wasn't until the latter part of that century, however, that casting out demons became a regular subject of discussion and a frequent feature of worship services for Protestants. The rise of demonic possession among evangelical Protestants corresponds roughly with the rise of exorcism in the Catholic Church. In both instances demonic possessions and exorcisms – or deliverances, as they are usually called in Protestant circles – flourished in the wake of the cultural event that was *The Exorcist*.

Perhaps the most influential practitioners of deliverance ministry were Frank and Ida Mae Hammond. Their 1973 book *Pigs in the Parlor: The Practical Guide to Deliverance* is regarded by many as a classic in the field. Like Malachi Martin's book, *Pigs in the Parlor* provides readers with a reference manual for identifying demonic possession and for bringing about deliverance. Importantly, the Hammond's criteria for determining the need for deliverance are of a decidedly less supernatural quality. Instead of focusing on such things as levitation and bodily contortions, the Hammonds focused on ethical and doctrinal features of demonic activity.

For example, the Hammonds offered seven ways to determine the need for deliverance from evil spirits. First, emotional problems may be a sign of demonic influence, specifically the presence of feelings of resentment, hatred, anger, fear and rejection. Second, demonic influence may show itself in the form of mental problems, namely mental torment, procrastination, indecision, compromise and doubt. (Ida Mae claimed to have received a special revelation about schizophrenia and reported, 'the Lord said, ". . . I want you to know that it is demonic. It is a nest of demon spirits, and they came into this person's life when she was very, very young."' (140)) Speech problems, including lying, cursing, criticism, mockery and gossip, offer a third sign. The fourth category is that of sex problems such as fantasy sex experiences, masturbation, perversions, lust, homosexuality, fornication, adultery, provocativeness and harlotry. The fifth indication of the need for deliverance is an addiction to drugs, alcohol or tobacco. Physical infirmities, including many chronic ill-nesses, may also be demon related. Finally, religious error is a sure sign of demonic infiltration.

In some cases the evidence of demonic presence is more explicit. An individual may exhibit serpentine manifestations such as rapid flicking of the tongue, narrowed snake-like eyes and writhing on the floor. The possessed may complain of numbness in the hands and exhibit extended and rigid fingers (usually a sign of the demons of lust, suicide or murder, the Hammonds reported). Demonic possession may be accompanied by loud unexplainable voices, strong unpleasant odors and the rhythmic movements of the possessed.

Likewise, the demon may manifest evidence of its presence as it leaves the victims. The Hammonds wrote:

> When evil spirits depart we normally expect some sort of manifestation through the nose or mouth. Undoubtedly the most common manifestation is coughing. The cough may be dry but it is often accompanied by the bringing up of phlegm. Phlegm may be brought up in excessive amounts. Similar material may be brought up through vomiting, drooling, spitting or foaming. Persons who receive ministry immediately following a big meal, have been observed to gag and retch violently and throw up large amounts of mucus without any traces of food. Rarely have we seen food substances brought up from the stomach. Infrequently small amounts of blood may appear. It is not unusual for this material to flow out of a person for an hour or longer. (62)

‹Demonic possession may be accompanied by loud unexplainable voices, strong unpleasant odors and the rhythmic movements of the possessed.›

Arguably the leading proponent of deliverance ministry working at the present time is evangelist Bob Larson. Larson made a name for himself in evangelical circles in the 1970s when he gained notoriety as an outspoken Christian critic of rock music. Most recently he has turned his attention to exorcisms. Like the Warrens before him, but to an even larger extent, Larson likes to perform his ministry in the eye of the news and entertainment media. He starred in the short-lived reality television program *The Real Exorcist* and has claimed to be working on a deal to take his performance to Las Vegas, where he would cast out demons on stage and in front of an audience, presumably in a Vegas casino.

For Larson, as for the Hammonds, demonic possession is as prevalent as the common cold. As a student in one of his exorcism workshops I mostly learned the many paths that can lead to demonic possession. The list of at-risk behaviors is a long one: listening to rock music, participating in new age practices, playing Dungeons and Dragons, using a Ouija board, practicing Wicca, practicing voodoo, experimenting with crystals or pyramid power, visiting a psychic, participating in Eastern religions, reading horoscopes and getting tattoos or piercings, just to name a few. In addition, demons may be the product of generational curses, passed down from parent to child, sometimes for many generations. Before the training session was over, everyone in the room admitted that they had clearly been exposed to demonic influence through one path or another. Fortunately, for a small offering, Larson volunteered to meet with his students one-on-one and deliver them from the shackles of possession.

In his *Larson's Book of Spiritual Warfare*, Larson noted that the theatrics associated with exorcism and reported by the Warrens and others are actually quite rare. He wrote,

> More than twenty years after Linda Blair played a fictional character whose head rotated 360 degrees as she spat out pea soup in the movie *The Exorcist*, people still ask me if what happened in that movie was accurately portrayed. Some scenes were reasonably authentic, but the more absurd demonic displays were pure Hollywood hype. I've seen more demonic supernaturalism than any living human I've known, but I have yet to witness arms and legs lengthened like rubber bands, heads spinning like tops, or bodies floating in the air. (388)

But, by his own account, Larson's experiences are not nearly as tame as his comments would indicate. He describes witnessing what he calls 'minor acts of levitation' in which a woman was 'thrown about a room as if unseen wrestlers were hurling her in a ring' (388). In another case, Larson describes a woman who was attacked by a 'sexual demon of incubus.' During the exorcism, the demon claimed to be planning to impregnate the woman with a demon-child. Larson writes, 'I watched her abdomen supernaturally swell until it expanded to the size of a full-term pregnancy' (389). Most terrifying of all, Larson reports watching as 'invisible claws' ripped across the body of a young woman, leaving scratches across her face, arms and legs. Wounds were revealed over the rest of her body by the blood seeping through her clothes.

The Protestant deliverance, it seems, can also be filled with theatrics, like the Catholic exorcism. Demons, it would appear, are ecumenical in their approach. They care not whose body they possess, whose head they spin, whose abdomen they stretch, whose house they haunt, whose bed they shake, whose skin they tear, whose souls they damn.

'Little pig, little pig, let me come in!'

Is this the sound the swine heard as Jesus cast the legion of demons their way? Did they resist? Did they object? 'Not by the hair of my chinny, chin, chin!' Or did they acquiesce, open their doors and let the demons in as they rushed madly into the sea? After all, it was not their enemy the wolf pounding at their hearts' doors. It was their fellow swine, their porcine brethren, their next of kin. When it comes to demons it is the pigs who are doing the knocking, the pigs peering in the windows, the pigs squealing from human throats, the pigs eyeing the parlor, its thick carpet and plush upholstery just waiting to be soiled. As it turns out, it is the little pig, little pig, that wants to come in.

Jesus cast demons into swine and it is in swine that they have remained. We can hear them squeal in fear and delight from the mouths of the possessed. We can see their 'foul, swinish smiles' on the face of Uncle Ponto and his kin. Jodie presses his snout to our living room windows, his red eyes gleaming, his hoof prints pressed deep in pure white snow. This little pig puts foul words in our children's mouths. This little pig makes us sick at the thought of all things holy. This little pig is a backseat driver, driving us mad with his insane chatter, his caricature face staring at us in the rearview mirror. This little pig befriends our children only to lead them astray. This little pig makes us lie and cheat and steal.

Demons, unlike ghosts, vampires and werewolves, are accepted by the orthodox within the Western religious tradition; they are accepted before they are cast out. The exorcist and the deliverance minister accept the reality of possessions and curses, of demons and devils. Demons thrive within the context of religion, it is there that they find their home. Indeed, the rejection of the reality of demons is one source of their power, one crack in the house of sticks, which allows them to come in and devour our lives. If other creatures of the night point to the holy in gestures silent and dark, demons squeal about it in churches and convents, under revival tents, in the village market and all the way home.

Ghosts haunt our mortal lives or, more accurately, we are haunted by our mortality. The shudder brought by the ghost is the shudder at our own future, our own ending, our unfinished business, our unrepented sins, our wasted lives. The vampire's horror lies closer to the surface, perhaps. With the vampire, we quake at our fleshly limits, at disease that destroys our health, at death that bloats and rots our bodies, at the fleshly passions that overthrow what we believe are our better rational and moral selves. The werewolf strikes us with the fear of the wolf, of nature wild and uncontrollable, nature lurking without the fire's circle and within. The wolf stalks the forest and strikes from our own beds. These creatures of the night point us to the awful mystery, the tremendous mystery, the wholly other; they are prophets of our doom, heralds of the coming destruction.

Demons, though – demons *are* the wholly other. Ghosts, vampires and werewolves are what we may surely become, the shadow self, the stinking corpse, the animal unleashed. Demons are from the other side. They take human beings and destroy them, transform them into something that they were not before, something foul and rotten, something evil. And the evil of the demon is not the natural evil of the werewolf: the evil that occurs when we humans give in to our baser natures. The evil of the demon is the evil that strikes against nature, that vomits on the priest, desecrates the elements, profanes the crucifix, utters words that are foul and obscene. The ghost is a wandering soul, but the demon is the soul prepared for hell, stinking of brimstone, blaspheming the creator.

The story of the demon is at one level the story of the good kid who turns bad, the gentle soul that learns to kill, the believer who does not lose faith but turns faith back upon itself, believing in the holy but rejecting it, hating it, loathing it. The story of the demon is, at another level, the story of pure evil, evil beyond comprehension, evil beyond motive or understanding, evil from the pit, evil too horrific to name, a Legion, an untold army of wickedness.

> This little piggy makes you live among the dead.
> This little piggy sends you crawling up the wall.
> This little piggy makes you kill your family.
> This little piggy murdered Annaliese.
> And this little piggy says 'Whee! Whee! Whee!' all the way home.

Speak of the Devil

Speak of the Devil and he will appear.

Folk proverb

If the devil does not exist, and man has therefore created him, he has created him in his own image and likeness.

Fyodor Dostoyevsky, *The Brothers Karamazov*

Give the devil his due.

William Shakespeare, *Henry IV, Part I*

I stood under a grove of trees in shadows cast by the moon and the flickering firelight.

Their black robes swallowed the light as they moved around the bonfire in concentric circles, each ring of shadows spinning in opposing directions. I listened to their chanting, watched their dark ritual, smelled their incense, felt their excitement. Lifting words of praise to Satanas, they turned, spinning round and round, raising the cone of power, sending its invisible energy rising to the star-filled sky.

I watched in silence, hardly daring to breathe. I felt as if I had been transported to some ancient world, witness to some primitive Celtic festival or some long-lost Atlantean rite. The air crackled with electricity and I felt drawn to them, as if the spinning vortex of power was pulling me in, perhaps to join them in their eternal circle, perhaps to send me tumbling forever into a black hole, into a rip in space, in time. I made myself move further away, creep deeper into the wooded glen. On the barren hilltop, in the full light of the moon, in the heat of the fire, they circled, faster and faster. Did I feel the air around me begin to move, pulled through the turbine of their turning engine? Did I see the power rise, the fire spark upward, the flame reach for the darkness between the stars? I wiped my sweaty palms on my blue jeans and waited, thinking for a moment that I should run down the hill to my car and drive away, thinking that something dark was being borne into the world this night.

Speak of the devil and he will appear.

Then, with an unspoken suddenness, it all stopped. The circles stood still. At just the moment that it seemed their ritual was going to cross the line into madness, into a place where the turning would never stop, their bodies spinning ever on through eternity, their chants rising higher and higher into the sky; at the very last instant, my car keys in hand, the cone of power collapsed, the air settled, the Brotherhood of Satan grew silent. Then one of them laughed. Not an evil laugh from the throat of a dark-robed villain, but a laugh of relief, of excitement, of joy.

I was no longer atop a pagan mountain, witnessing the birth of the world. I was on a hillside in a small town, a quiet residential street below me, houselights twinkling through the trees. I smelled fresh-cut grass, a hamburger on a grill, car exhaust. I dug an ice-cold beer from the bottom of a cooler and settled into a folding lawn chair, exhausted and exhilarated by what I had seen and by what I had learned. I wondered what the neighbors must think of this gathering of Satanists from around the United States, their bonfire blazing for all to see, their chants drowning out the chirp of cicadas.

Satanists have long been the enemy. Since the Dark Ages accusations of Satan worship have been leveled against enemies of the Church, dissenters, political rivals and those on the outskirts of society. In the fourteenth century, Philip IV of France accused the Knights Templar of Satanism and had them tortured until they confessed. In the late fifteenth century, the *Malleus Maleficarum* or *The Hammer of Witches*, written by Heinrich Kramer and Jacob Sprenger – both Dominican inquisitors – codified the charge of Satanic devotion and provided an arsenal of accusations to use against those deemed evil or demonic by the Church. In the wake of its publication, Satanists came out of the woodwork, out of the closet, out of the darkness into the light of accusation and shame. Kramer and Sprenger spoke of the devil and he appeared.

Based on testimony received under torture and on folktales and legends, the *Malleus Maleficarum* painted a horrible picture of witches and of the devil as the source of their power. Witches, it was claimed, came to their power through pacts with Satan himself. The devil was said to appear at the dark gatherings of witches where novices were presented to swear allegiance to the dark lord. At these meetings the initiates were asked whether they would reject the faith of the Church, forsake the Christian religion and reject the veneration of the sacraments.

> [I]f [the devil] finds the novice or disciple willing, then the devil stretches out his hand, and so does the novice, and she swears with upraised hand to keep that covenant. And when this is done, the devil at once adds that this is not enough; and when the disciple asks what more must be done, the devil demands the following oath of homage to himself: that she give herself to him, body and soul, forever, and do her utmost to bring others of both sexes into his power. (165)

Finally, the devil would insist that his new disciple make unguents from the bones and limbs of children, especially children who had been baptized. When this is done, the devil promised, his dark power would be shared with the witch, and her magic would be strong and true.

The *Malleus Maleficarum* reported that at least one accused witch had confessed to this evil deed. She claimed,

> We set our snares chiefly for unbaptized children, and even for those that have been baptized, especially when they have not been protected by the sign of the Cross and prayers (Reader, notice that, at the devil's command, they take the unbaptized chiefly, in order that they may not be baptized), and with our spells we kill them in their cradles or even when they are sleeping by their parents' side, in such a way that they afterwards are thought to have been overlain or to have died some other natural death. Then we secretly take them from their graves, and cook them in a cauldron, until the whole flesh comes away from the bones to make a soup which may easily be drunk. Of the more solid matter we make an unguent which is of virtue to help us in our arts and pleasures and our transportations; and with the liquid we fill a flask or skin, whoever drinks from which, with the addition of a few other ceremonies, immediately acquires much knowledge and becomes a leader in our sect. (167)

‘THEN WE SECRETLY TAKE THEM FROM THEIR GRAVES, AND COOK THEM IN A CAULDRON, UNTIL THE WHOLE FLESH COMES AWAY FROM THE BONES TO MAKE A SOUP WHICH MAY EASILY BE DRUNK.’

In addition to the public displays of allegiance to Satan, it was also reported that some witches were known to make their pact with the evil one in private.

> The other private method is variously performed. For sometimes when men or women have been involved in some bodily or temporal affliction, the devil comes to them speaking to them in person, and at times speaking to them through the mouth of someone else; and he promises that, if they will agree to his counsels, he will do for them whatever they wish. But he starts from small things ... and leads gradually to the bigger things. (168)

Such Faustian bargains, of course, are a staple of folklore and literature: morality plays meant to evoke a spirit of caution and circumspection. For Kramer and Sprenger, however, such bargains were decidedly real, yet another avenue for Satan's recruitment of disciples.

Kramer and Sprenger also described something that would become a common theme in the history of Satanism: desecration of the host, of the body of Christ. For example, they reported that 'a certain witch' received the host, only to remove it from her mouth and hide it in her clothing. After leaving Mass the witch placed the host in a pot along with a toad and buried it. Her actions were exposed when a workman heard what he thought were a child's cries coming from the ground. Suspecting infanticide, the workman reported his observations to the local authorities who, instead of rushing to the child's rescue, waited to see who might return to the scene of the crime. When the witch returned she confessed that she had followed the instructions of the devil and that the remains of the toad and host were to be used for magical purposes.

Such stealthy secreting of the host was, according to the authors, fairly common, prompting them to offer advice to those charged with serving the holy sacrament:

> For this reason all rectors of the Church and those who communicate the people are enjoined to take the utmost care when they communicate women that the mouth shall be well open and the tongue thrust well out, and their garments be kept quite clear. And the more care is taken in this respect, the more witches become known by this means. (187)

It is, of course, difficult to take the accounts of Kramer and Sprenger seriously, considering that they relied so heavily on testimony taken under torture or threat of torture. Many people of the time, however, took the accounts quite seriously and used *Malleus Maleficarum* as justification

for torture and abuse. Medieval Satanism is thus a double-edged source
of horror. We shudder once when we think of the crimes of which the
witches were accused and to which they confessed: the murder of children,
followed by the obscene boiling of flesh from their bones and the drinking
of the rich meaty soup; copulation by the light of the full moon with the
beast himself, the horned goat, the lord of the flies; the rejection of light in
favor of darkness; the promise of body and soul to the service of the great
worm. We shudder again when we think of how these horrors came to be
confessed: by torture both physical and psychological, by threats of torment
and empty promises never intended to be kept. Kramer and Sprenger
described the techniques that, surely, always produced a confession:

> [I]f after being fittingly tortured she refuses to confess the truth, [the
> judge] should have other engines of torture brought before her, and tell
> her that she will have to endure these if she does not confess. If then she
> is not induced by terror to confess, the torture must be continued on the
> second or third day, but not repeated at that present time unless there
> should be some fresh indication of its probable success. (346)

The crimes of the inquisitors were as bad as the crimes of which the
witches were accused. No, they were worse, because they were most
certainly real. What must it have been like to stand before the judges,
hungry, dirty and weary from pain? What must it have been like to hear
the charges read: the cursing of a friend by sinister means, the destruction
of crops, the forcing of needles into the heads of newborn children, the
consuming of human flesh, the consorting with the devil? In charges of
witchcraft, allegiance to Satan, horror builds upon horror, fear upon fear.

Fortunately, over time *The Hammer of Witches* ceased to carry weight with
Church authorities, and belief in witches and devils dwindled with the
advance of science. Accusations of Satanism outlasted the Inquisition,
however, flaring up now and again even in these 'more civilized' times.
In the 1980s, for example, a Satanism scare swept the United States and
Europe, characterized by charges of what became known as Satanic ritual
abuse (SRA). The scare was sparked in large part by the bestselling book
Michelle Remembers, in which Michelle Smith, assisted by her psychiatrist
Lawrence Pazder, narrated accounts of childhood abuse by Satanists.
Smith's memories were 'recovered memories', brought back to her through
counseling and hypnosis. Though later the subject of serious challenges to
the veracity of the accounts, *Michelle Remembers* nevertheless encouraged
other 'victims' of SRA to come forward and tell their stories.

In 1988, the evangelical Christian world became absorbed with stories of SRA recorded in the book *Satan's Underground* by Lauren Stratford. Stratford claimed to have been abused by a Satanic cult as a young adult. Held by a Satanist named Victor, she was told that a baby would be ritually murdered each week until she submitted to his will. At first refusing to join the worship of Satan, she finally broke after being locked inside a metal drum with the bodies of four dead infants, victims of her unwillingness to succumb to Victor's demands. Having finally agreed, she claimed to have participated in the sacrifice of another infant to Satan on Halloween night. She also stated that she had given birth to three children during her time of captivity, two of whom were killed on camera during the making of 'snuff' films, and one who was murdered as an offering to Satan. Stratford became a guest on Christian television and radio shows as well as on more mainstream television talk shows, and her account was taken very seriously by many people. In October 1988, ABC Television broadcast *Devil Worship: Exploring Satan's Underground*, hosted by Geraldo Rivera. The two-hour program brought the charges of SRA to the attention of an enormous audience. Like the stories of Michelle Smith, Stratford's accounts have been seriously challenged by later investigators.*

❰ROCK MUSIC, ESPECIALLY HEAVY METAL, WAS OFTEN ASSOCIATED WITH THE SATANISTS, SOME RECORDINGS EVEN SUPPOSEDLY INCLUDING HIDDEN, PRO-SATANIC MESSAGES THAT COULD BE UNCOVERED BY PLAYING THE RECORD BACKWARDS.❱

In the heyday of the scare, law enforcement officers were often trained in techniques for spotting evidence of SRA, and claims were made that tens of thousands of children and adults were being kidnapped, abused and murdered by Satanic cults. SRA charges were usually characterized by claims involving multiple young victims, usually victimized between birth and the age of six, as well as by multiple offenders, often including well-known community members such as law enforcement officers, clergy or elected officials. The abuse was also characterized by bizarre ritual behaviors, including chants, costumes, prayers, drug use, animal sacrifices, vampirism and cannibalism. Rock

---

* For an interesting exposé of Stratford's claims see 'Satan's Sideshow: The True Lauren Stratford Story' by Bob and Gretchen Passantino and Jon Trott, *Cornerstone*, Vol. 18, Issue 90 (1990), pp. 23–8.

music, especially heavy metal, was often associated with the Satanists, some recordings even supposedly including hidden, pro-Satanic messages that could be uncovered by playing the record backwards, a phenomenon known as 'backward masking.' According to the FBI, however, none of the charges of SRA was shown to have merit.*

Perhaps the most infamous U.S. case of SRA accusations was centered on the McMartin Preschool in California, where the entire staff of the daycare facility was accused in 1983 of participating in sexual and physical abuse motivated by Satanist beliefs. The charges in the McMartin case, like those recorded in the *Malleus Maleficarum*, would look laughable in hindsight if so much harm had not been done. Like the witches who stood before the Inquisition, these innocents stood before their accusers, charged with unspeakable evil. Though no guilty verdicts were reached by the court, the lives of the accused, and of the children who came to believe their own fabricated testimony, were irrevocably harmed. Once again, horror begat horror, fear begat fear.

Contemporary accusations of Satanism have not been limited to charges of ritual abuse, however. For the more conspiratorially minded, Freemasonry remains a popular target. Many of the current charges against the organization date from late nineteenth-century France and the work of Leo Taxil, a convert to Catholicism. Taxil claimed that Freemasonry represented a world-wide Satanist conspiracy. He articulated his charges in several books and before the Pope, who apparently took the charges somewhat seriously. Exposed as a fraud by A.E. Waite in his book *Devil Worship in France*, Taxil himself later recanted and confessed that his conversion to Catholicism had been a sham and his attack on Freemasonry meant to embarrass the Church. His confession, however, has not served to discourage those who continue to claim Satanic origins for the Masonic Orders.

William Schnoebelen, for example, claims to be a former Mason who came to his senses and abandoned the evil practices associated with the organization. He wrote in 1991's *Masonry: Beyond the Light*,

It could be said, with poetic license, that Freemasonry is the world's largest coven of witches. This statement would doubtless astound most Masons.

---

* See Kenneth V. Lanning, 'Investigator's Guide to Allegations of "Ritual" Child Abuse', Behavioral Science Unit, National Center for the Analysis of Violent Crime, Federal Bureau of Investigation, FBI Academy, Quantico, Virginia 22135 (1992). A copy of the report was found by this author at: www.religioustolerance.org/ra_rep03.htm.

However, appearances can be deceiving, and Masonry, like any secret society, has layers within layers – it is a Chinese puzzle box of evil.

Each box unveils a stronger increment of iniquity. Yet these 'boxes' remain shut to Masons who do not advance to higher levels. Since most Masons do not rise higher than the 32° in the Scottish Rite or the Knight Templar in the York Rite, they get no more than glimpses behind the veil. (142)

Following Taxil, Schnoebelen claims that American Mason Albert Pike was instrumental in creating a secret Luciferian rite within Masonry – the Palladium Rite. He accuses Waite of being a sorcerer and magician himself and claims that his criticisms of Taxil were driven by his own devotion to the dark paths. Schnoebelen offers by way of proof for the existence of the Palladium this first-hand testimony:

I was brought into Palladium Lodge (Resurrection, #13) in Chicago in the late 1970's and received the degree of 'Paladin' in that Lodge in 1981 . . . Evidently there was (and is) Palladium Masonry being worked in the 20th century.

I am ashamed to admit it, but I, myself, stood in Lodge and joined in the traditional Palladium imprecation, which is (translated from the French): 'Glory and Love for Lucifer! Hatred! Hatred! Hatred! To God accursed! accursed! accursed!' (192)

He also includes a copy of a certificate conferring the thirty-third degree of Masonry in the Palladium Brotherhood upon his wife Sharon. The document is signed by Brother David D. DePaul, Sovereign Grand Inspector Gen., 33°, Illuminatis Primus, Societe Des Illumines, Northern, U.S.A.

Schnoebelen also harks back to the medieval charges against the Knights Templar, and accuses Freemasonry of continuing the Satanic tradition of that ancient order. While recognizing that confessions were often gleaned by torture, he argues that there must indeed be a kernel of truth to the charges and accuses the Knights Templar, as well as modern Masons, of worship of the horned god, Baphomet. In support of his claim is the document conferring honors upon his wife in which the Ordo Templi Baphomet, the Ordre Du Palladium and the Ancient Order of the Knights of the Temple are listed as sponsoring organizations in her induction into the higher orders of Freemasonry.

The leader of the Brotherhood of Satan is Arch High Priest Druwydion Pendragon. Pendragon is a small wiry man with piercing eyes and a well-manicured goatee. On my visit to his gathering he wore a bandana to cover his hair, and a t-shirt and blue jeans. The two dozen or so people who were gathered in small-town America had traveled from all over the country to sit at his feet and learn the secrets of Satan, their cars parked helter-skelter in his front yard. The cone of power whose creation I had witnessed had burst forth on the hilltop behind Pendragon's modest home, beside a barn where a horned and bearded goat roamed the length of his chain. There was nothing on the surface that would indicate that Pendragon's home doubles as the Brotherhood of Satan's National Office. Not even the goat seemed out of place in this small country town.

After some pleading I persuaded Pendragon to allow me to attend the gathering of his followers. I received a conference discount at the local hotel (the only hotel in which I have ever stayed that posted a sign reading: 'Anyone caught smoking illegal substances in this motel will be escorted off the premises by the police'). I was told to register at the hotel as a member of the B.O.S. and, if asked, to say that the initials stood for the Brotherhood of the South. This little bit of subterfuge aside, however, there seemed little chance that the people in town didn't know what Pendragon was about. His neighbors, with a clear view of the dark rituals performed on the hillside, must have known. Indeed, one of those gathered told of a meeting in the recent past that had been interrupted by a group of locals caught spying from the woods. No doubt for the rest of their lives they would tell about the night they were chased away into the darkness by the black-robed followers of Satan. Other than that, however, all seemed quiet. I wondered how Pendragon managed to keep such a low profile. Considering all of the charges brought against Satanism, surely his group was not immune.

'It's simple,' Pendragon replied, 'I'm a thirty-third degree Mason. I out-rank everyone on the police force. Most of the city government comes to me for guidance. They don't harass me because they know who and what I am.'

The best-known image of Baphomet, the supposed horned god of Masonry and the Knights Templar, was produced by French occultist Eliphas Levi for his *Dogme et Rituel de la Haute Magie* (*Transcendental Magic: Its Doctrine and Ritual*) of 1854. Levi himself identified the image as the 'Goat of Mendes' or the 'Sabbatic Goat' and described its significance in this way:

> The goat . . . carries the sign of the pentagram on the forehead, with one point at the top, a symbol of light, his two hands forming the sign of

hermetism, the one pointing up to the white moon of Chesed, the other pointing down to the black one of Geburah. This sign expresses the perfect harmony of mercy with justice. His one arm is female, the other male like the ones of the androgyn of Khunrath, the attributes of which we had to unite with those of our goat because he is one and the same symbol. The flame of intelligence shining between his horns is the magic light of the universal balance, the image of the soul elevated above matter, as the flame, whilst being tied to matter, shines above it. The beast's head expresses the horror of the sinner, whose materially acting, solely responsible part has to bear the punishment exclusively; because the soul is insensitive according to its nature and can only suffer when it materializes. The rod standing instead of genitals symbolizes eternal life, the body covered with scales the water, the semi-circle above it the atmosphere, the feathers following above the volatile. Humanity is represented by the two breasts and the androgyn arms of this sphinx of the occult sciences. (300–1)

The image soon became associated with Baphomet, the god supposedly worshipped by the Templars and, though it was created in the mid-nineteenth century, came to be regarded by occultists as an ancient symbol. It was in this sense that the image and name was adopted by Aleister Crowley.

33. Aleister Crowley (1875–1947).

Crowley (1875–1947) was an English occultist who carefully cultivated the image of 'the wickedest man in the world.' At age twenty-three he joined the Hermetic Order of the Golden Dawn, an occult organization influenced by Eliphas Levi. In 1914, Crowley made his connection with the Knights Templar, and all of their reported heresies, clear when he became the leader of the Ordo Templi Orientis (The Order of Oriental Templars) and took the name Baphomet after their supposed deity.

In 1904, while traveling in Egypt, he wrote his most influential contribution to occult literature, *The Book of the Law*, the text of which Crowley claimed was revealed to him by the spirit Aiwass. The work, the very epitome of obscurity, is perhaps best summarized by these central claims:

39. The word of the Law is THELEMA.

40. Who calls us Thelemites will do no wrong, if he look but close into the word. For there are therein Three Grades, the Hermit, and the Lover, and the man of Earth. Do what thou wilt shall be the whole of the Law.

41. The word of Sin is Restriction. O man! refuse not thy wife, if she will! O lover, if thou wilt, depart! There is no bond that can unite the divided but love: all else is a curse. Accursed! Accursed be it to the aeons! Hell.

42. Let it be that state of manhood bound and loathing. So with thy all; thou hast no right but to do thy will.

43. Do that, and no other shall say nay.

44. For pure will, unassuaged of purpose, delivered from the lust of result, is every way perfect. (30–1)

'Thelema' became the term Crowley used to describe his own brand of occult philosophy and magic. The term, along with his philosophy of 'do what thou wilt,' had their sources in the work of François Rabelais (1494–1553) and his fictional abbey of Thélème. Crowley's Thelema is a humanistic philosophy, bearing the mark of Nietzsche's rejection of ethical monotheism in favor of personal will and existential freedom.

Crowley's theory of magic, or – as Crowley would have it – 'magick' was based in part on the Enochian Keys of John Dee (1527–1608). Dee, like Crowley, claimed that his knowledge came from the spirit world, specifically from angelic beings that he had the ability to summon through his assistant Edward Kelly. These angelic revelations were given in the Enochian language, supposedly a language that pre-dated ancient Hebrew. The Enochian Keys are spells and charms that reportedly allow their users to call upon the aid of spiritual beings. Crowley's own experiences with the Enochian Keys were recorded as *The Vision and The Voice* or *Liber 418*, in which he described the Enochian or Angelic language,

> It is not a jargon; it has a grammar and a syntax of its own. It is far more sonorous, stately and impressive than even Greek or Sanskrit and the English translations, though in places difficult to understand, contain passages of a sustained sublimity that Shakespeare, Milton and the Bible do not surpass . . . There are nineteen of these Keys: the first two conjuring the element called Spirit; the next sixteen invoke the Four Elements; each sub-divided into four; the nineteenth, by changing two names, may be used to invoke any one of what are called the thirty 'Aethyrs' or 'Aires'. The genuineness of these Keys, altogether apart from any critical observation, is guaranteed by the fact that anyone with the smallest capacity for Magick finds that they *work*. (7)

Crowley's philosophy and lifestyle proved to have a lasting influence on Western society. His drug use and experimental attitude toward sex were clearly a rich source for the counter-culture of the 1960s. Likewise, his insistence that 'will' occupy the central place in human morality ('do what thou wilt shall be the whole of the law!'), along with the importance of Enochian magic in his system, proved critical to the birth of modern Satanism.

It is hard to see how Crowley himself could be understood as a Satanist, however. While he adopted the name and image of Baphomet and referred to himself as the 'Beast' of Revelation, complete with an appropriation of '666' as his own symbolic number, he showed no clear affinity for the figure of Satan, Lucifer or the devil. Crowley, it might be argued, was too thoroughly pagan to be a Satanist. However, Crowley was an occultist, and as much

⟨HIS DRUG USE AND EXPERIMENTAL ATTITUDE TOWARD SEX WERE CLEARLY A RICH SOURCE FOR THE COUNTER-CULTURE OF THE 1960S.⟩

as some forms of Satanism have adopted the occult as part of their theory and worship, he may be seen as a foundational figure in the movement.

Undoubtedly, Anton LeVey, founder of the Church of Satan, was heavily influenced by Crowley, but not by Crowley alone. LeVey's heritage is perhaps more clearly related to the Hellfire clubs of eighteenth-century England. These organizations, described by Chris Matthews in his *Modern*

Satanism: Anatomy of a Radical Subculture, were an intentional mockery of Christianity, including its Satanic elements. Matthews writes, 'In truth, these clubs had little to do with the dark arts and everything to do with drunkenness and sexual excess, but as drunkenness and sexual excess were the traditional specialties of the devil, the association was inevitable' (16). Preceding Crowley in the adoption of the Thelemic motto, 'do what thou wilt,' these clubs flaunted their disdain for Christianity by mockingly adopting the symbols of its enemy. Matthews writes of Sir Frances Dashwood's Club, founded in 1746:

> In irregular meetings on occasions such as Walpurgis Night in 1752, it conducted elaborate and blasphemous ceremonies. Rafts were floated down the Thames with members dressed in monk's robes. The group's private abbey was adorned in inverted crosses and lit with dark candles, and a Black Mass was conducted with the naked body of an aristocratic lady serving as an altar. Masked, naked nuns were also involved, most likely prostitutes shipped down the Thames from London. (17)

The Satanism of the Hellfire clubs was primarily a mockery of Christianity accomplished through the adoption of behaviors whose wickedness Christianity had used as charges against its enemies. There is little evidence that there was any sincere Satan worship in eighteenth-century London, no more than there is evidence that the Knights Templar were guilty as charged. Satan, the great enemy of the Church, was rather embraced in an effort to ridicule the Church. Satan, the old worm, became – as in the work of Milton, Goethe, Shelley and Byron – a heroic figure because of his refusal to bow the knee to a tyrannical God.

Speak of the devil and he will appear.

It was clearly in the spirit of the Hellfire clubs that Anton LaVey, born Howard Stanton Levey, launched the Church of Satan on Walpurgis Night in 1966, its headquarters at LaVey's Black House on California Street in San Francisco. In 1969 LaVey published *The Satanic Bible* and brought the organization's philosophy to the world. Burton Wolfe, in the introduction to the original edition of the book, summed up the Church of Satan pretty well,

> In the summer of 1966, a few newspapers in the San Francisco Bay Area began to take notice of a body of Devil-worshippers headed by a former circus and carnival lion handler and organist, Anton Szandor LaVey. Their practice of the black arts was nothing new in the world. It had traces in

voodoo cults, a Hell-Fire Club that existed in 18th-Century England, a Satanic circle led by Aleister Crowley in England a century later, and the Black Order of Germany in the 1920's and 1930's. But two aspects of the San Francisco group made them different from their predecessors: they were blasphemously organized into a church, the First Church of Satan, instead of the usual coven Satanism and witchcraft lore; and they carried on their black magic openly instead of underground.

Wedding, baptism, and funeral ceremonies dedicated to the Devil were held in the Church of Satan, with the press invited.

The Satanic Bible begins with 'The Nine Satanic Statements':

1. Satan represents indulgence, instead of abstinence!

2. Satan represents vital existence, instead of spiritual pipe dreams!

3. Satan represents undefiled wisdom, instead of hypocritical self-deceit!

4. Satan represents kindness to those who deserve it, instead of love wasted on ingrates!

5. Satan represents vengeance, instead of turning the other cheek!

6. Satan represents responsibility to the responsible, instead of concern for psychic vampires!

7. Satan represents man as just another animal, sometimes better, more often worse than those that walk on all-fours, who, because of his 'divine spiritual and intellectual development', has become the most vicious animal of all!

8. Satan represents all of the so-called sins, as they all lead to physical, mental, or emotional gratification!

9. Satan has been the best friend the church has ever had, as he has kept it in business all these years! (33)

Thereafter, the bible is divided into four books: the Book of Satan, the Book of Lucifer, the Book of Belial and the Book of Leviathan. The Book of Satan consists of a collection of Nietzschean aphorisms clearly meant to offer a challenge to Christianity and traditional morality, such as,

I request reason for your golden rule and ask the why and wherefore of your ten commandments.

Before none of your printed idols do I bend in acquiescence, and he who saith 'thou shalt' to me is my mortal foe!

I dip my forefinger in the watery blood of your impotent mad redeemer, and write over his thorn-torn brow: The TRUE prince of evil - the king of slaves!

Behold the crucifix; what does it symbolize? Pallid incompetence hanging on a tree.

'Love one another' it has been said is the supreme law, but what power made it so? Upon what rational authority does the gospel of love rest? Why should I not hate mine enemies – if I 'love' them does that not place me at their mercy? He who turns the other cheek is a cowardly dog! (35–6)

The Book of Lucifer is a series of short essays expressing a decidedly humanist philosophy: humanity creates its own nature and destiny, religion is a delusion, the universe is uncaring and unaware. LaVey recognized the humanist nature of this philosophy but insisted that Satanism is more than humanism.

'Satanism is based on a very sound philosophy,' say the emancipated. 'But why call it Satanism? Why not call it something like 'Humanism' or a name that would have the connotation of a witchcraft group, something a little more esoteric – something less bla-tant.' There is more than one reason for this. Humanism is not a religion. It is simply a way of life with no ceremony or dogma. Satanism has both ceremony and dogma. (46)

> **❛SATANISM IS BASED ON A VERY SOUND PHILOSOPHY.❜**

Dogma and ceremony are crucial, LaVey argued, because humanity – particularly at this stage of our development – cannot accept the humanist message in a purely rational way. We are emotional beings and thus need to have our philosophy acted out in ritual and presented as a metaphor in myth and dogma.

Despite the need for dogma and ritual, LaVey made it clear that Satanism was not just another form of religion; it did not just substitute one deity for another. He wrote,

Most Satanists do not accept Satan as an anthropomorphic being with cloven hooves, a barbed tail, and horns. He merely represents a force in nature – the powers of darkness which have been named just that because no religion has taken these forces *out* of the darkness. Nor has science been able to apply technical terminology to this force. It is an untapped reservoir that few can make use of because they lack the ability to use a tool without having to first break down and label all the parts which make it run. It is this incessant need to analyze which prohibits most people from taking advantage of this many faceted key to the unknown – which the Satanist chooses to call 'Satan'. (54)

And,

The popular concept of the black mass is thus: a defrocked priest stands before an altar consisting of a nude woman, her legs spread-eagled and vagina thrust open, each of her outstretched fists grasping a black candle made from the fat of unbaptized babies, and a chalice containing the urine of a prostitute (or blood) reposing on her belly. An inverted cross hangs above the altar, and triangular hosts of ergot-laden bread or black-stained turnip are methodically blessed as the priest dutifully slips them in and out of the altar-lady's labia. Then, we are told, an invocation to Satan and various demons is followed by an array of prayers and psalms chanted backwards or interspersed with obscenities . . . all performed within the confines of a 'protective' pentagram drawn on the floor. If the Devil appears he is invariably in the form of a rather eager man wearing the head of a black goat upon his shoulders. Then follows a potpourri of flagellation, prayer-book burning, cunnilingus, fellatio, and general hindquarters kissing – all done to a background of ribald recitations from the Holy Bible, and audible expectorations on the cross! If a baby can be slaughtered during the ritual, so much the better; for as everyone knows, this is the favorite sport of the Satanist!(77)

According to LaVey, however, this is just a fiction invented by the Church to accuse its enemies of great crimes, or by perverts who could justify the creation of such debauched scenes only by claiming thereby to describe the evils of the Church's enemies. 'Devil worshippers,' LaVey claims, were created by the Church.

According to LaVey, a true Satanist celebrates a Black Mass as a kind of 'psycho-drama,' as a way of freeing oneself from the confines of a 'sacred' ritual by parodying it, in much the same way as it was parodied in the Hellfire clubs, and, LaVey claimed, by the Great Beast himself, Crowley. LaVey wrote, 'Crowley obviously spent a large part of his life with his tongue jammed firmly into his cheek, but his followers, today, are somehow able to read esoteric meaning into his every word' (79). The true Satanist, unlike the Church-created devil worshippers, are self-actualized men and women who forge their own destiny, follow their own path, live their own lives and regard 'do what thou wilt' as the 'whole of the law.'

Part three, the Book of Belial, consists of a description of the philosophy and techniques of Satanic magic and rituals, including sex rituals, rituals of compassion and rituals of destruction. Part four, the Book of Leviathan, contains invocations and commentaries on the Enochian Keys. Among these is an 'Invocation Employed Toward the Conjuration of Destruction,' a prayer intended to bring a curse upon one's enemies.

I call upon the messengers of doom to slash with grim delight this victim I hath chosen. Silent is that voiceless bird that feeds upon the brain-pulp of him (her) who hath tormented me, and the agony of the is to be shall sustain itself in shrieks of pain, only to serve as signals of warning to those who would resent my being.

Oh come forth in the name of Abaddon and destroy him (her) whose name I giveth as a sign. Oh great brothers of the night, thou who makest my place of comfort, who rideth out upon the hot winds of Hell, who dwelleth in the devil's fane; Move and appear! Present yourselves to him (her) who sustaineth the rottenness of the mind that moves the gibbering mouth that mocks the just and strong!; rend that gaggling tongue and close his (her) throat, Oh Kali! Pierce his (her) lungs with the stings of scorpions, Oh Sekhmet! Plunge his (her) substance into the dismal void, Oh mighty Dagon!

I thrust aloft the bifid barb of Hell and on its tines resplendently impaled my sacrifice through vengeance rests!

Shemhamforash! Hail Satan! (108)

Of course, with LaVey's philosophy in mind, it is hard to read these invocations and spells as more than elements of a 'psycho-drama' meant to assist the individual in expressing anger and hatred toward an enemy and thereby freeing them from the guilt imposed upon them by the confines of the Christian faith.

Current High Priest of the Church of Satan, Magus Peter H. Gilmore, has made the humanistic and atheistic philosophy clear in his essay 'Satanism: The Feared Religion.' Gilmore writes,

As you can see, there are no elements of Devil worship in the Church of Satan. Such practices are looked upon as being Christian heresies; believing in the dualistic Christian world view of 'God vs. the Devil' and choosing to side with the Prince of Darkness. Satanists do not believe in the supernatural, in neither God nor the Devil. To the Satanist, he is his own God. Satan is a symbol of Man living as his prideful, carnal nature dictates. The reality behind Satan is simply the dark evolutionary force of entropy that permeates all of nature and provides the drive for survival and propagation inherent in all living things. Satan is not a conscious entity to be worshipped, rather a reservoir of power inside each human to be tapped at will. Thus any concept of sacrifice is rejected as a Christian aberration – in Satanism there's no deity to which one can sacrifice.*

* * *

The atheistic nature of the Church of Satan was challenged in 1975 when LaVeyan disciple Michael Aquino left the church after leveling charges of corruption at LaVey. Aquino's new organization, the Temple of Set, retained some philosophical connections with the church but moved in a more occult direction, more in the tradition of Crowley than LaVey. Like Crowley and his revelation from Aiwass, Aquino claimed a revelation from the Ancient Egyptian god Set. Aquino traced the worship of Set to pre-dynastic Egypt, where Set was originally regarded as a stellar deity. Set fell into disfavor, according to Aquino, with the cult of Osiris and Isis, who cast the god as the evil principal at work in the universe. The Hebrews, upon escaping from Egyptian captivity, took the idea of Set, or Satan, with them. Christians further vilified Set, and added to him characteristics from the Roman mystery cults, such as Pan's horns and hooves.

❨A FUNDAMENTALISM AS MINDLESS AND BRUTISH AS THAT OF THE MIDDLE AGES.❩

Aquino rejects any notion that there has been a secretive cult throughout history devoted to the worship of Satan and sees Satanic scares in the Middle Ages and in the present day as the product of Christian Churches' attempt to scare their faithful into submission and to eliminate enemies and challengers through accusations of deals with the devil. Aquino describes the Satanism scare of the late twentieth century as an 'eruption' of

a fundamentalism as mindless and brutish as that of the Middle Ages. Now, as before, it needed a scarecrow – and 'Satanism' was a word with an appropriately scary sound. Christian fanatics who knew [and cared] nothing whatever about *actual* Satanism suddenly embarked upon passionate [and financially profitable] campaigns brandishing the scarecrow before credulous followers.†

---

* From the Church of Satan website, at www.churchofsatan.com/Pages/Feared. html.

† This and following quotations are from 'Temple of Set General Information and Admissions Policies, March 2003.'

According to Aquino, one consequence of the elevation of 'Satanism' as the enemy of the Church was the rise of those who embraced the label of devil worshippers.

> Complicating the situation was the perennial impulse among alienated youth and antisocial elements to deliberately shock society by flaunting its bogymen. If prudish elements of the community were going to terrify themselves with 'scarecrow Satanism', then Heavy Metal rock music would affect this same image, as would the occasional psychotic criminal and teenage gang. Fundamentalists happily showcased such aberrations as 'proof' of the scarecrow's existence.

Speak of the devil and he will appear.

Aquino rejects the notion that the Temple of Set is just another example of this adoption of the Christian enemy as a god, however. While theistic in a way that the Church of Satan is not, the temple does not worship Satan, but rather the ancient deity known as Set, although Set was the pattern for the Christian Satan. In Aquino's view, the Temple of Set is not a parody of Christianity but rather an embracing of the ancient ways that Christianity helped to destroy.

Aquino distinguishes the theism of the temple from other forms of religion by arguing that other religions represent the primitive longing for humanity to feel at one with the universe. This is often sought through various forms of white magic. The Temple of Set, however, rejects this longing for union with the whole and instead stresses the kind of individualism and humanism common to Crowley and LaVey. This is the realm of the Black Magician.

> The Black Magician, on the other hand, rejects both the desirability of union with the Universe and any self-deceptive antics designed to create such an illusion. He has considered the existence of the individual *psyche* – the 'core you' of your conscious intelligence – and has taken satisfaction from its existence as something unlike anything else in the Universe. The Black Magician desires this *psyche* to live, to experience, and to continue. He does not wish to die – or to lose his consciousness and identity in a larger, Universal consciousness [assuming that such exists]. He wants to *be*. This decision in favor of individual existence is the first premise of the Temple of Set.

The worship of Set, for Aquino, is clearly not the worship of Satan or the devil, but in some sense it is also not really the worship of Set. It is the worship of the individual.

* * *

If, as Gilmore and Aquino both claim, devil worship is just a fiction created
by the Church in an attempt to, literally, demonize their opponents, then it is
perhaps not surprising that the cult of the Dark Lord has enjoyed a healthy
life in the fictional world of literature and film. One of the most influential
examples of this is Joris-Karl Huysmans' 1891 novel *Là-Bas*, translated into
English as both *Down There* and *The Damned*. *Là-Bas* is the story of the
novelist Durtal, who, while researching the Satanism of the Middle Ages,
discovers its thriving existence in late nineteenth-century France.

Following the trail of Satan, Durtal unearthed accounts of the Black
Mass practiced in the seventeenth century, where women would flock to a
fallen priest in order to participate in the apostasy as 'in our times women
flock to have their fortunes told with cards.' In these ceremonies the women
would lie down naked on the altar table and hold the altar candles aloft
throughout the service. One notorious priest, Abbé Guibourg, created his
own dark host for use in the sacrament.

> Generally a child was kidnapped and burnt in a furnace out in the country
> somewhere, the ashes were saved and mixed with the blood of another child
> whose throat had been cut, and of this mixture a paste was made resembling
> that of the Manicheans of which I was speaking. Abbé Guibourg officiated,
> consecrated the host, cut it into little pieces and mixed it with this mixture
> of blood and ashes. That was the material of the Sacrament. (54)

Obsessed with the idea that such activities could still be alive at the
dawn of the twentieth century, Durtal arranged to attend a contemporary
Black Mass with his lover. Held in an abandoned and derelict chapel, the
ceremony at first nauseated Durtal, who was overcome by the humid,
moldy air and nearly impenetrable darkness that filled the place. Finally, a
choir boy lit candles, allowing the altar to become visible.

> It was an ordinary church altar on a tabernacle above which stood
> an infamous, derisive Christ. The head had been raised and the neck
> lengthened, and wrinkles, painted in the cheeks, transformed the grieving
> face to a bestial one twisted into a mean laugh. He was naked, and where
> the loincloth should have been, there was a virile member projecting from a
> bush of horsehair. In front of the tabernacle the chalice, covered with a pall,
> was placed. The choir boy folded the altar cloth, wiggled his haunches, stood
> tiptoe on one foot and flipped his arms as if to fly away like a cherub, on
> pretext of reaching up to light the black tapers whose odour of coal tar and
> pitch was now added to the pestilential smell of the stuffy room. (222)

Durtal observed the priest, Docre, enter the chapel, wearing a scarlet hood adorned by two horns of red cloth. He knelt before the altar and began to say Mass, revealing that he was wearing nothing under his robe. His chasuble, also blood red, was adorned with an image of a black goat, presenting his horns in challenge. The priest then stood before the image of Christ, hurling blasphemies and insults. Then,

> One of the choir boys knelt before him with his back toward the altar. A shudder ran around the priest's spine. In a solemn but jerky voice he said, 'Hoc est enim corpus meum,' then, instead of kneeling, after the consecration, before the precious Body, he faced the congregation, and appeared tumefied, haggard, dripping with sweat. He staggered between the two choir boys, who, raising the chasuble, displayed his naked belly. Docre made a few passes and the host sailed, tainted and soiled, over the steps.
>
> Durtal felt himself shudder. A whirlwind of hysteria shook the room. While the choir boys sprinkled holy water on the pontiff's nakedness, women rushed upon the Eucharist and, groveling in front of the altar, clawed from the bread humid particles and drank and ate divine ordure. (227)

The chapel became a madhouse. Women screamed and convulsed on the floor. Choir boys presented themselves to the men for pleasure. A little girl howled like a dog. A woman held the chalice between her legs like some profane phallus. And the priest, the priest was the worst of all.

> Durtal, terrified, saw through the fog the red horns of Docre, who, seated now, frothing with rage, was chewing up sacramental wafers, taking them out of his mouth, wiping himself with them, and distributing them to the women, who ground them underfoot, howling, or fell over each other struggling to get hold of them and violate them. (228)

If there is a classical modern depiction of the Black Mass, it is Huysmans'. Indeed, much of what the average person thinks of when they think of Satanism is probably found in the pages of this novel. While it might not be the origin of the many stereotypical features of Satanism, it certainly condenses them into a thoroughly modern form. The Satanists are a secret underground cult, centered around a charismatic leader. Their adoration of Satan is juxtaposed by their hatred and mockery of Christianity. The host is desecrated. Sexual deviancy runs rampant. The priest, Docre, even wears a red hood with devil horns, like Anton LaVey. Only, of course, Huysmans' priest is sincere in his adoration of Lucifer; for him it is much more than psycho-drama. It is not just Satanism, it is devil worship.

34. Mia Farrow in *Rosemary's Baby* (1968) (William Castle Productions).

The relationship of LaVey to fictional portrayals of Satanism, of course, ran both ways. It was, after all, less than a year after the Church of Satan made a big media splash that Ira Levin's 1967 novel *Rosemary's Baby* was published. The novel, and the even more influential 1968 film by Roman Polanski, helped to bring Satanism into the contemporary world. The tale of Rosemary and Guy Woodhouse, as portrayed by Mia Farrow and John Cassavetes, is a classic tale of urban, twentieth-century horror.

In the novel and subsequent movie, the young couple move into an apartment building, where they meet a group of lovely older neighbors who seem to want only the best for them. Soon after becoming pregnant, however, Rosemary begins to suspect that something awful has happened to her and that something terrible is growing inside her womb. Over time, Rosemary comes to the truth that Guy has made a terrible, though tragically classic, deal with the devil. Guy has offered his wife's womb in exchange for success in business. Drugged and abducted by her innocent-seeming neighbors, Rosemary was impregnated by Satan himself. The child that she carries is the spawn of the devil.

Putting aside the obvious portrayal of the fears any expectant parent faces in relation to their unborn child, *Rosemary's Baby* is the story of an underground cult of Satan worshippers, and of their role in Satan's plan to dominate the world. Its contemporary setting and the normalcy of the cult members adds to the horror of the earlier tales. These Satanists live in a modern apartment building and hold cocktail parties. Satan wears a suit, a tie. Evil, it is implied, could be anywhere. No one can be trusted.

While *Rosemary's Baby* is arguably the best of Hollywood's attempt to frighten viewers by appeals to the Satanic menace, it is certainly not the only one. As early as 1934, Boris Karloff and Bela Lugosi starred in *The Black Cat*, about stranded honeymooners trapped in the home of a priest of Satan. *The Seventh Victim* appeared in 1943, about a Satanic cult in Greenwich Village. *The Devil's Hand*, a tale of a modern-day Satanic cult, was released in 1963. In 1971, the elderly Satanists of *Rosemary's Baby* returned in *The Brotherhood of Satan*. In this film the senior Satanists kidnap children and introduce them to the worship of Satan in a scheme to restore their own lost youth. Two years later, 1973's *Satan's School for Girls*, a made-for-TV movie, featured two of Charlie's Angels in a tale about a Satanic cult at a girls' school. In 1975, *Race with the Devil* featured Peter Fonda on the run from Satanists after witnessing a ritual murder. In the same year, *The Devil's Rain* starred Ernest Borgnine, William Shatner and John Travolta.

The fictional portrayal of Satanists, whether in film or on the page, plays its part in the ever-turning circle. Unsubstantiated charges against the innocent turn around to reveal the real thing, itself a parody of the former. *Malleus Malificarum* spins around to reveal the Hellfire clubs and the Church of Satan. The Hellfire clubs and the Church of Satan set to spinning *Là-Bas*, *Rosemary's Baby* and the *Brotherhood of Satan*. These fictions in turn spin more fiction – the much more dangerous fiction of *Michelle Remembers* and *Satan's Underground*.

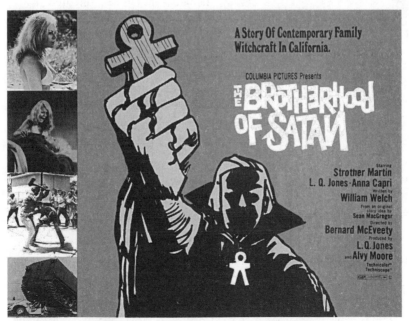

35. Poster for *The Brotherhood of Satan* (1971) (Columbia Pictures).

Speak of the devil and he will appear.
But is none of it real? Is Satanism merely a moon-cast shadow?
Don't we have to give the devil his due?

William Schnoebelen is one of those Christians who warn of the pervasive threat from Satanists, not LaVeyan humanists engaged in psycho-drama and not Setian individualists, but real honest-to-God Satanists. In his book *Lucifer Dethroned*, Schnoebelen describes his descent into Satan worship in the late 1970s and his subsequent conversion to Christianity. Following a bit of dabbling with the Church of Satan which left him unfulfilled, Schnoebelen was introduced to 'hardcore' Satanism through the journal of a Satanist group called the Order of the Black Ram. Of special interest to him was an article written by someone calling himself 'Orion'* and claiming the title 'Ipsissimus, High Priest and King of the Morning Star,' a title Schnoebelen calls the highest rank in all magic, a title so advanced that its bearer has 'literally become a god incarnate' (110).

According to Schnoebelin's account, Orion claimed in the article that there was a secret pact between God and Lucifer to pretend to be enemies in order to allow humans to have free choice between them. Those who choose God are bound for Heaven. Those who choose Lucifer, bound for Hell. The dichotomy between the two afterlives is not what it seems, however. It is not true that Heaven is a place of reward while Hell is a place of punishment. Instead, Schnoebelen says, 'Heaven would be for the mellow, do-nothing types – foreclosed personalities whose idea of fun was a church picnic and hot game of horseshoes. Hell would be a place of great challenge and excitement, with rock music, non-stop sex, drugs and total freedom of artistic expression' (110). Orion, wrote Schnoebelen, claimed that this arrangement came about in part because 'God did not want the malcontents making his heavenly citizens fret.'

Schnoebelen was intrigued, 'Bells started going off inside. This explained so many philosophical questions everyone had about the nature of evil and free will! I was supremely impressed and immediately wrote this Orion . . . a letter telling him so' (111). Before long, Schnoebelen and Orion arranged a meeting. Schnoebelen described their first encounter and says that Orion was

---

* Identified as 'Orias' by Frater Barrabbas in his blogged account of his time with Schnoebelen (http://fraterbarrabbas.blogspot.com/2010/02/descent-into-madness-chronology-of_23.html).

a small fellow, both in height and build, and was dressed like a biker, with a battered brown fedora that looked like something Indiana Jones threw away. . . .

Orion was handsome, in a roguish way, although his face and demeanor were somehow ferret-like. He had obviously not been to any finishing schools, or many starting schools either. Could this be the fellow whose pen had produced such profound thoughts. (112–13)

Orion told Schnoebelen that he had been orphaned while very young and raised by his stepfather, who was a devoted Freemason. At some point, Orion ran away from home and headed to California.

There, he tried the Church of Satan, but thought them too 'white.' He got involved with biker Satanists and moved around the coast with the Hell's Angels for awhile, slicing up cats and women and raising hell. He showed me his arms, which were crawling with tattoos of devils heads and skulls. (113)

Exposed to real Satanism, Orion soon came under the influence of a man calling himself 'Adrian' who claimed to be the head of a secret organization, 'a Pentagon or NORAD of Satanic power,' located near Los Angeles. Adrian, Orion claimed, was so rich and powerful that he was feared by the southern California and Hollywood elite. Adrian was very impressed with Orion, believing that he represented the fulfillment of Satanic prophecy. He adopted Orion in a ceremony 'on a hillside ringed with lightning' (115). To elevate the power three virgin girls were crucified upside down during the ceremony.

In Schnoebelen's account, Orion explained that blood was essential for the practice of real magick. 'For minor magick, a hamster or cat was all that was needed, but the High Art called for human blood to be spilled out upon the ground. "Good to the last drop!" he chortled' (115). He went on to explain that the shedding of blood was an integral part of the symbiotic relationship between God and Lucifer. For Christians the holiest act is to be martyred for the faith. For Satanists, the holiest act is to murder a Christian.

He told me that almost every quarter of the year the body of a young girl – usually a Christian child – turned up in a river near his home, slain by obviously Satanic means. Yet nothing was ever done.

He said the authorities knew who was doing it, but dared not touch them because of how powerful they were. In fact, many of the authorities were Satanists in secret! How else could they rise to positions of authority. (117)

Intrigued by Orion's claims, Schnoebelen decided to take the dark oath and pledge his allegiance to Satan. At a ceremony in Chicago, Schnoebelen knelt before Orion and promised to serve the Dark Lord. Soon thereafter Orion encouraged his new convert to participate in blood rituals so that he could get ready for 'the Big One,' the sacrificial slaughter of a human being. Seeing Schnoebelen's wariness, Orion sought to comfort him.

'Don't worry. A lot of brothers get nervous about their first one. It's kinda like sex, the first time's the trickiest. But we have our methods.' He smiled darkly, and seemed ready to erupt into another fountain of giggles.

> ❮A LOT OF BROTHERS GET NERVOUS ABOUT THEIR FIRST ONE. IT'S KINDA LIKE SEX, THE FIRST TIME'S THE TRICKIEST.❯

'We make sure you get a candidate for the oblation *who's more than willing* – some chick who's old enough or doped up enough to not scream too much – and who is offering herself willingly as a gift to the Master. Those kind are a breeze. They get off on dying, little brother! They can't wait for you to plunge the dagger into their heart.'

Orion smiled in a way that would have seemed angelic on any other face. 'It's like they say: "Death is the ultimate trip. That's why they save it till last."' (173–4)

Apparently, Schnoebelen never did participate in 'the Big One,' his Christian conversion intervening and pushing Orion out of his life.

Schnoebelen does try to answer questions that might arise if one were to take Orion's claims seriously, as he does. For example, one might want to know why there is so little evidence for Satanic murders. 'Where have all the bodies gone?' as Schnoebelen puts it.

This is a comparatively easy one to answer. Satanists, like all 'good' witches, are devout believers in recycling! I know this sounds like a grisly joke in poor taste, but actually, very little of the human bodies that are sacrificed are wasted.

Without going into all the gory details, much of the culture of shamanism (the Paleolithic ancestor of Satanism) revolves around the consumption of body parts for magical reasons. Little, if anything, is left to waste. This is true in most satanic 'denominations.' Even the human bones are highly prized artifacts of magical virtue. Many times such bones are worn or carried much like Native Americans carry bones of their sacred totem animals. (192)

Schnoebelen also reports that his 'superiors in the Satanic Brotherhood,' by which I assume he means Orion, claimed that Satanists will often corrupt or blackmail a funeral director, who will help them dispose of human remains.

The question of where Satanists acquire their victims is another question deemed 'all too easy to answer' by Schnoebelen. Infants are particularly prized and quite easy to acquire. Schnoebelen tells us that his 'satanic mentor,' who I again take to be Orion, observed that 'Few commodities in the world are as easy, as cheap or as pleasant to produce as a baby' (194). Babies are acquired, according to Schnoebelen, from several sources. Some may be purchased from drug-addicted parents. Some, though a rare few, may be kidnapped. Finally, some are conceived and born within the Satanic organization. With no record of their existence, their murder is all the more risk-free. Schnoebelen claims to have received training as a midwife for the express purpose of helping with the delivery of these doomed babies. Adult victims, on the other hand, may be members of the Satanic organization itself who are being punished for some misdeed. Homeless people are another source of adult victims. Finally, some victims, particularly women, are kidnapped.

The third objection Schnoebelen responds to is the question, 'Why aren't these people caught and prosecuted?' There are multiple reasons for this. The Satanists, as he already said, do a good job of getting rid of the evidence. Sometimes their familiar spirits warn them of impending police investigations, thus allowing them time to prepare. Most importantly, however, is the fact that many Satanists are:

> 'pillars' of the local community – doctors, lawyers, judges, clergy and even police. They are not people with whom most police chiefs would wish to tangle without a lot of good, hard evidence. Such evidence is not usually forthcoming. Even if it is turned up, the coven can often send fire elementals (demons) to burn it up or otherwise consume it right in the evidence locker before the case can come to trial.
>
> Beyond that, often the first people in a town which a coven will try and co-opt will be people in law enforcement and the judiciary. They 'convert' them to the Brotherhood by the same methods mentioned concerning funeral directors, as well as through lower-level networks of Brotherhood influences such as the Masonic Lodge. The presence of such people virtually assures that no such case will ever be prosecuted. (198)

William Schnoebelen disagrees with those within the Church of Satan and the Temple of Set who claim that there is no hidden cult of Satan worship stretching back into the distant past, and defends those who have claimed that Satanism poses a genuine threat to life and faith. In Schnoebelen's view, there is more to Satanism than Hellfire clubs and psycho-drama. Real Satanism, devil worship, is not a fiction created by the Church, he argues. It is real and it has a pervasive, albeit secretive, presence in our society. Satanic ritual abuse is real. Human sacrifice is real. We have reason to be afraid. Schnoebelen knows this to be true because he was a part of it. He was a member of the dark brotherhood, a student of Orion. His information comes from the highest source, the Ipsissimus himself.

According to Schnoebelen, covens and brotherhoods in big cities and small towns carry out their dark rituals, not for show like LaVey and his kin, but in darkness. They are not pretending. They are not performing a mytho-poetic drama. They are not worshipping themselves or some impersonal force at the heart of the universe. They are worshipping Satan, Lucifer, the Dark Lord, Beelzebub, Baphomet, the Deceiver, the Fallen One, the Devil himself. They bring curses upon their enemies and acquire dark power for themselves. They perform acts of perversion. They shed the blood of innocents. They defile the host.

They speak of the devil and he appears.

Druwydion Pendragon stood before the crude altar. The black candles flickered in the evening breeze. Around him the Brotherhood of Satan waited.

He turned to face the congregation, holding something aloft in his left hand. Then he spoke.

'Behold, the pale Nazarene!'

It was the host, the Body of Christ, that he held aloft. He smiled and quickly took it out of sight behind his back. 'Is he defiling it, wiping his ass with the host?' I wondered to myself. I could not tell for sure. His smile remained.

According to Pendragon's website, the Brotherhood of Satan should not be confused with LaVey's church, for the brotherhood preceded the Church of Satan by millennia: 'Before the public formation of the Church of Satan in San Francisco, Ca. by Dr. Anton LaVey there existed in both Europe and the U.S.A. secretive Satanism whose members did not advertise their membership. This form of Satanism still exists and even now is undergoing reorganization.'* The brotherhood, it is claimed, has existed since the earliest of times under different names. Originally called the Brotherhood of Darkness and Shadows, it was the very first known secret society. Its lineage can be traced from 'a highly secretive Satanic movement that was called among the higher ups, the Black Brotherhood or more simply The Brotherhood.'

The website claims that the current incarnation of the brotherhood, made public for the first time under Pendragon's leadership, is backed and supported by powerful 'Generational Bloodline families that have long existed in the Shadows of the Underworld of Darkness.' The Brotherhood of Satan, under Pendragon's guidance, is the new public arm of this still-secretive organization. The organization has gone public in order to seek new members: 'The Brotherhood of Satan is the reorganization project of the Brotherhood Illuminati Council and is the vehicle created by us to manifest this Satanic reality: "The total restoration of the throne of SATAN on Earth and the Unification of Satan's true family."'

The Brotherhood of Satan is 'the new Brotherhood generation,' secretly sponsored by the 'old Brotherhood generation.' This secret sponsoring organization is made up of powerful individuals, including members of the film and music industries and extends throughout other occult and esoteric organizations, including Freemasonry.

> Real Satanists operate quietly and secretly and we do not have need or desire to tell the whole world who we are. We get more done by remaining in the Shadows of Darkness and Secrecy and operating behind the scenes.
> We are quite simply, Hell on Earth.

In addition to claiming ties to the ancient brotherhood – ties that give the Brotherhood of Satan (or BOS) claim to the term *generational* Satanism – the group articulates other important distinctions between themselves and other Satanic organizations. Perhaps most important is the fact that the BOS regards Satan as a real entity. Satan is a personal being towards whom the worship of the group is directed. Thus, this generational Satanist organization is also *theistic*. Unlike the Church of Satan, it believes in and worships the devil.

According to the brotherhood, Satan or 'Satanas' is,

---

* This and following quotations are from 'An Introduction to the Brotherhood of Satan,' at www.brotherhoodofsatan.com/pdf/BOSFYI.pdf.

the Force in all living things upon planet earth, He is OUR motivating power that pushes everything into existence as well as pulling everything out. He is both Creation and Destruction to the Brotherhood Satanist.

❛CHRISTIANITY HAS ALWAYS ENJOYED PERVERTING NATURE AND NATURAL PRACTICES. THEY ALSO LIKE TO TRY TO TELL US TO ABSTAIN FROM OUR CARNAL NATURE AND IT IS SATAN THAT TEMPTS US TO INDULGE.❜

The Serpent of the Brotherhood devouring its tail while its body grows with strength and wisdom. Satan IS NOT A SPIRITUAL BEING THAT TEMPTS HUMAN KIND TO SIN for sin to the Brotherhood Satanist does not exist. To us, what they call sin is a NATURAL instinct latent in all human beings. Christianity has always enjoyed perverting Nature and natural practices. They also like to try to tell us to abstain from our carnal nature and it is Satan that tempts us to INDULGE. It is the Brotherhood view that christianity is opposed to Life and our living and ENJOYING IT. Satan to us is the only true power that teaches us that WE SHOULD FOLLOW OUR OWN TRUE NATURE. It is the Nature of The Brotherhood that we see Satan as a part of Nature not anti-nature. He is more to us as Brotherhood members than just a mere scapegoat of christianity. He has both our lives and our souls.*

Another aspect of Satan is represented by the name 'Lucifer,' 'the ancient Roman God that is directly related to the direction of the East and element of Air.' Lucifer is the light bearer, the angel of light, and represents enlightenment and ancient wisdom.

He also is another aspect of Eternal Darkness as is Satanas in that He must yet exist IN THE DARKNESS ITSELF. It is only there that the true Brotherhood Satanist will find Lucifer Inviticus [sic] as He is fondly referred to as by The Brotherhood past and present. He then becomes our Spiritual Evolution within that very Darkness which we as well as He exists in. Lucifer the Inviticus demands that we do not bow down in servitude to follow the Will of The Pale Nazarene but rather to excel to Goddesshood and Godhood upon the Planet Earth which is part of His Universal Domain.

---

* This and the following quotations are from 'The Brotherhood of Satan's Perspective on Satan and Lucifer', at www.brotherhoodofsatan.com/pdf/bospsl. pdf.

While Satanas represents carnality, the flesh and animal nature, Lucifer represents knowledge, illumination, rebellion, intelligence and pride.

For the brotherhood, Satanas and Lucifer are always associated with each other. In order to have light, there must be darkness: 'The Light of Lucifer can be found in no other place but the Darkness of Satanas.' The brotherhood recognizes unity in the duality of Satanas and Lucifer, worshipping the two in one as 'the great Satanas–Luciferi.' A brotherhood Satanist seeks to live a life of balance between the two ways: between darkness and light, between the natural and the rational, between the fleshly and the intellectual.

This attempt at balance perhaps explains the brotherhood's official position on the most horrible charge brought against Satanism: human sacrifice. While the group recognizes the importance of blood sacrifice in traditional Satanist ritual, in the brotherhood this is limited to the few drops of blood used to sign the blood oath of loyalty to Satanas and the brotherhood. 'The BOS does not condone animal or human sacrifice, many of our members are animal and human rights activists and some are even advocates for children and adults.'* The dark need for blood is balanced by the understanding of the value of life in all its forms.

It took only a little research for me to find another name associated with Druwydion Pendragon. He is also David Daniel De Paul, identified on a website devoted to the Knights Templar as 'Grand Master, Ancient Order of Knights of the Temple of Solomon, Baphomet Preceptory.' A telephone conversation with William Schnoebelen confirmed that this is the same David De Paul who signed Sharon Schnoebelen's certificate of advancement to the level of thirty-third degree Mason. Schnoebelen also confirmed that David De Paul is the man he identified in *Lucifer Dethroned* as Orion. Suddenly it all made sense.

David De Paul is Druwydion Pendragon. Druwydion Pendragon is Orion.

Speak of the devil and he will appear.

Does this confirm what Schnoebelen writes about Satanism? Is it possible that the tales of the secret Satanic underground are true, that the worst fears of Christian society have been real all along? I have seen the desecration of the host, but what am I not seeing? What is kept hidden from all but the select few?

---

* From 'The Brotherhood of Satan (BOS) Frequently Asked Questions (FAQ)', at /www.brotherhoodofsatan.com/faq.php#quiz2.

Pendragon's Brotherhood of Satan disavows the murders and sacrifices that Schnoebelen's Orion claimed were all too real. Does Schnoebelen misrepresent what Orion told him thirty years ago, or does Pendragon misrepresent what he actually believes and practices today? Or maybe Orion duped Schnoebelen – maybe none of his tales of murder and dark magic is real. Tell the truth and shame the devil, but when you're dealing with the devil, how do you tell the truth from the lie?

Speak of the devil and he will appear.

We humans are drawn to the darkness, to the sinister, to the left-hand path. In its shadow the divine takes form and shudders to life. It is in the fear, Otto said, that we first find faith. It is in the darkness, the brotherhood claims, that we first see the light. The darkness becomes the boundary of our community. It tells us who we are, what we believe, who we love and how we live. It also tells us what we are not, what we deny, who we hate and who to kill. The darkness is powerful. It is terrible. It is deep. We speak its name (Baphomet, Lucifer, Satanas) in order to deny it, but in speaking its name we call it forth from the pit, we bring it to be, like God speaking the world into existence. We call our enemies devils and become devils ourselves, committing the very deeds that we condemn: killing the innocents, defiling the body and blood.

Drawn to the darkness, we find power there. In fear and trembling we find faith and pride. Satan cast out is a rebel strong and brave, opposing tyranny, battling overwhelming odds to seek freedom and life. In Hellfire clubs and Satanic churches it is this Satan that is worshipped, this devil that is admired. It is this devil that inspires Crowley's will and LaVey's humanism. This devil brings light as well as darkness, knowledge as well as the pleasures of the flesh.

Speak of the devil and he will appear.

And so he did. From the Middle Ages when witches were said to gather to celebrate the Black Sabbath and to bow before Satan, when servants of the Dark One stole infants to make their sinister unguents and power their evil spells, through the centuries of accusations of Satanic evil on the part of Templars, Masons, Catholics and kings, to the modern world of Satanic ritual abuse, backward masking and dark conspiracies, this has been true.

Speak of the devil and he will appear.

Kramer and Sprenger spoke the appearance of the Hellfire clubs and of Huysmans' damned, who in turn spoke the appearance of Aleister Crowley and Anton LaVey. Crowley and LaVey spoke the appearance of Rosemary

Woodhouse and Michelle Smith, who in turn spoke the appearance of Schnoebelen and Orion, who stand in balance – like Satanas and Lucifer – spinning forth the cone of power, the magic circle.

The Black Mass drew to a close. The dark rites had been performed. The elemental spirits had been summoned. The faithful had stood in the magic circle, protection against forces of the universe so powerful that they are beyond even Pendragon's total control. Only I existed outside the protective ring, face to face with the spirit of Satanas and Lucifer, with the forces of the earth, air, fire and water.

The host was passed among the people. It is not the body of Christ, not the sign of the pale Nazarene, but something else, something the participants received with a gusto that could never be expressed at the sight of the pasty unleavened bread of Mass. They enjoyed it. They went back for more.

A part of me was shaken by the stories of old, stories of the witches' stew made from the babies killed with their sharp needles and their poisoned ointments, stories of the blood of innocents baked into the host by the fallen priest, stories of the host defamed and spat upon the ground. But this was not the scene from Là-Bas: the writhing minions of Satan slobbering over the foul crumbs they find on the floor. This was not LaVey's grandly staged ritual: a naked woman offering her body as the altar of Satan. This was simple human community, the sharing of bread, the joy of eating together.

Pendragon brought the service to a close and then walked out of the circle and towards me. He held out the vessel that contained the host. I'm sure I looked frightened for a moment, unsure of what to do, but he smiled with a devilish twinkle in his eye. He said, 'It's Devil's Food cake, have some.'

I did.

Conclusion
Out of the Whirlwind

Then the LORD answered Job out of the whirlwind . . .

Job 38:1

From the far north they heard a low wail of the wind, and Uncle Henry and Dorothy could see where the long grass bowed in waves before the coming storm. There came now a sharp whistling in the air from the south, and as they turned their eyes that way they saw the ripples in grass coming from that direction also.

Suddenly Uncle Henry stood up.

'There's a cyclone coming, Em,' he called to his wife.

L. Frank Baum, *The Wonderful Wizard of Oz*

One does not kneel before a cyclone or the blind forces of nature, not even before Omnipotence merely as such. But one does kneel before the wholly uncomprehended Mystery, revealed yet unrevealed, and one's soul is stilled by feeling the way of its working, and therein its justification.

Rudolf Otto, *The Idea of the Holy*

The cyclone twists and turns through the sepia landscape, following a senseless path across the flat prairie, moving randomly and without purpose, yet coming ever closer to the tiny farmhouse and its rickety barns. Chickens and horses scurry, the tumbling tumbleweeds scatter before the spinning cone of power, farm hands and family rush for the cellar, seeking shelter down under the ground from the cyclone, the tornado, the whirlwind.

Dorothy arrives too late to escape into the cellar with Uncle Henry and Aunt Em, and her pleas for help go unanswered through the heavy wooden door. Once locked from inside, the door does not open until the storm has passed, no matter how loud the cries, or how fierce the pounding. Dorothy's knock is one knock that is not answered. Could they simply not hear her or did they fear that she had already been forever scarred by the winds, flesh ripped away, leaving nothing but her skeleton like a cartoon cat caught in the sinister trap of a cartoon mouse? Did they wonder what kind of thing might be knocking? Did they think 'sometimes dead is better' and try to wish her away? Dorothy keeps calling for her family, but no one answers. They are long buried in the ground. Abandoned when the cyclone strikes, except by her faithful dog Toto, it is no wonder that Dorothy retreats to a fantasy land, where the wicked are wicked but the good are forever true.

In the early sepia scenes of 1939's *The Wizard of Oz*, the small Kansas farmhouse of Dorothy Gale, her Uncle Henry and her Aunt Em is lifted from the ground by a twisting cyclone, a tornado tearing across the prairie. Dorothy, knocked senseless by an imploding window frame, is transported to the land of Oz, a land of green-skinned witches, red poppies and yellow brick roads. The violent winds of the storm blow Dorothy from the dreary world of a dry and desolate farm, a dust-bowl disaster, to a poly-chromatic fairy land of Technicolor dreams come true.

The makers of *The Wizard of Oz* chose to shoot the Kansas scenes of the movie in black and white and through a sepia filter in order to emphasize the contrasts between the everyday world of Kansas and the magical world of Oz – contrasts also found in Baum's original novel.

> When Dorothy stood in the doorway and looked around, she could see nothing but the great gray prairie on every side. Not a tree nor a house broke the broad sweep of flat country that reached to the edge of the sky in all directions. The sun had baked the plowed land into a gray mass, with little cracks running through it. Even the grass was not green, for the sun had burned the tops of the long blades until they were the same gray color to be seen everywhere. Once the house had been painted, but the sun blistered the paint and the rains washed it away, and now the house was as dull and gray as everything else. (12)

Dorothy's aunt and uncle, long residents of this gray land, are said to have taken the gray hues of the landscape upon themselves.

When Aunt Em came there to live she was a young, pretty wife. The sun and wind had changed her, too. They had taken the sparkle from her eyes and left them a sober gray; they had taken the red from her cheeks and lips, and they were gray also. She was thin and gaunt, and never smiled now. When Dorothy, who was an orphan, first came to her, Aunt Em had been so startled by the child's laughter that she would scream and press her hand upon her heart whenever Dorothy's merry voice reached her ears; and she still looked at the little girl with wonder that she could find anything to laugh at.

Uncle Henry never laughed. He worked hard from morning till night and did not know what joy was. He was gray also, from his long beard to his rough boots, and he looked stern and solemn, and rarely spoke. (12–13)

Could anything more horrible than the swirling storm have blown into these gray lives, the stinging winds blowing away the last of the topsoil, scattering the livestock, lifting their home from the ground and sending it spinning upward into the dark and angry clouds, taking the little girl Dorothy with it, ripping her from their hearts and lives?

36. Dorothy and the cyclone from *The Wizard of Oz* (1939).

Of course tornadoes don't really pick up farmhouses with such gentleness and deposit them and their occupants safely back to earth in fairy lands. And, of course, the victims of such storms are not singled out for their evil and wickedness as was the Wicked Witch of the East. Crushed by a farmhouse falling from the sky, we can confidently say that she never knew what hit her. Not that such whirling vortices couldn't remove a house from the earth; it is just that putting it back together again would be as difficult a challenge as reconstituting Humpty Dumpty after his great fall. All the king's horses and all the king's men couldn't put that house, or that life, back together again.

I grew up in the storm-ravaged southeastern United States and was taught early to fear the tornado. Schoolhouse drills sent us into the hallways with our heads between our knees. Midnight weather alerts awakened the family with a shrill alarm, sometimes sending us scurrying next door to huddle in the cellar with our neighbors: too many people packed into too small a space, hail knocking on the door like Dorothy's fists, wind toppling pine trees, lightning crashing on a dark and stormy night.

Now tornado sirens wail out a warning at any time of day or night. Their volume rises and falls – when one grows soft another grows louder. In the middle of the night, jarred from a deep sleep, it is the end of the world, Gabriel blowing his horn, the four horsemen of the apocalypse approaching with fire and fury. I flip on the television to see where the monster has been spotted by the radar beams that seek it out, revealing its tell-tale outline like the invisible creature of Altair IV illuminated by the force field of the C57-D in *Forbidden Planet*. Sometimes the beast is miles away and I stumble back into bed with the television on. Sometimes it is barreling down on top of us and the kids must be awakened and hustled downstairs and into the cellar; our Maggie, like Toto, always threatening to make us give chase as we try to lead her to safety. There we wait for the wind and rain and, finally, for the sound of the 'all-clear' siren that sends us back to bed.

But others are not so lucky.

I am completing this book only days after such monsters swept across the earth just miles from my home. The tornadoes did indeed pick up houses, but they did not bring them back down to earth with a gentle bump. Instead, they were dropped in bits and pieces all over the landscape fifty miles away. People died by the hundreds, not only the wicked, but the righteous as well. Dread Cthulhu, Oz the Gweat and Tewwible, stirred and walked the earth and left destruction in his wake. The whirlwind is, of course, just one of his many forms. He lives in the earthquake and tsunami, in pestilence and disease, in flood and famine. But it is the tornado that keeps me up at night, that costs me sleep, that makes me shudder in fear. I have heard too many stories from family and friends about the way it spins across the land, like a living thing, a force beyond comprehension, leaving only destruction in its wake. I have seen the twisted tree trunks, the flattened houses, the cars scattered hither and yon across highways and the open fields.

When Yahweh Elohim finally answered the pleas of Job for answers, he spoke to him out of a whirlwind. When a response was finally given to Job's incessant queries about the meaning of life and the reason for suffering, it came from the mighty wind, the whirling tornado, the spinning cyclone. Job's children had been killed by a whirlwind that blew out of the dessert and destroyed their dwelling. It was from that whirling storm that the LORD decided to speak.

For Rudolf Otto, the story of the voice from the whirlwind was a profound expression of the numinous in the Old Testament, perhaps the most profound in all the history of religion. He wrote,

> In the 38th chapter of Job we have the element of the mysterious displayed in rare purity and completeness, and this chapter may well rank among the most remarkable in the history of religion. Job has been reasoning with his friends against Elohim, and – as far as concerns them – he has been obviously in the right. They are compelled to be dumb before him. And then Elohim Himself appears to conduct his own defense in person. And He conducts it to such effect that Job avows himself to be overpowered, truly and rightly overpowered, not merely silenced by superior strength. (78)

In Otto's reading of Job 38, God does not offer a rational defense of his ways in response to Job's questioning, not even the response that says, 'My ways are higher than your ways. I have my own reasons that are too complex for your understanding.' In contrast, according to Otto, God's response 'relies on something quite different from anything that can be exhaustively rendered in rational concepts, namely, on the sheer absolute wondrousness that transcends thought, on the *mysterium*, presented in its pure non-rational form' (79).

Otto was particularly struck by the litany of natural examples that Job's God brings to mind: the eagle with keen eyes to spot her defenseless prey, who feasts on the carrion of man and beast, and whose young drink not gentle milk but swallow flesh and blood; the ostrich who allows its eggs

37. 'Job Confessing his Presumption to God Who Answers from the Whirlwind'
by William Blake (1804).

to be trampled underfoot; the behemoth and the leviathan, monsters
that prowl the earth and swim the sea. The eagle, according to Otto, 'is in
truth no evidence for the *teleological* wisdom that "prepares all cunningly
and well", but is rather the creature of *strangeness* and *marvel*' (79). The
ostrich is 'a crucial difficulty rather than evidence of wisdom, and it affords
singularly little help if we are seeking *purpose* in nature' (79). The behemoth
and leviathan 'would be the most unfortunate examples that one could
hit upon if searching for evidences of the purposefulness of the divine
"wisdom"' (80). Instead,

> They, no less than the previous examples and the whole context, tenor, and
> sense of the entire passage, do express in masterly fashion the downright

stupendous, the well nigh daemonic and wholly incomprehensible character of the eternal creative power; how, incalculable and 'wholly other,' it mocks at all conceiving but yet can stir the mind to its depths, fascinate and overbrim the heart. (80)

Otto went on to describe a scene from a story by May Eyth, involving the building of a bridge to span a river. Otto writes,

In spite of endless difficulties and gigantic obstacles, the bridge is at length finished, and stands defying wind and wave. Then there comes a raging cyclone, and building and builder are swept into the deep. Utter meaningless seems to triumph over richest significance, blind 'destiny' seems to stride on its way over prostrate virtue and merit. (81)

Before this devastation the characters of Eyth's story kneel. Not, Otto insists, before the blind forces of nature or even before omnipotence itself, but before 'the wholly uncomprehended Mystery.' (81)

Theodicy is the attempt to justify the ways of the divine in human terms. Theodicy seeks to explain why bad things happen to good people, why bad things happen at all. Job was looking for such a justification: some reason that would help him make sense of the whirlwind that swept across the dessert and slaughtered his family. Otto argued that Job was never given such a reason. Instead, the voice of the divine spoke to him from the heart of the cyclone and offered no justification at all. The answer was not 'I have my reasons but they are too deep for you to understand,' but rather 'I am beyond reason. I am completely other. I am a mystery. In my presence, people tremble.' For Otto, this trembling is at the heart of religion, the most primitive religious response, the most basic spiritual movement. We shudder before the inexplicable, before the mysterious, before the wholly other. The religious impulse rises in the face of the whirling storm as the pulse races and the knees buckle in fear and trembling, but it is not simply the fear of death and destruction. The religious impulse rises as humans contemplate what it means to live in a world where cyclones tear through barnyards, whirlwinds destroy families and tornadoes wreak havoc and destruction. This shudder arises not only on a dark and stormy night but also in the bright light of day, whenever the human heart confronts the wholly other, the thing beyond understanding, the eerie, the great and the terrible.

There is an ancient response to life in the world: a purely human response, rooted, no doubt in our evolutionary history and our biology as much as in our culture. Our hearts race, the color drains from our faces, our flesh crawls, our skin tingles, our hair stands on end. We shudder. This is not the fear bred into us as prey fleeing before predators – the terror of the rabbit at the sight of the hawk. It is a different fear, a deeper fear. It strikes us when we are at our safest, when there is no external threat at all, when we least expect it, when we are least prepared for it.

We use words such as these to describe it: eerie, creepy, weird, spooky, spectral, unearthly, macabre, ominous, numinous. In the shadows we catch sight of deeper shadows still, moving ever toward us in the dark. Something is fleetingly witnessed across the open field or in the dense forest, something neither human nor beast. We feel a strange breath upon our neck. We swear that we saw a coffee cup move, a book close by itself, a window close of its own accord. We catch a look in the eyes of a stranger – or even worse, a friend – that makes us catch our breath, a look, if not of menace, then of the unknown or the unexpected. Strange ancient chants come to us on the wind, through our open windows, as if from some distant, distant time, some primitive past, some foreign future. These things make us shudder because they are the unknown, the mysterious. They are outside our reality, beyond our accepted world. They make no sense, have no explanation, reveal us for what we are: unknowing children, primitive beings, unsure for a moment that the world is as it seems, that we are who we think we are.

These moments of creepy terror provide the rich soil from which religion springs. Ghosts become gods, demons become deities. The awful becomes the awesome. But the terror, of course, remains. Often on the fringes, and sometimes in the heart of faith, the monsters prowl. Ghosts haunt. Vampires rise from the grave. Werewolves hunt their prey. Demons corrupt the innocent.

The ghost of Condie Cunningham, engulfed in flames, runs on and on, along hallways, round corners, down stairs and across the world. The bloated thing with the missing nose and the rotting flesh moves in the darkness of the grave, digs its way to freedom, dresses in a nice suit of clothes and tries to pass itself off as the living. The beast, in the form of a man, waits lurking in the shadows to spring upon its unsuspecting prey. The demon leers from the backseat of the car, from the living room window, from the face of a loved one. The Satanist defiles the sacred and bows down before the profane.

Perhaps these ghouls and specters are more then they seem. Perhaps they are more than survivors from a superstitious past, more than the product of fancy and fiction. Perhaps they continue to haunt, and stalk, and hunt, and possess us, even though we should all know better, because today, as in the past, they offer us glimpses of the wholly other, glimpses of the tremendous mystery, the *mysterium tremendum*, glimpses of the holy. These creatures of the night, these phantoms, haints, specters and ghouls that make us shudder and shake, these ghosts, vampires, werewolves and demons point us to the mystery that lies beyond the locked door.

In the dead of night, when everything is quiet, if you listen carefully, you can hear them knock.

Bibliography

Anson, Jay (1977) *The Amityville Horror* (New York, Pocket Star Books).

Barber, Paul (1988) *Vampires, Burial and Death: Folklore and Reality* (New Haven, CT, Yale University Press).

Baring-Gould, Sabine (2008) *The Book of Werewolves* (Forgotten Books).

Baum, L. Frank (1900) *The Wonderful Wizard of Oz* (Chicago and New York, George M. Hill Company).

—— (1917) *The Lost Princess of Oz* (Chicago, Reilly & Benton Company).

Bayless, Raymond (1967) *The Enigma of the Poltergeist* (West Nyack, NY, Parker Publishing).

Belanger, Michelle (2003) *The Vampire Ritual Book* (Michelle Belanger).

—— (2004) *The Psychic Vampire Codex* (San Francisco, CA, Weiser Books).

—— ed. (2007) *Vampires in Their Own Words: An Anthology of Vampire Voices* (Woodbury, MN, Llewellyn Publications).

Blackwood, Algernon (2008) *The Empty House and Other Ghost Stories* (Cornwall, Stratus Books).

Blatty, William Peter (1971) *The Exorcist* (New York, HarperCollins).

Blum, Deborah (2006) *Ghost Hunters: William James and the Search for Scientific Proof of Life After Death* (New York, Penguin Press).

Brittle, Gerald Daniel (1980) *The Demonologist: The Extraordinary Career of Ed and Lorraine Warren* (New York, Prentice Hall).

Bulwer-Lytton, Edward George (1830) *Paul Clifford* (New York, J. & J. Harper).

Calmet, Augustine, (1850) *The Phantom World* (London, Richard Bentley).

Cavendish, Richard (1967) *The Black Arts* (New York, Penguin).

Clarke, Barbara (2005) *Practical Vampyrism for Modern Vampyres by Lady CG* (LaVergne, TN, Lulu).

Conan Doyle, Arthur (1930) *The Edge of the Unknown* (New York, G. P. Putnam's Sons).

—— (2006) *The History of Spiritualism* (Middlesex, Echo Library).

Coudray, Chantal Bourgault du (2006) *The Curse of the Werewolf: Fantasy, Horror and the Beast Within* (London, I.B.Tauris).

Crowley, Aleister (1998) *The Vision and the Voice* (Boston, MA, Red Wheel/Weiser).

—— (2004) *The Book of the Law* (York Beach, ME, Red Wheel/Weiser).

Cuneo, Michael W. (2001) *American Exorcism: Expelling Demons in the Land of Plenty* (New York, Doubleday).

DeLarue, Paul (1956) *The Borzoi Book of French Folk Tales*, trans. Austin E. Fife (New York, Alfred A. Knopf).

Endore, Guy (1933) *The Werewolf of Paris* (New York, Farrar & Rinehart).

Fortune, Dion (2001) *Psychic Self-Defense: New Edition* (San Francisco, CA, Weiser Books).

Gerard, Emily de Lazowska (1885) 'Transylvanian Superstitions,' in *The Nineteenth Century*, vol. XVII, ed. James Knowles (London, Kegan, Paul, Trench & Co.).

Ginzburg, Carol (1992) *The Night Battles: Witchcraft and Agrarian Cults in the Sixteenth and Seventeenth Centuries* (Baltimore, MD, Johns Hopkins University Press).

Hammond, Frank and Ida Mae (1973) *Pigs in the Parlor* (Kirkwood, MO, Impact Christian Books).

Holzer, Hans (1997) *Ghosts: True Encounters with the World Beyond* (New York, Black Dog and Leventhal).

—— (2003) *The Ghost Hunter's Favorite Cases* (New York, Barnes and Noble Books).

Huysmans, J.-K. (2001) *The Damned*, trans. Terry Hale (New York, Penguin Books).

Jacobs, W.W. (1902) 'The Monkey's Paw,' in *The Lady of the Barge* (London and New York, Harper & Brothers).

Jackson, Shirley (1959) *The Haunting of Hill House* (New York, Penguin Books).

James, Henry (2007) *The Turn of the Screw and Other Short Novels* (New York, Signet Classics).

James, M.R. (1905) *Ghost Stories of an Antiquary* (London, Edward Arnold).

James, William (1985) *The Varieties of Religious Experience* (New York, Penguin Books).

Joshi, S.T. (1999) 'Introduction,' in *The Call of Cthulhu and Other Weird Stories* (New York, Penguin Books).

Kendrick, Walter (1991) *The Thrill of Fear: 250 Years of Scary Entertainment* (New York, Grove Weidenfeld).

Kiely, David M. and Christina McKenna (2007) *The Dark Sacrament: True Stories of Modern-Day Demon Possession and Exorcism* (New York, HarperCollins).

King, Stephen (1981) *Danse Macabre* (New York, Berkeley Books).

—— (1983) *Pet Sematary* (New York, Pocket Books).

Konstantinos (2007) *Summoning Spirits: The Art of Magical Evocation* (Woodbury, MN, Llewellyn Publishers).

—— (2008) *Vampires: The Occult Truth* (Woodbury, MN, Llewellyn Publishers).

Kramer, Heinrich and James Sprenger (2008) *Malleus Maleficarum*, trans. Montague Summers (Charleston, SC, Forgotten Books).

Kuzmeskus, Elaine M. (2007) *Séance 101* (Atglen, PA, Schiffer Publishing Ltd.).

Larson, Bob (1999) *Larson's Book of Spiritual Warfare* (Nashville, TN, Thomas Nelson).

LaVey, Anton Szvandor (2005) *The Satanic Bible* (New York, Avon Books).

Laycock, Joseph (2009) *Vampires Today: The Truth about Modern Vampires* (Westport, CT, Praeger).

LeFanu, J. Sheridan (2010) *Carmilla* (London, Bibliolis).

Levi, Eliphas (1942) *Transcendental Magic: Its Doctrine and Ritual* (Whitefish, MT, Kessinger Publishing).

Levin, Ira (2010) *Rosemary's Baby* (New York, Pegasus).

Lovecraft, H.P. (2001) 'The Call of Cthulhu,' in *Black Seas of Infinity*, ed. Andrew Wheeler (New York, Science Fiction Book Club).

—— (2005) 'Supernatural Horror in Literature,' in *At the Mountains of Madness: The Definitive Edition* (New York, Modern Library).

Lupa (2007) *A Field Guide to Otherkin* (Stafford, Megalithica Books).

Martin, Malachi (1976) *Hostage to the Devil* (New York, HarperCollins).

Matthews, Chris (2009) *Modern Satanism: Anatomy of a Radical Subculture* (Westport, CT, Praeger).

McDonald, Beth E. (2004) *The Vampire as Numinous Experience* (Jefferson, North Carolina, McFarland and Co.).

Otto, Rudolf (1923) *The Idea of the Holy* (London, Oxford University Press).

Partridge, Christopher and Eric Christianson, eds. (2009) *The Lure of the Darkside: Satan and Western Demonology in Popular Culture* (London, Equinox).

Peck, M. Scott (2005) *Glimpses of the Devil* (New York, Free Press).

Perrault, Charles (1922) *Fairy Tales of Charles Perrault*, trans. Christopher Betts (London, George Q. Harrap & Co.).

Polidori, John William (1819) *The Vampyre: A Tale* (London, Sherwood, Neely & Jones).

Post, Eric G. (1946) *Communicating with the Beyond: A Practical Handbook of Spiritualism* (New York, Atlantic Publishing).

Prest, Thomas Preskett (2004) *Varney the Vampire or the Feast of Blood*, vol. 1 (Whitefish, MT, Kessinger Publishing).

Price, Harry (1940) *The Most Haunted House in England* (London, Longmanns).

—— (1946) *The End of Borley Rectory* (London, Harrap).

Russo, Arlene (2005) *Vampire Nation* (Woodbury, MN, Llewellyn Publications).

Schnoebelen, William (1991) *Masonry: Beyond the Light* (Ontario, CA, Chick Publications).

—— and Sharon (1993) *Lucifer Dethroned* (Ontario, CA, Chick Publications).

Sitwell, Sacheverell (1988) *Poltergeists: An Introduction and Examination followed by Chosen Instances* (New York, Dorset Press).

Skal, David J. (1993) *The Monster Show: A Cultural History of Horror* (New York, W.W. Norton & Co.).

Slate, Joe H. (2008) *Psychic Vampires: Protection from Energy Predators and Parasites* (Woodbury, MN, Llewellyn Publications).

Smith, Michelle and Lawrence Pazder (1980) *Michelle Remembers* (New York, St. Martin's Press).

Stevenson, Robert Louis (1886) *Strange Case of Dr. Jekyll and Mr. Hyde* (London, Longman, Green & Co.).

Stoker, Bram (2007) *Dracula* (New York, Signet Classics).

Stratford, Lauren (1991) *Satan's Underground* (Gretna, LA, Pelican Publishing Co.).

Summers, Montague (1933) *The Werewolf in Lore and Legend* (London, Kegan Paul, Trench, Trubner & Co.).

Swedenborg, Emanuel (1903) *Heaven and Hell* (Boston, Swedenborg Printing Bureau).

Tylor, E.B. (1874) *Primitive Culture: Researches into the Development of Mythology, Philosophy, Religion, Language, Art and Custom* (New York, Henry Holt and Co.).

Waite, A.E. (1896) *Devil Worship in France* (London, George Redway).

Williamson, Jack (1948) *Darker Than You Think* (New York, Tom Doherty Associates).

Wilson, Colin (1971) *The Occult* (New York, Random House).

Index